T0383441

# RACISM

Racism has a long history and its devastating impacts continue to spark heated, moral and political debate and give rise to social movements and widespread protest. This accessible primer provides a cogent introduction to the study and confrontation of racism in the twenty-first century, making use of key insights from sociology and other social sciences.

Drawing on a range of scholars, including from the radical black tradition and the Global South, this book explores key issues in racism studies. Putting racism into historical context, Moran explains the modernity of racism and its creation through European colonialism and imperialism, racial capitalism, and the development of racist hierarchies stimulated by colonialist exploitation as well as pseudoscientific and Enlightenment thinking centred upon white supremacy. Moran also discusses the intersectional, structural, institutional and systemic nature of racism, and the connections between race, racism and nationalism evident in the explosion of right-wing nationalist populism around the world. The book also investigates how the self and subjectivity are involved in racism and contribute to the reproduction of racism as a system, before considering whether there are new, cultural forms of racism, and how we can account for Islamophobia and other racisms described as new, such as colour-blind racism, post-racial racism and racism without racists. Crucially, the book explores anti-racist social movements (such as Black Lives Matter) and how racism has been challenged, and discusses how accounts of race and racism can be given without reproducing the category of race as a 'natural' organiser of people, groups, and identities.

This book will appeal to the general reader and students in the humanities and social sciences with an interest in the continuing impact of racism, racial identities, migration, multiculturalism, ethnic and racial studies, nationalism and identity studies.

**Anthony Moran** is Associate Professor in Sociology and Director of Graduate Research in the School of Humanities and Social Sciences at La Trobe University, Australia. His teaching and research explore ethnicity and race; racism; multiculturalism; nationalism and national identity; migration; settler/Indigenous politics; and Australian political culture. He is author of *Australia: Nation, Belonging, and Globalization* (Routledge, 2005) and *The Public Life of Australian Multiculturalism: Building a Diverse Nation* (2016); co-author of *Ordinary People's Politics: Australians Talk about Life, Politics, and the Future of Their Country* (2006); and co-editor of *Trust, Risk and Uncertainty* (2005).

# KEY IDEAS

Series Editor: Anthony Elliott

Designed to complement the successful *Key Sociologists*, this series covers the main concepts, issues, debates, and controversies in sociology and the social sciences. The series aims to provide authoritative essays on central topics of social science, such as community, power, work, sexuality, inequality, benefits and ideology, class, family, etc. The books adopt a strong 'individual' line, as critical essays rather than literature surveys, offering lively and original treatments of their subject matter. The books will be useful to students and teachers of sociology, political science, economics, psychology, philosophy, and geography.

**WELFARE CONDITIONALITY**
*BETH WATTS AND SUZANNE FITZPATRICK*

**THE STRANGER**
*SHAUN BEST*

**SECULARIZATION**
*CHARLES TURNER*

**UNIVERSAL BASIC INCOME**
*BRIAN MCDONOUGH AND JESSIE BUSTILLOS MORALES*

**REFUGIA**
RADICAL SOLUTIONS TO MASS DISPLACEMENT
*ROBIN COHEN AND NICHOLAS VAN HEAR*

**POSTCOLONIAL EUROPE**
*LARS JENSEN*

**EXCEPTIONALISM**
*LARS JENSEN AND KRISTÍN LOFTSDÓTTIR*

**CONSUMPTION**
*JOHN STOREY*

**SEXUALITY (5TH EDITION)**
*JEFFREY WEEKS*

**CLASS**
*NICK STEVENSON*

**HAPPINESS (2ND EDITION)**
*BENT GREVE*

**RISK (3RD EDITION)**
*DEBORAH LUPTON*

**RACISM**
*ANTHONY MORAN*

For a full list of titles in this series, please visit www.routledge.com/Key-Ideas/book-series/SE0058

# RACISM

**Anthony Moran**

Routledge
Taylor & Francis Group
LONDON AND NEW YORK

Designed cover image: © Shutterstock

First published 2024
by Routledge
4 Park Square, Milton Park, Abingdon, Oxon OX14 4RN

and by Routledge
605 Third Avenue, New York, NY 10158

*Routledge is an imprint of the Taylor & Francis Group, an informa business*

© 2024 Anthony Moran

*British Library Cataloguing-in-Publication Data*
A catalogue record for this book is available from the British Library

*Library of Congress Cataloging-in-Publication Data*
Names: Moran, Anthony, author.
Title: Racism / Anthony Moran. Description: Abingdon, Oxon ; New York, NY : Routledge, 2024. | Series: Key ideas | Includes bibliographical references and index.
Identifiers: LCCN 2023026075 (print) | LCCN 2023026076 (ebook) | ISBN 9781032212975 (hbk) | ISBN 9781032212968 (pbk) | ISBN 9781003267690 (ebk)
Subjects: LCSH: Racism.
Classification: LCC HT1521 .M629 2024 (print) | LCC HT1521 (ebook) | DDC 305.8—dc23/eng/20230808
LC record available at https://lccn.loc.gov/2023026075
LC ebook record available at https://lccn.loc.gov/2023026076

ISBN: 978-1-032-21297-5 (hbk)
ISBN: 978-1-032-21296-8 (pbk)
ISBN: 978-1-003-26769-0 (ebk)

DOI: 10.4324/9781003267690

Typeset in Bembo
by Apex CoVantage, LLC

For my mother Patricia, for Claudia and Liam, and in memory of my father Bernie

# CONTENTS

# ACKNOWLEDGEMENTS

Series editor Anthony Elliott encouraged me to take up the challenge of writing this book and has provided me with much needed encouragement as I have gone about it. I thank him also for his gentle art of persuasion that kept me focused on the task amidst the other exacting tasks of academic life. Thank you to the three anonymous reviewers for Routledge who provided invaluable critique of my initial proposal for this book, which provoked me to rethink my approach to the topic. And thank you to Routledge's editors for their flexibility when this took me longer than planned to complete.

Thank you to my colleagues in the Department of Social Inquiry at La Trobe University, for many stimulating discussions over coffee and in seminars; and to my diverse undergraduate and postgraduate students, who continuously alert me to the importance of this book's topic, and have stimulated me to keep puzzling over what racism means and about its impacts. In particular, I would like to thank Raelene Wilding, Martina Boese and Nicholas Smith, who I have taught with on the topics of race, racism, ethnicity and multiculturalism for many years, and for many ongoing discussions that inform this book.

Huge thanks, as always, to Claudia, who has provided continuous encouragement and support and listened to my various doubts as I researched and wrote, as did our son Liam, who I also thank for his stimulating discussions and 'take' on things. I thank my broader family and friends for being there.

# INTRODUCTION
## WE ARE NOT POST-RACIAL – THE
## TENACITY OF RACISM

How do sociologists, and social scientists more generally, define and explain racism? This would seem to be a good starting point for this book, but it is also a difficult way to start, given that racism has been defined in various ways, and different aspects of it have been given more emphasis or less emphasis, depending on theorist or empirical examples. Is there a distinction between old and new racism? Or is there just one concept or object of study that we call racism, which then has different variants, expressed in different ways in different contexts? Racism involves beliefs, emotions, attitudes, stereotypes and ideologies, but it also needs to be understood as systemic. This point has been made by many social scientists (for example, Carmichael[1] and Hamilton 1967; Sivanandan 1982; Bonilla-Silva 1997; Feagin 2006; Omi and Winant 2015 [1986], as well as many others discussed in this book) and it has also been the message of political activists and social movements. It has been the major message of Black Lives Matter, which became a truly global movement in 2020, with major public protests in many countries sparked by brutal police perpetrated murders and killings in the US, most prominently of African American George Floyd in Minneapolis. Black Lives Matter made 'structural' or 'systemic' racism and 'intersectionality' (another key term used and discussed in this book) mainstream ideas and rallying points. Racism is not just about individual attitudes, prejudices, beliefs, phobias – it is about the very structure of society, driving systemic problems such as police violence and the killing of African Americans and other non-whites in the US, mass incarcerations of people of colour (including Indigenous people

DOI: 10.4324/9781003267690-1

and people of African backgrounds in my country, Australia), and all manner of racial disparities in housing, education, employment, health and the criminal justice system throughout the world, but especially in white-dominated societies.

As many theorists, leaders and anti-racism activists have emphasised, we are still firmly in the racist historical moment. Many doubt that we will ever be free of racism, which has a powerful capacity to transform itself under new conditions and in response to the challenges of anti-racism and its social movements. Indeed, though significantly challenged on a global scale since the end of World War Two (Barkan 1993; Bonnett 1999), racism remains as a pervasive structure of inequality, discrimination and violence, devastating the lives of countless people, especially, though not only, in white-dominated societies. Though this may seem obvious to many readers, I emphasise it in the face of false claims that societies have moved beyond racism, into an era of post-race enlightenment in the post-civil rights era. And that is also the stance of this book.

This book is primarily concerned with the contribution of sociology to studying racism. Critics have noted that much of mainstream sociology has neglected the study of racism, or pushed it into an area of specialisation, rather than seeing it as central to the understanding of society, power, opportunity and inequality (see Meer and Nayak 2015). This book argues that 'race' and 'racism' are central to understanding contemporary societies and politics, and thus are central to sociology. It is crucial for any student studying sociology that they develop an understanding of how race and racism (like other central sociological concepts such as class, gender, sexuality, ethnicity, religion, age, disability, etc.) shape contemporary societies in a global context. Not only students, but academic researchers too.

But how do we think about racism? From what positions do we discuss racism? What does structural racism mean, and what are its effects? How is subjectivity engaged in racism? Are there 'new racisms'? This book provides various accounts of and ways of thinking about and theorising racism, considered as a highly contextualised phenomenon. It asks how we can *think with* and at the same time *think against* race? In other words, how can we give accounts of race and racism without succumbing to the reproduction of the category of race as a seemingly natural key organiser of people, groups, identities (a question posed by Kwame Anthony Appiah, Robert Miles and Paul Gilroy, among many others)?

## DEFINING RACE AND RACISM

Raymond Williams, in the first edition of his famous book *Keywords*, had no separate entry for 'race', but instead included it in the entry for 'nationalist' (Nonini 1999). There he notes that the word 'race' is of 'uncertain origin' but is in common use in English from the sixteenth century, meaning 'common stock', and that 'racial' had mostly positive connotations in its nineteenth-century usage, but that, in the same period, it also gathered up much more negative and discriminating meanings, largely through scientific explanation of 'arbitrary' categorisations of race. He also states that '*racial* community' is often used by nationalists in claims about nation and its boundaries (Williams 1976, pp. 178–179). Williams' (1983) second and expanded edition of *Keywords* did include a separate entry on 'racial'. He noted here that race came into the English language through the French word 'race' and the Italian 'razza', and its early meanings were about a line of 'descent' as in 'race and stock of Abraham' (from 1570), and they related also to blood, and the already-mentioned 'stock'. It was also associated with species of plants and animals in the late 1500s. In 1580 there is mention of the 'human race', and later meanings included as a 'group of human beings in extension and projection from' the sense of 'descent', as well as the meanings associated with species of plants and animals. The entry then went into a longer discussion of what happened with 'race' in the nineteenth century, when scientific classification got mixed up with political and social theories – the major example he refers to is Arthur de Gobineau's (1915) *The Inequality of Human Races* (first published in French in 1853–1855) – and that the concept was always fuzzy and confusing, and took disastrous directions once there were conceptions of distinctions within a species, as in 'races of man'. Though 'race hatred' was used as a term in the nineteenth century, words such as 'racialism' come into use only in the early twentieth century, and 'racialist' in 1930, later shortened to 'racism' and 'racist'– and these terms were entirely hostile and negative in connotation (Williams 1983, pp. 248–250).

In racial thinking as expressed in writing and science, it is important to recognise, as Banton emphasises, that 'as new modes of explanation of human variation have arisen, so the word "race" has been used in new ways, but the old uses have often continued side by side with the new ones' (Banton 2000, p. 51). For example, Banton traces a broad historical shift in the meaning of race, in many European languages, from commonality of 'descent' or 'character' in the eighteenth century, with a focus on individuals and distinguishable social strata, to a transformed view of race as 'type' in the nineteenth century (also transferring the concern with character to a concern with 'national character'). Racial typology emerged among a group of racial thinkers as something that fixed groups of people as separate races – 'man' (as per the contemporary language) was a 'genus divided into types which in effect were species' (Banton 2000, p. 55). Under the influence of Darwinian thought in the late nineteenth and early twentieth centuries, race came to be understood in terms of subspecies that had emerged in different environments, under the influence of selective adaptation. But, in social analyses, adaptation gave way to the view that social evolution was less about adaptation than it was 'a story of man's progress to superior modes of living' (Banton 2000, p. 57), with Europeans at the top of the evolutionary scale. However, Banton points out that, in the popular mind, 'race as type' was still easier to grasp in the twentieth century, where race as subspecies was too scientifically abstract.

Though race thinking became an important way of explaining the world in the eighteenth and nineteenth centuries, as noted above 'racism' as a term only came into common usage (in the English language) as late as the 1930s, to describe the theories and practices of the Nazis in Germany (Fredrickson 2002, p. 5). The negative views of 'others', the perception of superiority and inferiority, and the hierarchical and oppressive societal practices that we now refer to as racism have been around for much longer than the term that we now use to describe them.

Robert Miles (1989) defined racism mainly as an ideology (in Marx's sense, as distorted representation of human beings and of social relations) within a social formation (with economic, political and ideological levels), and explained it via processes of signification and representations (always contextualised in particular social, political and economic relations), through which racialised selves and others were defined and demarcated. Ideology was a continuous social production, in which subjects are actively involved but at the same time reconstitute themselves in relations of self and other. Ideologies were 'the accumulated, taken-for-granted, and often contradictory set of assumptions and beliefs that are employed by people to impose an ideological structure upon the social world, within which they then act' (Miles 1989, p. 70). 'Representations' were those concepts, images and associations that cohere in symbolic frameworks that then orient subjects' relations within the world, including the world of others, and that orient actions. Signification was the 'representational process' through which representations were made and 'meanings . . . attributed to particular objects, features and processes, in such a way that the latter are given special significance, and carry or are embodied with a set of additional, second order features'. It was a 'process of depicting the social world and social processes, of creating a sense of how things "really are"' (Miles 1989, p. 70). It was therefore a historical, creative, transformative process that involves production, invention, selection and combination. It is inevitably a site of contestation and domination where certain images and meanings capture the hearts and minds of subjects who are then guided by them in their actions.

These representations had real effects: they were embodied in institutions; they could shape economic relations (including labour markets) in important ways, positioning people in advantaged and disadvantaged situations (e.g. in education and housing markets), and keeping racialised peoples and groups there, reproducing societies of domination over time (Miles 1989; see also Miles 1982). They were not merely ad hoc rationalisations for already existing relations of domination. Rather, they feed into and shape the very formation of these relations which they legitimise (Miles 1989, p. 101). As Miles explained, the images that Europeans had of colonial others were central to the actual transformation of economic and social relations brought about in colonised areas, a process also famously analysed by Edward Said (1978) as 'orientalism'.

Arguing against what he saw as 'conceptual inflation', Miles proposed a more stringent definition of racism than he perceived in many writings of the time. First, it must involve an ideology (explicit or implicit) about the existence of biologically determined groups of people (these did not necessarily have to rely on distinguishable phenotypical differences like skin colour, a point made by Miles and Brown [2003, p. 6], reflecting on the racist violence and genocide in the former Yugoslavia and in Rwanda in the 1990s). Second, that these groups of people, called races, are in that ideology arranged in a hierarchy based on notions of superiority and inferiority. And third, it involves practices of domination (which the ideology provokes and supports). Though the first two dimensions refer to representation and signification – to the ideational aspect of racism – the third points to a broader understanding of racism, which includes practices and, by implication, institutions. However, as I explain in Chapter 2, Miles was loathe to adopt a concept like 'institutional racism', unless it was very carefully argued. Yes, ideologies infused institutions and gave them shape – so there can be racist institutions. But the phenomenon of institutional racism, he argued, did not make sense unless the people who engaged in those institutional practices were driven, in some way, by racist beliefs and attitudes, or at least their afterlife infused institutional practices – in other words, by racist ideology (Miles 1989; see also Miles 1982, Ch. 4).

Anthias and Yuval-Davis (1993, p. 8) challenged Miles's definition because, in their view, it precluded inclusion of the 'new racism' – which focused on the inferiorisation of culture – and also failed to capture other experiences of exclusion that they would characterise as racism – the experiences of refugees and migrant ethnic groups who were deemed outsiders to a nation. They argued for broadening the meaning of racism and associating it with a very broad category of ethnic groups (which 'races' were a version of):

> We believe that the specificity of racism lies in its working on the notion of ethnic groupings. It is a discourse and practice of inferiorizing ethnic groups. Racism need not rely on a process of racialization. We believe that racism can also use the notion of the undesirability of groups, in the form in which they exist. This may lead to attempts to assimilate, exterminate or exclude. These may be justified in terms of the negative attribution given to culture, ethnic identity, personality as well as 'racial' stock. For example, anti-Muslim racism in Britain relies on notions of the 'non-civilized' and supposedly inferior and undesirable character

of Islamic religion and way of life, rather than an explicit notion of biological inferiority.

As we will see in Chapter 5, there has been considerable development since the early 1990s on what Anthias and Yuval-Davis termed 'anti-Muslim racism', captured by the term Islamophobia.

Anthias and Yuval-Davis argued that, while there were legitimate analytical distinctions to be made between racism, xenophobia and ethnocentrism, the latter two could also be instances of racism when power intervenes: 'Indeed the question of power and racist effects is central to our own definition of racism' (Anthias and Yuval-Davis 1993, p. 8). They also challenged Miles's strict demarcation of institutional racism, arguing that we can judge whether an institution or practice is racist in terms of its racist effects, despite any forms of intentionality on the part of actors or explicit policies (Anthias and Yuval-Davis 1993, p. 9; see also Anthias 1999). In addition they state that:

> Our view is that all those exclusionary practices that are formulated on the categorization of individuals into groups whereby ethnic or 'racial' origin are criteria of access or selection are endemically racist. Further, our view is that racist practices are also those whose outcome, if not intention, is to work on different categories of the population in this way.
>
> (Anthias and Yuval-Davis 1993, p. 11)

Howard Winant (1998) noted that, although there was something that we could term racism (sharing certain fundamental qualities) that has existed for several centuries, it has significantly transformed across time, and this change was partly stimulated by contesting racial projects, a concept that he had developed earlier with his collaborator Michael Omi, in their book *Racial Formation* (Omi and Winant 2015, first published in 1986). The theory of racial formation involved a conceptual distinction between race and racism – not all ideas, expressions and identities related to race are racist, and not all 'racial projects' are racist. He argued for a definition of racism that is not that different to Miles's definition as explained above: '*Today, a racial project can be defined as racist if it creates or reproduces a racially unequal social structure, based on essentialized racial categories; if it essentializes or naturalizes racial identities or significations, based on a racially unequal social structure; or both'* (Winant 1998, pp. 760–761; italics in original).

In this book, I generally adopt this broad definition of racism put forward by Miles and Omi and Winant, recognising also that the systemic nature of racism has to be at the forefront of the account. Racism is not just about racist representations and racist prejudice, but is also about the systemic ways that lives are structured and racialised in racist systems, that also have global reach. Indeed, as Michelle Christian (2019, p. 170) has argued, the world racist system ushered in by white supremacy and colonialism is one in which there is a global racial hierarchy of nations: 'countries and groups continue to be transnationally racialized . . . and must contend with the "transnational assemblage". . . of racist logics and projects that interact and intersect in local spaces.' The structure of racism (as theorised by Bonilla-Silva 1997), Christian argues, needs to be theorised in a world systems approach, rather than studied primarily as relations within nations. In this proposed approach, 'the global and historical components to racialized social systems foregrounds the totality of the racial structure as always globally connected, if locally realized' (Christian 2019, p. 181).

In this book, I draw upon a range of thinkers including many African American and other non-white and Global South scholars, to highlight different ways to think about racism – in the main restricting myself to sociological approaches. The field of race and racism studies has always been a contentious one. As asked earlier, where do race and racism sit in the sociological lexicon? While they should be in the mainstream of sociology, not siphoned off as an extra, vital but specialist stream of sociology, mainly handled in specialist journals and books, they are often neglected in mainstream sociological accounts of modern societies. As many racism scholars, including critical race theory scholars who are often from non-white backgrounds have argued, race and racism should be right at the centre of sociology, combining intersectionally with other axes of domination, inequality and discrimination, such as class, gender, sexuality, ethnicity, religion, disability, etc.

There has been a long tradition, especially among African American scholars (see Bhambra 2014), as well as, increasingly, among non-white scholars from across the globe and scholars who either identify or are identified as people of colour, Indigenous and from the Global South, to see the workings of race and racism as central to the operation of mainstream, white-dominated societies, for the entire modern era that sociology emerges from and studies as its main focus – the societies that emerged via the great change from predominantly agricultural to industrialised societies. For some, race and racism are central to most if not all social phenomena, including politics. As African American philosopher and theorist of racism Charles W. Mills writes, 'White supremacy is the unnamed political system that has made the modern world what it is today' (Mills 1997, p. 1).

This argument has been approached in several different ways: Du Bois' (1986) famous argument in *The Souls of Black Folk* that 'the problem of the Twentieth Century is the problem of the color line'; the arguments about 'racial capitalism' pioneered by major African American thinkers such as Cedric Robinson ([1983] 2000), and which have been championed by other scholars (Virdee 2019; Issar 2021), and by the Black Lives Matter movement, emphasising the ways that race made modernity; and indeed Stuart Hall, who came to see race as one of the major foci of categorization of differences in the modern/postmodern world (Hall 2017), and who referred to racial modernity, as did his former student Paul Gilroy, who argued for seeing modernity as 'racialized modernity' to emphasise ways that racism and racial categories permeate the contemporary modern world (Gilroy 1993, 2000). Scholars such as Barnor Hesse (2007) have also theorised the contours of 'racialized modernity', arguing for the central tropes of European (in a signifying chain including 'Christian', 'Whiteness', 'the West') and non-European as organising race and racism, since the sixteenth century, as Europe began to establish its colonialist system. The centralising of race, racism, colonialism and imperialism has also been seen by many non-white and Global South scholars as a challenge to the Eurocentrism and 'methodological whiteness' (Bhambra 2014, 2017) of sociology. There have been increasingly loud calls to decolonise sociology – and one of the most important aspects of this challenge has been the call to recognise non-Western thinkers and epistemologies (Mbembe 2016; Savransky 2017) and to decentre Europe and North America and adopt a much more global perspective in terms of what is studied, how it is studied, and by whom it is studied. Sociology has been too dominated by the world view of white, European or American males (Rattansi 2021; Mbembe 2015).

As a white Australian settler-colonial scholar, this is a difficult challenge when writing a book on racism. On the other hand, as a white person living in a white-dominated world, of which I am a major beneficiary, such discomfort is necessary and justified. And I also feel morally obliged to research and study racism, as part of a collective effort to find ways to challenge and overcome racism. The call from decolonising non-white scholars is not for white scholars to vacate the field (racism is too important a topic for a sociologist to step back and simply leave the subject area to the labour of others, from non-white backgrounds, to research and analyse), but is a challenge to be self-reflective in terms of how they study racism and to realise the necessary limits to their understanding that their white racial positioning entails. There are deeper insights into the workings of racism that many non-white scholars have revealed, based on the intersection between their lived experience in racist systems, societies and their own workplaces and their intellectual labour, some of which I attempt to convey in this book.

In Chapter 1, I consider the historical emergence of racism as a global phenomenon, spreading out from Europe, and shaped and inspired by modern forms of thinking including race categorisation and racial hierarchy, by capitalism (or racial capitalism), imperialism, colonialism and slavery, and the ideology and practices of white supremacy. A key argument is about the modernity of racism. In the final section of the chapter, I focus upon challenging questions (for example, from postcolonial and other scholars) about the broad connections between modernity, Enlightenment and racism.

Chapter 2 discusses the crucial insight of black feminist theorists about the intersectionality of racism (considering especially intersections of race, class, gender and sexuality, and scholars such as Crenshaw, Patricia Hill Collins, bell hooks, among others), which in itself produces a systemic account of racism. Beginning with Carmichael and Hamilton's (1967) famous argument from *Black Power*, I then discuss a series of theoretical attempts to explain and theorise the institutional, structural and systemic nature of racism, examining structural racism (Bonilla-Silva), racial formation (Omi and Winant), systemic racism and the white racial frame (Feagin), and everyday racism (Essed), which links the micro and macro experiences of racism.

The intersectionality of race, racism, nation and nationalism is critically discussed in Chapter 3. Here I discuss the main arguments of a range of scholars, centred on George L. Mosse's arguments about historical and contextual connections between race, nationalism and sexuality, Benedict Anderson's argument about the connections between class and racism, rather than between racism and nationalism, and Étienne Balibar's complex arguments about racism as nationalism's 'supplement', as standing behind nationalism's 'fictive ethnicity', and as always also involving sexism. I draw upon examples of settler-Australian nationalism, and late nineteenth- and early twentieth-century Chinese nationalism. The chapter concludes with a discussion about the links between racism and right-wing nationalist populism.

Chapter 4 engages with the subjectivities of racism – how do we understand racism at the level of individuals and groups caught up in its dynamics? Psychoanalytic contributions to the understanding of racism are discussed, including the work of the Frankfurt school, the classic, seminal work of Fanon (1968), *Black Skin, White Masks*, and other key contributions. Many sociological approaches are focused on the roles of discourses that position racial and racist subjectivities, and which individuals engage with in sometimes transformative ways. I discuss some key examples of studies of white and black subjectivities. In addition to these approaches, the chapter also makes a case for examining racial subjectivity through the lens of Bourdieu's concept of habitus: racialised habitus as a set of racial dispositions deeply embedded in individuals and societies.

Chapter 5 discusses different theories and ways of thinking about 'new racism' (first theorised by Martin Barker), 'cultural racism', 'differentialist racism', 'racism without racists', 'color-blind racism' and 'post-racism'. The chapter discusses a range of examples where these phenomena gain expression, from the US, France, the UK, Australia, Singapore and Japan. Focusing on Islamophobia in the last section, I develop an argument about what is both old and new about it.

In Chapter 6, I discuss the difficulties for sociologists and other social scientists who analyse the impacts of 'race' yet need to avoid reinforcing false beliefs about race: in other words, how can we think with and against race? A range of approaches are discussed, including arguments about replacing race with other terms, such as ethnicity, or majority/minority, or 'colour differentiation'. Can we, and societies, ever shift 'beyond race'? The resounding answer in the present circumstances of ongoing systemic racism is 'no'. In a discussion of this theme, I analyse implications for race and racism of demographic changes projected to result in the rise of majority-minority populations, and of the significance of 'mixed-race' populations for experiences of racism. I discuss utopian visionings 'beyond race', such as embracing an ethic and language of 'planetary humanism', as argued by Paul Gilroy. Finally, when discussing the prospects for dismantling racism, I address the possibilities of emancipatory 'racial reconstruction' and 'racial democracy'.

In a brief conclusion I return to the main themes of the book, and also provide some final thoughts on challenging racism in the present, reflecting on the impact of the civil rights movement in the past and the Black Lives Matter movement in the present.

## NOTE

1 The author Stokely Carmichael later changed his name to Kwame Ture.

## REFERENCES

Anthias, F. 1999, 'Institutional Racism, Power and Accountability', *Sociological Research Online*, vol. 4, no. 1 http://www.socresonline.org.uk/4/lawrence//anthias.html.

Anthias, F. and Yuval-Davis, N. 1993, *Racialised Boundaries: Race, Nation, Gender, Colour and Class and the Anti-Racist Struggle*, Routledge, London.

Banton, M. 2000, 'The Idiom of Race', in L. Back and J. Solomos (eds), *Theories of Race and Racism: A Reader*, Routledge, London and New York, pp. 51–63.

Barkan, E. 1993, *The Retreat of Scientific Racism: Changing Concepts of Race in Britain and the United States Between World Wars*, Cambridge University Press, Cambridge and New York.

Bhambra, G.K. 2014, 'A Sociological Dilemma: Race, Segregation and US Sociology', *Current Sociology*, vol. 62, no. 4, pp. 472–492.

Bhambra, G.K. 2017, 'Brexit, Trump, and "Methodological Whiteness": On the Misrecognition of Race and Class', *The British Journal of Sociology*, vol. 68, issue S1, pp. S214–S232.

Bonilla-Silva, E. 1997, 'Rethinking Racism: Toward a Structural Interpretation', *American Sociological Review*, vol. 62, no. 3, pp. 465–480.

Bonnett, A. 1999, *Anti-Racism*, Routledge, London.

Carmichael, S. and Hamilton, C.V. 1967, *Black Power: The Politics of Liberation in America*, Penguin Books, Harmondsworth.

Christian, M. 2019, 'A Global Critical Race and Racism Framework: Racial Entanglements and Deep and Malleable Whiteness', *Sociology of Race and Ethnicity*, vol. 5, no. 2, pp. 169–185.

de Gobineau, A. 1915, *The Inequality of Human Races*, trans. A. Collins, William Heinemann, London.

Du Bois, W.E.B. 1986, *Writings, W.E.B. Du Bois*, Library Classics of the United States, Viking Press, New York.

Fanon, F., 1968, *Black Skin, White Masks*, MacGibbon and Kee, London.

Feagin, J. 2006, *Systemic Racism: A Theory of Oppression*, Routledge, New York.

Fredrickson, G.M. 2002, *Racism: A Short History*, Scribe Publications, Melbourne, Victoria.

Gilroy, P. 1993, *The Black Atlantic: Modernity and Double Consciousness*, Harvard University Press, Cambridge, Massachusetts.

Gilroy, P. 2000, *Against Race: Imagining Political Culture Beyond the Colour Line*, Belknap Press of Harvard University Press, Cambridge, Massachusetts.

Hall, S. 2017, *The Fateful Triangle: Race, Ethnicity, Nation*, edited by K. Mercer, Harvard University Press, Cambridge, Massachusetts, and London.

Hesse, B. 2007, 'Racialized Modernity: An Analytics of White Mythologies', *Ethnic and Racial Studies*, vol. 30, no. 4, pp. 643–663.

Issar, S. 2021, 'Listening to Black Lives Matter: Racial Capitalism and the Critique of Neoliberalism', *Contemporary Political Theory*, vol. 20, no. 1, pp. 48–71.

Mbembe, A. 2015, 'Decolonizing Knowledge and the Question of the Archive', Public Lecture, Wits Institute for Social and Economic Research (WISER), University of the Witwatersrand (Johannesburg), https://wiser.wits.ac.za/system/files/Achille%20Mbembe%20%20Decolonizing%20Knowledge%20and%20the%20Question%20of%20the%20Archive.pdf.

Mbembe, A. 2016, 'Decolonizing the University: New Directions', *Arts & Humanities in Higher Education*, vol. 15, no. 1, pp. 29–45.

Meer, N. and Nayak, A. 2015, 'Race Ends Where? Race, Racism and Contemporary Sociology', *Sociology*, vol. 49, no. 6, E-Special Issue 2, pp. NP3–NP20.

Miles, R. 1982, *Racism and Migrant Labour*, Routledge and Kegan Paul, London.

Miles, R. 1989, *Racism*, Routledge, London.

Miles, R. and Brown, M. 2003, *Racism,* 2nd edn, Routledge, London.

Mills, C.W. 1997, *The Racial Contract*, Cornell University Press, Ithaca, and London.

Nonini, D.M. 1999, 'Race, Land, Nation: A(t)-Tribute to Raymond Williams', *Cultural Critique*, No. 41, Winter, pp. 158–183.

Omi, M. and Winant, H. 2015 [1986], *Racial Formation in the United States*, 3rd edn, Routledge, New York.

Rattansi, A. 2021, 'A Postcolonial/Decolonising Critique of Zygmunt Bauman: A Response to Dawson', *Thesis Eleven*, vol. 167, no. 1, pp. 141–144.

Robinson, C. [1983] 2000, *Black Marxism: The Making of the Black Radical Tradition*, University of North Carolina Press, Chapel Hill, North Carolina, and London.

Said, E. 1978, *Orientalism*, Pantheon Books, New York.

Savransky, M. 2017, 'A Decolonial Imagination: Sociology, Anthropology and the Politics of Reality', *Sociology*, vol. 51, no. 1, pp. 11–26.

Sivanandan, A. 1982, *A Different Hunger*, Pluto Press, London.

Virdee, S. 2019, 'Racialized Capitalism: An Account of its Contested Origins and Consolidation', *The Sociological Review*, vol. 67, no. 1, pp. 3–27.

Williams, R. 1976, *Keywords: A Vocabulary of Culture and Society*, Fontana, London.

Williams, R. 1983, *Keywords: A Vocabulary of Culture and Society*, revised and expanded edition, Fontana, London.

Winant, H. 1998, 'Racism Today: Continuity and Change in the Post-Civil Rights Era', *Ethnic and Racial Studies*, vol. 21, no. 4, pp. 755–766.

# HOW MODERN IS RACISM?

The argument in this chapter is that race, as understood today, is a modern conception and 'world view' (Smedley 2007), and that racism as a phenomenon is also modern. Of course, people have noticed differences between human populations for much longer periods, dating far back in history. We can find accounts of the peculiarities of different peoples in Herodotus' (1972) *The Histories*, written around 430 BC. There is no doubt that prejudices about other peoples have been around for as long as humanity has been around; and, also, that these prejudices have been a major cause of conflicts and violence throughout history. But such prejudices and practices are not the same as what we conceive as racism.

Consider, for example, what is known about Ancient Egyptian, Greek and Roman civilisations. Historians inform us that such civilisations did not have a notion of distinct races (Hannaford 1996; Solomos and Back 1996, p. 33; Smedley 2007). Most of the differences noticed between people could be explained by their social and political organisation, not their biology or their skin colour. Egyptians, Greeks and Romans lived in a multi-ethnic world, and, through their migrations and conquering of other peoples, they lived among many different-looking people. Though different skin colours were noticed, these ancient peoples did not seem to place any great significance on such physical differences, even if, in 'some ancient literature', denigration of physical attributes of 'alien others', like skin colour, is found (Smedley 2007, pp. 14–15). Different skin colour was explained mainly by the effects of different environments (Miles and Brown 2003, pp. 23–24), not by race. Though

DOI: 10.4324/9781003267690-2

slavery was an established practice, one did not have to be black to be a slave, and many black Africans were soldiers and esteemed warriors. In fact, throughout its long history, dating back thousands of years, slavery either did not require explicit justifications, or justifications were on religious or other grounds, and were not about race. The justifications only became racial in the last decades of the eighteenth century and during the nineteenth century, when the slave trade was being challenged by critics and abolitionists (Wilson 1957; Smedley 2007, Ch. 9).

Ethnocentrism is a much older phenomenon than racism (Fredrickson 2002; Smedley 2007). Ancient Egyptian, Greek and Roman civilisations made 'ethnocentric' rather than 'racial' judgements about people. Ethnocentrism involves beliefs about one's own group's superiority, but, unlike racism, it does not hold that people from another group can never become like 'us'; ethnocentrism can also be vicious, involves fears about others and provokes violence – but it entails the possibility that, through socialisation and integration, people very different to 'us' can become like 'us' and therefore accepted into 'our' society. Beliefs about race and racism take the opposite view – the differences are permanent, not socially and culturally acquired, and therefore someone from a different 'race' can never be like 'us', and never truly belong to 'our' group (Hirschman 2004; Smedley 2007). In racial societies, people can be fundamentally similar in terms of culture and religion (for example, when viewed by outsiders), and yet be separated by sharp racial boundaries; when a racial world view prevails, people who look similar can nevertheless be distinguished by having an unseen 'racial essence' (Smedley, 2007, pp. 33–34). This way of thinking, feeling and being in the world is more modern than ethnocentrism. It has been inspired by modern ways of thinking, including biological and other scientific forms of classification and argument. The social and political context in which 'race thinking' emerged also had a powerful shaping influence on its ideas and outcomes. Racism drew on, and then refashioned in its own terms, a long history of religious, philosophical and scientific thought, as well as the views of different peoples constructed and absorbed from a wide variety of sources including literature, travelogues and journals of exploration. It is tied in intricate ways to: imperial expansion, colonisation and slavery; modern developments in science; the massive changes wrought by capitalism since the fifteenth century; the impact of the Enlightenment; the formation of nation-states and the development of new forms of state practices, including those concerned with the management of people (see Foucault 1978; Goldberg 2002; Omi and Winant 2015); and the emergence of national consciousness.

This chapter traces some of this history, the gradual emergence of beliefs about race, and the development of racism. I discuss and analyse the arguments about the connections between the Enlightenment, modernity, racism and white supremacism, including claims by critics that these connections were *intrinsic*. I argue that the ideals of the Enlightenment and modernity, while embedded in and sometimes supporting white supremacism and racism, should not be dismissed, with reference also to black radical scholars whose work argued for the true expression of those ideals.

## HISTORY OF RACE THINKING AND RACISM

The fundamental context for the rise of race thinking, and of racism, was European colonial expansion from the fifteenth century onward – which brought Europeans into closer and more continuous contact with the diversity of humanity throughout the globe. Europeans' thinking about differences arose in a context of domination, and this shaped their beliefs about their own superiority. When they saw people very different to themselves, living in different types of societies, following different customs and laws, looking very different physically, sometimes living in situations with very little technological development (Adas 1989) and closer to nature – what should they make of them? Did they have souls? Were they even human like Europeans? Or were these so-called 'savages' somehow sub-human – more like apes, for example? Why did some of these peoples not read or write? Why did they live so differently? In some cases, why did they seem to live in lawless, brutal societies? (Adas 1989; Arendt 1986).

Throughout history, groups have thought about who they were by virtue of images of, and relations with, 'others'. In a dialectic of self and other, representations of the Other are always at the same time representations of the self (Miles 1989). Drawing upon an earlier European contrast between the 'wild man' and the 'civilized European', under the influence of puritan forms of Christian repression of sensuality the European self was counterposed to the wild man who came to represent untamed and aggressive sexuality. In the colonial encounter, these images of the wild man were then associated with black Others (Miles 1989, p. 20).

One of the prominent intellectual obsessions of Europeans in the eighteenth century had been the problem of physical differences between people and how these could be explained. The age of exploration and expansion had intensified this concern. Yet religion, especially Christianity, still fundamentally shaped European views of non-European others in the eighteenth century; there was a need to reconcile physical and cultural differences between peoples with the biblical/Judeo-Christian doctrine of the descent of humanity from two common parents (for a comprehensive account of the relationship between biblical and other religious myths and racism, see Hannaford 1996, Ch. 4). Thus, for theologists, the Tower of Babel and other biblical myths about the Canaanites or the sons of Ham were used to explain the different appearances, and especially colour differences, between peoples. For scientists in the eighteenth century, the unity of 'man' (humanity) was still sacrosanct; differences could be explained by the impact of different environments. To argue for different species of 'man', even in the late eighteenth century, could be politically dangerous and opened one to the accusation of atheism and blasphemy (Gossett 1997, pp. 33–34, 44).

In understanding the modern emergence of racism, some theorists have pointed to the secularisation or disenchantment of the West, and of the related rise of a 'mechanistic' world view. This broad shift had important implications for the development of different sciences, releasing them from biblical strictures. The study of animal, plant and human life – which came to be known as biology (the term was invented in Germany around 1800; Appiah 2019a, p. 111) – and the systems of classification produced out of such study were central to the development of racism. Some authors have argued that racism is a part of the rationalisation process that Max Weber saw as the underlying central feature of modernity (Rubenstein 1975; Bauman 1989). The processes of distantiation/bureaucratisation, of making things abstract, codifying social life into smaller manoeuvrable and modifiable units that Weber analysed made racism possible (Goldberg 1993).

Thinkers in the eighteenth century were obsessed with classification (Adas 1989) – of both the natural world and also of different types of humanity – and this was the beginning of early modern racial thinking, as scientists attempted to place different human populations into different categories. They also tried to show where the true differences lay – was it about colour, head shape, physical size, intelligence and aspects of character (for example, were some races more emotional or less emotional?).

Carl Linnaeus (1707–1778), an eighteenth-century Swedish taxonomist and a trained physician, who was also strongly religious and believed that he could find a natural order to everything in the universe from the simplest to the most complex structures, produced one of the early scientific classifications of human variety. In his famous 1735 text, *Systema Naturae* (Linnaeus 1935, known in English as *System of Nature*), he did not use the term race, but instead the scientific terms *genus*, *species*, and *varietas* (Banton 2015, p. 13). He believed in biblical descent, and thus that the different varieties of humans (as mentioned, he did not call these races) that he classified had all come from the one initial source: Adam and Eve. The varieties became distinct from each other through interaction with different natural situations. There were seven varieties of the species *homo sapiens*: six diurnal – *ferus* (four-footed, mute and hairy), *americanus* (red, choleric, erect), *europeaus* (white, ruddy, muscular), *asiaticus* (yellow, melancholic, inflexible), *afer* (black, phlegmatic, indulgent), and *monstrosus* (included dwarfs, giants, and lazy Patagonians). There was one nocturnal variety – *Homo sylvestris* (troglodytes or cave-dwellers, orangutan). From this description by Linnaeus, it is clear that, in the late eighteenth century, the line between man and apes could not be easily drawn – and, for many, it was not clear which side of this line the so-called 'pygmies' and 'Hottentots' of the African continent inhabited (see Banton 1998, p. 20). The skin colour of the four main varieties, europeaus, americanus, asiaticus, and afer, were the result of different climates, not different origins, and skin colour for Linnaeus did not point to essential difference; these four varieties were also repeated in racial science in the nineteenth century, but with conclusions about race separation and permanence of type that Linnaeus did not share (Müller-Wille 2015).

Though Linnaeus did not explicitly refer to these different varieties as belonging to a hierarchy, his use of terms to describe them implied superiority and inferiority – and this is certainly the way that his varieties were later taken up by anthropologists of race, as was his distinction between skin colours mapping on to these varieties (Müller-Wille 2015). The descriptions in the tenth edition of *System of Nature* (published in 1758) were more elaborate, describing types of character, emotion and relationship to governance. Europeaus was described in more positive terms, and afer or Africanus in much more negative terms. However, his varieties were fluid, and his notations suggest that he kept changing his mind about the descriptions, including adding some very negative descriptions of some subvarieties of white Europeans, like Swedes, and some very positive description of Americanus (Native Americans), under the influence of images of the noble savage (Müller-Wille 2015).

Other important taxonomists included Comte de Buffon who, in 1749, used the term 'race' in his classification, but the meaning of race was not much different to variety, and he also described these varieties existing within a unified human species (Smedley 2007, p. 171). He proposed the varieties Laplanders (the Polar Race), Tartars or Mongolians, southern Asiatics, Europeans, Ethiopians, and Malays. Their physical differences had emerged through migration to different climates, and also the effects of different cultures on physical attributes (Smedley 2007, p. 171).

Blumenbach, a German anatomist known as the father of anthropology, is important for racial thinking especially because of the racial categories (initially described as varieties, and only later as 'races') that he established, and that became standard classifications repeated in many later typologies. In his famous book *On the Natural Variety of Mankind* (1775) Blumenbach postulated five types – Caucasian, Mongolian, Ethiopian, American and Malayan – but these different kinds of humans only differed in degree; they were all part of a unified human species – the types (later 'races') were not separate creations but had diverged from each other over time. And though Blumenbach did not arrange the different human types/races into a definite hierarchy, his own cultural prejudices were evident in some of his descriptions; for example, he described the ideal type of the white 'Caucasian' as the most beautiful of the races and the original form from which the other races diverged or degenerated (Fredrickson 2002, pp. 56–57). It was Blumenbach who claimed that the white, Caucasian type had its origins in the Caucasus (in Russia) and spread outwards from there (Gould 1996); in other words, that humans had initially been white, but had become other races with different skin colours through interaction with different climates. It was Blumenbach's general classification that stuck among later racial thinkers and racial scientists.

As the eighteenth century gave way to the nineteenth century, scientific thinkers started to free themselves of biblical prescriptions; eventually, this allowed thinkers to argue against the unity of humanity (humans were not all descended from Adam and Eve). In the nineteenth century, race theories developed alongside the development of biological science, and its sub-branch physical anthropology. Other knowledges fed into racism: aesthetics and pseudosciences, such as physiognomy, craniology and phrenology, were drawn upon by racist thinkers to prove claims of inherent superiority and, later (e.g., as in eugenics), of superior health of particular 'races' (Mosse 1978; Banton 1998).

In terms of the development of racism one of the crucial doctrines that gained prominence in the early decades of the nineteenth century was that of 'polygenism', which gradually came to replace 'monogenism', and other popular notions of the unity of the human species. Polygenism argued that the different races had emerged from distinct biological pools; thus, the belief in the common parents of biblical lore was, for some thinkers, undermined. Though this theory did not necessarily stipulate the racial superiority of any one group, it was important mainly because, as Hannah Arendt has argued, it 'arbitrarily isolated all peoples from one another by the deep abyss of the physical impossibility of human understanding and communication'. It also fuelled the fear of miscegenation, since the 'hybrids' formed through a mixing of races were not truly human beings as they did not belong to a single race; they were 'a kind of monster whose "every cell is a theater of civil war"' (Arendt 1986, pp. 177–178). For some polygenists, 'full-blooded' 'Negroes' and other non-whites were not human either (Gossett 1997, p. 54).

A further development of racism came in the latter half of the nineteenth century, with the rise of social Darwinism, which superseded polygenism in public opinion. This was a contradictory movement of social thought (Banton 1977, Ch. 5), but in the hands of some of its 'scientific' practitioners it provided clearer, more direct, and firmer proof of a racial hierarchy, in which Europeans positioned themselves at the superior level. It entailed notions of progress and of the survival of the fittest (coined by Herbert Spencer in his *The Principles of Biology*, from 1864), which were at once both a justification and an explanation for the experiences of imperialism and colonisation. Moreover, it even gave a moral fervour to the active overthrowing of one 'inferior' race by a 'superior' one. This theory built on the older theory of the Great Chain of Being (which had its roots in Ancient Greece and reached its full flowering in the seventeenth and eighteenth centuries) and Linnaeus' immense classificatory scheme. The Great Chain of Being and Linnaean classification had been fervently embraced by many intellectuals in the eighteenth century in their efforts to reintroduce system, order and hierarchy during a period of turmoil and massive social upheaval. Under the influence of Christianity, all human beings had tended to be set on the same level within the Great Chain, between beasts and godly creatures as creations of God. But the widespread enthusiasm for the principles of fixity, gradation, hierarchy and natural order entailed by the Great Chain in the late eighteenth century laid the groundwork for the view of racial hierarchy embraced in the nineteenth century, once the view of the unity of man, and the explanation of Creation in Genesis, came under sustained attack. Under the influence of revolutionary upheaval and the reaction to it, the debate on slavery, which focused attention on the character of the 'Negro', the search for the source of nationhood and for what held a given community together, and the development of science (especially biology and, in the second half of the nineteenth century, social Darwinism and eugenics), this understanding was transformed into the view of a hierarchy of biologically defined and fixed races (Lovejoy 1971; Jordan 1969, Ch 6; Gossett 1997; Arendt 1986; Miles 1989, pp. 31–35). As Jordan (1969, p. 228) wrote in *White Over Black*, it 'was no accident that the Chain of Being should have been most popular at a time when the hierarchical arrangement of society was coming to be challenged'.

Imperialism (which intensified as a system across the globe as the mood of expansionism gripped Europe in the late eighteenth century), the European experience in Africa and America, the immense struggle, conflict and moral dilemmas involved in the slave trade – all these contributed to the shaping of the Enlightenment view of the 'equality of all men', meaning the equality of all white men, situated at the top of the hierarchy of unequal races (Mills 1997).

In this respect the argument concerning the link between the collapse of feudal society and the rise of racism (including racial anti-Semitism) has explanatory power. The movement for equality and the 'natural rights of man' proclaimed in the French and American revolutions, came hard up against the fact of imperial domination of 'coloured' populations, including slavery. As Louis Hartz (1964) argued in *The Founding of New Societies*, where feudal society could accommodate the repression of whole groups of people as belonging to categories within a hierarchy without recourse to a concept like race, the more open, and ostensibly less hierarchical, post-feudal society produced a compelling need to find arguments to support the repression of such categories of people – if such dominative social structures were to persist (see also Todorov 1986). The Enlightenment concern with rationality instantiated the subject of reason as *the* human subject. Rationality distinguished the human from the brute. The level of rationality could be inferred from the level of cultural and technological development—or civilisation—achieved by a given people. Scales of humanity, as I argued above, had become widely accepted by the late eighteenth century. This opened the way, in the light of pervasive images and perceptions of other, usually conquered, coloured peoples, for the key Enlightenment and liberal utilitarian thinkers to fall prey to the assumptions of racism when accounting for, and even justifying, the subjection and exploitation of other non-European peoples (Poliakov 1982). The greatest happiness of the greatest numbers—the key axiom of utilitarians—meant something different when non-European peoples were added to the equation. Their happiness counted for less than that of their more rational and enlightened counterparts (Goldberg 1993, pp. 26–28).

Reflecting on the long period of European colonial imperialism from the fifteenth century onward, involving the development of a massive slave trade, Winant (2001, p. 49) has written: 'By the early eighteenth century the existence of a divided, racialized world, a word system distinguishing systematically between persons and slaves, between Europeans and "others", between white and non-white, was a generally acknowledged, comprehensive phenomenon.' Racism was embroiled in imperialism; it also came to the fore as both the justification for the brutal age of high imperialism, and as an explanation for the 'shattering experience' of contact with black Africa. Hannah Arendt has argued that, if not for the terrible deeds of Europeans during the scramble for Africa in the nineteenth century, racial thinking might have evaporated from the European mind. But Europeans as moral beings had to find suitable justifications for their own brutality; to this end, the vision of racial superiority, and the perception of Africans as less than human, were irresistible and compelling temptations (Arendt 1986, pp. 183–184). The European flight from guilt, one might argue, exacerbated projective processes and European aggression; a guilt so powerful that it drove a vicious cycle of extreme idealisation of the European self, and denigration of non-European others.

The European experiences in Africa were shocking in other ways too. The 'dark tribes' were somehow inexplicable and, from a European perspective, thoroughly degraded—a naked, godless Other. Blackness had symbolised evil, death and the satanic for centuries among Europeans, especially among the English (see Smedley 2007). This chain of meaning was offloaded onto dark-skinned peoples; dark skin was for many Europeans repulsive, and reverberated with fantasies of sin, evil and uncontrolled impulses. Whiteness symbolised purity and restraint. Authors like Frantz Fanon and Joel Kovel, working from a psychoanalytically informed historical and social perspective, have argued that, for the European, these peoples represented an irreconcilable otherness that European culture had, over the course of centuries, suppressed within itself and from which it sought to flee. At the same time, dark-skinned peoples represented, for the European, a state of instinctual freedom to which he or she *unconsciously* desired to 'return'. 'The civilized white man', Fanon (1968, p. 165) argued, 'retains an irrational longing for unusual eras of sexual license, of orgiastic scenes, of unpunished rapes, of unrepressed incest.' A rigid division between the intellectual and the sexual in Western cultures – most evident in Puritanism – was reproduced in different forms, in divisions between culture and nature, or civilisation and savagery. White Europeans needed to believe in these divisions because of the peculiarity of their cultural development and instinctual renunciation (Kovel 1970, 1995). They projected their own fears of disintegration, of lapsing back into a 'primitive state', onto native others. Colonisers viewed the 'natives' as hardly separable from nature at all, equating their apparently different relationship to nature with being not-quite-human – as if what defined being human was a vigorous separation from, and hostility towards, a nature that must be subdued and dominated (Arendt 1986, p. 192).

Racism provided emotional and identity certainty when all certainties had been undermined during the period of massive upheaval in Europe and the colonised regions from the fifteenth century onward. Moreover, the emergence of racism was closely tied to the development of national consciousness (Balibar 1991). Mosse (1978, p. 94) has argued that, especially in central Europe, 'the language and history of the people was used to explore its racial origins, and the virtues of a race were ascribed to the qualities of its roots'. The sources for racism were always much deeper than the intellectual probings and postulations of science. Races, like nations, were meant to have mythological and spiritual roots lost in the mists of time. Races, like nations, were timeless. Racists, though drawing sustenance from scientific explanations where these were useful, would never be held by scientific rigor. In the last decades of the nineteenth century and the early decades of the twentieth century, racism was, for some individuals and political movements, a mystical national religion (Mosse 1978, pp. 94–95).

This was certainly true of the influential racist theorists such as the Frenchman Comte de Gobineau who, in his widely read mid-nineteenth century work *The Inequality of Human Races* (de Gobineau 1915), saw race as the major explanation of history and of the rise and fall of civilisations, and lamented the decline of the white race through race mixing. Houston Stewart Chamberlain, a virulent anti-Semite, proselytized a spiritual, mystical racism combined with social Darwinism. His work *Foundations of the Nineteenth Century* (first published in German in 1900) sold over 200,000 copies, and he became a fundamental author read by many Nazis, including Hitler (Mosse 1981, Ch. 5; Chapoutot 2015). Such figures, however, were anti-Enlightenment and anti-modernity.

The historian Patrick Wolfe (2016) has argued that colonialism, in varying forms, produced different racial regimes and different categorisations of races. His broad framework was 'land and labour', which resulted in distinctive ways of racialising. African American slaves in the USA, wanted for their labour in plantation colonialism, maintained their black race status even through mixed descent; they were a continuously self-replenishing labour force for the slave-holding society. However, the Indigenous people subject to settler-colonialism and its strategies were typically surplus in terms of labour – it was their land that was wanted and stolen, setting up a 'logic of elimination', expressed, for example, in claims about the absorbability of Native American or Australian Aboriginal blood into the 'white race', and subsequent strategies for absorption and assimilation that would remove them as a distinct people and their claims to sovereignty. As Wolfe (2016, p. 5) argues, 'race is colonialism speaking, in idioms whose diversity reflects the unequal relationships into which Europeans have co-opted conquered populations'. Race and racial regimes have spread across the world, but they are a European invention.

## RACIAL CAPITALISM

The argument outlined above about colonialism and racism, and its periodisation, is also about the rise and global expansion of capitalism. This raises an important question. Is capitalism by its very nature racial or racist? Marx, and associated Marxist critics of capitalism, have not developed convincing theories about racism and, in fact, racism has not typically been central to their critique (but see Miles 1982). There is an assumption among Marxist theorists that capitalism, as a transformative and revolutionary force, sweeps away 'fixed' and particularistic identities, and identities and categories of race would also fit this scenario, as people are drawn into a homogeneous mass of proletarian workers experiencing 'free wage labour'. According to African American critic and advocate of the theory of racial capitalism, Cedric Robinson, 'racialism' has been a central feature of social organisation in Western civilisation since the feudal period, and Marxism has 'little or no theoretical justification . . . for . . . [its] existence' (Robinson [1983] 2000, p. 2). One Marxist assumption has been, for example, that racism is a ruling-class strategy to divide the working class. Robinson argues that capitalism developed as racial capitalism. Race was not an accidental addition to capitalism's expansion, but central to it. For example, he notes that 'the Atlantic slave trade and the slavery of the New World were integral to the modern world economy' and that their 'relationship to capitalism was historical and organic rather than adventitious or synthetic' (Robinson [1983] 2000, p. 4).

Charting the fitful rise of capitalism during the feudal period of Europe, he argues for the way that it involved racialisation of groups marked out for different forms of exploitation within the economic and social system (Robinson [1983] 2000, p. 26):

> The tendency of European civilization through capitalism was thus not to homogenize but to differentiate – to exaggerate regional, subcultural, and dialectical differences into 'racial' ones. As the Slavs became the natural slaves, the racially inferior stock for domination and exploitation during the early Middle Ages, as the Tartars came to occupy a similar position in the Italian cities of the late Middle Ages, so, at the systemic interlocking of capitalism in the sixteenth century, the peoples of the Third World began to fill this expanding category of a civilization reproduced by capitalism.

One of Robinson's main arguments, then, is that 'racial ordering' was a key and long-standing feature of European civilisation for many centuries (including the deeply racialised feudal order, in his view) and that it therefore was integral to the capitalist economic and social relations that gradually developed and expanded across the globe. Race was thus not a super-structural phenomenon, but rather intrinsic to the economic system of capitalism as it developed; it was not simply a political tactic of divide and rule, but fundamentally a key structural organisation that produced capital accumulation. Whereas Marx and, later, Marxists concentrated on the relation between capital and 'free labour' as the central dynamic of capitalism, ignoring the race dimensions of capitalism, Robinson argued instead that transatlantic slavery and other exploitation of black and Third World labour were central structural features of capitalism and intrinsic to its success as an economic system (see also Fraser 2016). And, in the view of many later critics who have taken up the argument about racial capitalism, including social movements like Black Lives Matter, race remains central to the capitalist economy the world over; capitalism is fundamentally an economic system that relies upon and works through racial categorisation. As one such critic has recently written, 'the capitalist economy is constituted by a racial logic' (Issar 2021, p. 58):

> Instead of separating analyses of capitalism, particularly capital's logic, from analyses of racial domination, it is necessary to grasp the ways the capitalist world system, since its inception, has been powered by a racialized dialectic of exploitation and expropriation. From this perspective, racial domination structures capital's violence, and is visibly expressed in the exploitation and expropriation dialectic, the social division of labor, and the creation of . . . 'global surplus humanity'.
>
> (Issar 2021, p. 63)

## IS 'MODERNITY' INEVITABLY RACIST?

It has been established that race and racism were European inventions of the past few hundred years, with terrible effects within societies and globally, especially for those deemed inferior races. I want to confront here a question that is not only an intellectual one, but one that has important political implications, including for the prospects of anti-racism. Is the Enlightenment, and Western thinking more generally, and the modernity that it gave rise to and shaped, so enmeshed with racism that it can never be disentangled from its racist origins? Thus, is the Western thinking associated with the Enlightenment *fundamentally* white racial thinking, irrevocably tied to white supremacism? Or did Western thinking – including understandings of the role of reason and science, democracy, liberty and equality and, by extension, modernity – also provide resources that challenged racism? Is modernity itself inevitably racist, and thus can racism as a system only ever be overcome if the main structures of modernity and its main patterns of thought are dismantled? Some critiques of racism in the 1980s and 1990s, and also more recent decolonising theory, would seem to suggest that the answer is yes – that modernity itself must be in some way overcome.

For example, Zygmunt Bauman (1987, 1989, 1992) argued in some of his writing that modernity and racism were inextricably interwoven. Not only was racism a *normal* feature of modernity, but it also expressed the very ethos and spirit of modernity, which was a 'gardening culture' that looked for weeds (races) which were weeded out in pursuit of perfectible society (indicating the incredible hubris of modernity in terms of its belief in its capacity to transform human society according to a utopian vision). Racist genocides like the Holocaust and other genocides of the twentieth century did not betray the modern ethos – they 'were the most consistent, uninhibited expression of that spirit' (Bauman 1989, p. 93). This would suggest that modernity could not provide the resources to overcome racism; but Bauman provided no account of where such resources might come from – for example, other modes of non-Western thought – and also had no comment on the prospects of anti-racism.

There are also arguments that see modernity and Enlightenment themselves as intrinsically racist. Winant (2001, p. 19), in *The World is a Ghetto,* posits that race was the central structuring element of modernity:

> Race has been a constitutive element, an organizational principle, a praxis and structure that has constructed and reconstructed world society since the emergence of modernity, the enormous historical shift represented by the rise of Europe, the founding of modern nation-states and empires, the conquista, the onset of African enslavement, and the subjugation of much of Asia.

Winant argues against thinking about 'race' as a side product of something else (class would be an example). Instead, he sees race as 'a key causative factor in the creation of the modern world. Imperialism's creation of modern nation-states, capitalism's construction of an international economy, and the Enlightenment's articulation of a unified world culture, I argue, were all deeply racializing processes' (Winant 2001, p. 19). And though he says he is not a racial determinist – race does not underlie and explain everything about the modern world – on the other hand, 'Modernity . . . is a global racial formation project' (Winant 2001, p. 20). He then sets out to 'show how, from the dawn of the modern world to the middle of the twentieth century, the ongoing dilemmas of democratization, economic equality, and the recognition of human distinctiveness continue to be deeply shaped by racial logic' (Winant 2001, p. 22). Furthermore:

> To the extent that it deployed cultural instrumentalities – of inter-pretation, of representation, of identification that made use of racial discourse – modernity was a culturally based racial project as much as it was an economically and politically based one. To iden-tify human beings by their race, to inscribe race upon their bodies, was to locate them, to subject them, in the emerging world order.
>
> (Winant 2001, p. 30)

Winant also has an argument that, while there was resistance and racial reform in the twentieth century, 'white supremacy' survived, and perhaps in some ways became stronger: 'it could be said to have gained some real new strength from the very racial reforms that it had been forced to initiate' (Winant 2001, p. 33). The argument here is about the powers of 'color-blind racism' (see my longer dis-cussion of this in Chapter 5) to provide new, powerful forces for the continuation of white racial supremacy:

> The rearticulation of (in)equality in an ostensibly color-blind framework emphasizing individualism and meritocracy, it turns out, preserves the legacy of racial hierarchy far more effectively than its explicit defence . . . Similarly, the reinterpretation of racialized differences as matters of culture and nationality, rather than as fundamental human attributes somehow linked to pheno-type, turns out to justify exclusionary politics and policy far better than traditional white supremacist arguments can do.
>
> (Winant 2001, p. 35)

Winant argues that after the achievements of the civil rights and decolonisation movements, anti-racism has been stalled – in part because of claims that racism has already been overcome – in the colour-blind arguments in the US, the '"non-racialist" rhetoric of the South African Freedom Charter', the claim about 'racial democ-racy' in Brazil and racial differentialist arguments in Europe. The vison of racial justice has also stalled globally (Winant 2000, p. 183). He is pessimistic that 'race' will ever be transcended, or that the world will ever move beyond race, though he retains some hope that racial stratification might one day become a less prominent feature of the world, that hierarchy will become less salient, and that racial injustice and inhumanity might become less blindly accepted. Here he suggests that 'race' could be just one element, like religion or language, as an accepted 'part of the human condition' (Winant 2000, p. 183).

Goldberg (1993), in *Racist Culture*, also provided a trenchant critique of modernity for its inextricable link with racism. In a reading of key Enlightenment figures, he argues that ideas about equality and reason were always, inherently, exclusionary – sections of humanity were deemed irrational or less rational than their white European counterparts, and thus not deserving of equal treatment. In fact, he argued, the discourse of equality produced the discourse of races. This argument draws upon a similar argument made by authors including Hartz (as discussed above), who discussed the way that race was invented as feudal society broke down, as a way to produce and justify new hierarchies in an imperial and colonising world that was emerging around a series of centralised European nation-states, to control the spread of equality to all peoples, and to justify new forms of colonial domination. The relationship between modernity and racism ran deep – to the very underpinning precepts of modernity's 'discursive formation' (as per Foucault):

> the preconceptual elements or primitives of racialized discourse and of the conditions, implications, and practices that they inform are embedded in social discourses central to and legitimised by practices and relations constitutive of modernity . . . [These include] . . . classification, order, value and hierarchy; differentiation and identity, discrimination and identification; exclusion, domination, subjection, and subjugation; as well as entitlement and restriction.
>
> (Goldberg 1993, p. 49)

Decolonising theory, which has become increasingly prominent in the last decade or so, but also has its sources in works by writers such as Frantz Fanon (1968, 1971) and Aimé Césaire (1972), has been understandably hypercritical of the West, sometimes resulting in a complete disavowal of 'Western thinking' and of any positive side to modernity, which is instead seen as an unmitigated disaster, especially for colonised peoples, including Indigenous people. Lakota author Vine Deloria Jr provided early versions of this argument in works such as *Custer Died for Your Sins* (Deloria Jr 1969), where he vigorously critiqued Western civilisation and advocated the teaching of Indigenous traditions, religions, epistemologies and world views to young Indigenous people, which, he argued, were in important ways superior to Western thinking and civilisation. In *God is Red*, Deloria Jr (1973) argued that the Indigenous world view was incommensurable with much of Western science and religion, and he went on in other works to challenge the very metaphysical bases of Western thought (1979, 1997, 1999). It was racism and colonialism that stood behind Western refusals to accept the validity of other non-Western knowledges, he argued (Deloria Jr 1997, Ch. 2). Indigenous Australian scholar Eileen Moreton-Robinson (2004) has also posited incommensurability between Indigenous knowledge and epistemologies and white knowledge and epistemologies, whose universalism she rejects. A recent article from an Indigenous Australian scholar Yin Paradies (2020) engages in a complete dismissal of modernity, arguing for an overcoming of modernity as the only political stance that would make possible planetary survival. Citing a series of devastating statistics related to people and climate, he claims that it is crucial to engage in 'truth telling' that:

> means telling the unsettling truth about the dangers of modernity for global life, including its deeply atrophied capacity to provide people with a collective existential purpose. . . . An understanding of modernity's wrongs means not only knowledge of its past impacts but also apprehending how it continues to destroy our present/futures, and then acting to prevent this in ways that are more than merely metaphorical.
>
> (Paradies 2020, p. 439)

There are, however, powerful critics of modernity and Enlightenment figures who have sought to retain some kind of emancipatory vision of the Enlightenment, and of the possibilities contained within strands of modernity.

The philosopher Charles W. Mills (2008) has argued that we need to rethink the whole Western philosophical tradition by directly confronting the powerful ways that it was shaped and constructed by racism. In particular, he critiques the dominant doctrines of liberalism, arguing that 'racism is not an anomaly in an unqualified liberal universalism but generally symbiotically related to a qualified and particularistic liberalism' (Mills 2008, p. 1382). He has argued that the 'social contract' was always a 'racial contract' – the key Enlightenment, liberal thinkers never imagined an equal humanity, but instead envisaged a world of equality for white men, and forms of unequal treatment and domination of other, coloured peoples. This is not surprising, given that this thinking emerged in close association with, and often directly supporting, Western colonialism and imperialism: 'Racism, racial self-identification, and race thinking are then not in the least "surprising", "anomalous", "puzzling", incongruent with Enlightenment European humanism, but *required* by the Racial Contract as part of terms for the European appropriation of the world' (Mills 1997, p. 122; italics in original.).

Mills makes a powerful case, arguing that the racial contract has underpinned Western societies and supported white supremacy, and that it developed various strategies that blinded these societies, especially once racism was challenged, to their own histories of racism, and their refusal to give up the immense privileges and power of white supremacy. The whole Western tradition, the West's conquest of the rest of the world, and its continuation of economic and military domination of the world, need to be understood as racial conquest. Race, Mills argues, needs to become the central concept in political theory: 'Political theory is in part about who the main actors are, and for this unacknowledged polity they are neither the atomic individuals of liberal thought nor the classes of Marxist theory but races' (Mills 1997, p. 113).

Though Mills is a strong critic of the Enlightenment as an instigator of the Racial Contract and white domination of the world, he is not on the other hand anti-Enlightenment. He broadly accepts Habermas' (1987) position on the unfinished project of the Enlightenment and modernity, while strongly criticising Habermas for his race blindness and silence. He is 'pro-Enlightenment' and 'anti-postmodernist', aiming at creating a world that achieves 'racial justice'. This is ideology critique, which accepts that there can be a truer picture of the world, revealed through critique and argument (Mills 1997, p. 129). He considers the racial contract as revelatory theory:

> The 'Racial Contract' throws open the doors of orthodox political philosophy's hermetically sealed, stuffy little universe and lets the world rush into its sterile white halls, a world populated not

by abstract citizens but by white, black, brown, yellow, red beings, interacting with, pretending not to see, categorizing, judging, negotiating, allying, exploiting, struggling with each other in large measure according to race – the world, in short, in which we actually live.

(Mills 1997, pp. 130–131)

Mills has also argued that white racism has been fundamental as a structure of domination shaping the modern world. He gives it an important place, but does not regard it as the only such structure of domination. Class and gender, which have much longer histories than race, have also been fundamental shaping forces – but race is of particular relevance because, he argues, it is the most modern of the three (Mills 2007, p. 273):

Class and gender as structures of domination and subordination long precede the modern world; it is race that is distinctively modern and that explains, at least in rough outline, the shape of the globe and the nature of its players. Neither class nor gender domination as such explains the most striking fact about modernity: that Europe, Europeans and European settler-states dominate the planet, privileging whites globally, and that racial Self- and Other-identification has been central to the social psychology of the world over the past few hundred years, tending to trump (contra orthodox Marxism) other identities in times of conflict.

Mills also does not claim that the capacity for racism is inherent in white people, and in white people only, and 'there should be no essentialist illusions about anyone's intrinsic "racial" virtue' (Mills 1997, p. 128).

Mills stands in a long line of black dissident intellectuals, trained in Western thinking, but also outsiders and critics, attuned to the unfulfilled promise of the grand narratives of modernity, and yet challenging it, in a sense, also from within, demanding that it hold itself up to its proclaimed ideals of democracy, equality, universality (including universal humanity) and progress. W.E.B. Du Bois, as Paul Gilroy explains, was a major early figure in this line of dissenting black intellectuals, trained thoroughly in Western thinking, a major sociologist using sociological tools to penetrate and undermine the ideological justifications and pretensions of racist societies. Frantz Fanon was another, who, while trenchantly critiquing the racism and exploitation of white racism, and its colonial appropriations, was nevertheless an heir to Western traditions of thinking and argument, and explicitly advocated for a truer, universal humanity, emerging from anti-colonial revolutionary practice:

> Fanon's call for the institution of an anticolonial and nonracial universalism is a significant gesture that reveals his links to the modern political traditions of the western world even in his greatest gestures of disavowal. What is most important about this stance is his insistence that this precious universalism can only be bought at the price of a reckoning with colonial modernity. It takes shape only in the process of facing the antinomies of modernity revealed in social order of the colony, which was emphatically not that of the metropole until the Nazi genocide brought it back home.
>
> (Gilroy 2000, p. 71)

Contemporary figures in that line of dissenters include Gilroy himself and Kwame Anthony Appiah, who describes himself as a child of the Enlightenment. Appiah (2019b) in a recent essay reviewing a book that claims that rationality inherently produces irrationality (with the book thus critiquing the pretension to reason of the Enlightenment), argues that the racism and negative stereotypes voiced by key Enlightenment figures such as Kant, Voltaire, Hume and many others reflect that they were men of their time, in this respect. Of greater interest, he argues, are the strong arguments that they (and many other Enlightenment figures) made against imperialism and slavery at the time that these systems ruled the world (see also Todorov 1986). He also alerts us to the 'Radical Enlightenment', explored in Jonathan Israel's (2002, 2006) history of Enlightenment figures, suggesting that the Enlightenment was a complex phenomenon, with many different thinkers, some holding strong views about the unity of humanity. Similarly, Kenan Malik (2008), also drawing on Israel's history, has pointed out that many members of the Radical Enlightenment were anti-racist in approach, inspired by visions of equality of all humanity, and were also virulently anti-slavery. In addition, many argued that all of humanity was capable of the reason that the Enlightenment so venerated (Malik 2008,

Ch. 4) – thus, contra Goldberg's argument, reason as a concept and vison for humanity was not inevitably constructed out of its opposition to the unreason of the non-white world. Scientific classification and the perception of differences, as a whole way of seeing, did not lead inevitably to racial classification in hierarchies of superiority and inferiority (Malik 2008, p. 84). In a recent article Vartija (2021) has also argued that some theorisation on race among Enlightenment figures cannot be explained by racism, but it reflects an attempt to discuss human varieties in the context of nature and deep time, and it did not always coincide with arguments about inequality of these varieties. Vartija (2021, p. 605) also highlights the complexity of the Enlightenment: 'contrary to detractors and defenders of a certain version of the Enlightenment, the philosophes' reflections on human diversity cannot be reduced to either a racist European supremacy or a straightforward egalitarianism'. In *The Lies that Bind*, Appiah (2019a, p. 115) reminds us of important counter-figures such as Abbé Grégoire 'the great French revolutionary and anti-slavery campaigner' who, in 1808, wrote a book extolling the achievements of black Africans, supporting his claim of the equality of the 'races' and the fundamental unity of all humanity, and which he sent to Thomas Jefferson as a response to Jefferson's famous claim in *Notes on the State of Virginia* ([1785] 2016) that Africans were not capable of high levels of cultural achievement.

## CONCLUSION

This chapter has outlined a case for seeing racism as a modern phenomenon that emerged as a world system of white supremacist domination, historically shaped and created through European colonialism, imperialism, slavery and capitalism. The chapter has discussed the emergence of race thinking and racism, in particular in the eighteenth and nineteenth centuries, and discussed the ambivalent ties to the Enlightenment and to the 'unfinished project of modernity'. As such, racism has been an immense shaping force of the modern world, socially, politically, economically and culturally. As I show in the next chapters, and as we move to contemporary times and ongoing manifestations of racism, this complex phenomenon has many dimensions.

# REFERENCES

Adas, M. 1989, *Machines as the Measure of Men: Science, Technology, and Ideologies of Western Dominance*, Cornell University Press, Ithaca and London.

Appiah, K.A. 2019a, *The Lies That Bind: Rethinking Identity*, Profile Books, London.

Appiah, K.A. 2019b, 'Dialectics of Enlightenment', *The New York Review*, 9 May 2019.

Arendt, H. 1986, *The Origins of Totalitarianism*, André Deutsch, London.

Balibar, E. 1991, 'Racism and Nationalism', in E. Balibar and I. Wallerstein (eds), *Race, Nation and Class: Ambiguous Identities*, Verso, London, pp. 37–67.

Banton, M. 1977, *The Idea of Race*, Tavistock Publications, London.

Banton, M. 1998, *Racial Theories*, 2nd edn, Cambridge University Press, Cambridge.

Banton, M. 2015, *What We Now Know About Race and Ethnicity*, Berghahn Books, London and New York.

Bauman, Z. 1987, *Legislators and Interpreters: On Modernity, Postmodernity and Intellectuals*, Polity Press, Cambridge.

Bauman, Z. 1989, *Modernity and the Holocaust*, Cornell University Press, New York.

Bauman, Z. 1992, *Mortality, Immortality and Other Life Strategies*, Polity Press, Cambridge.

Blumenbach, J.F. 1775, *De Generis Humani Varietate Native Liber [On the Natural Varieties of Mankind]*, in *The Anthropological Treatises of Johann Friedrich Blumenbach and the Inaugural Dissertation of John Hunter*, ed. and trans. Thomas Bendyshe, London: Longman, Green, Longman, Roberts, & Green, 1865, pp. 65–144.

Césaire, A. 1972, *Discourse on Colonialism*, trans. J. Pinkham, Monthly Review Press, New York.

Chapoutot, J. 2015, 'From Humanism to Nazism: Antiquity in the Work of Houston Stewart Chamberlain', *Miranda*, 11, viewed 15 May 2023, http://journals.openedition.org/miranda/6680.

de Gobineau, A. 1915, *The Inequality of Human Races*, trans. A. Collins, William Heinemann, London.

Deloria Jr, V. 1969, *Custer Died for Your Sins: An Indian Manifesto*, University of Oklahoma Press, Norman, Oklahoma.

Deloria Jr, V. 1973, *God Is Red*, Grosset & Dunlap, New York.

Deloria Jr, V. 1979, *The Metaphysics of Modern Existence*, Fulcrum Publishing, Wheat Ridge, Colorado.

Deloria Jr, V. 1997, *Red Earth, White Lies: Native Americans and the Myth of Scientific Fact*, Fulcrum Publishing, Wheat Ridge, Colorado.

Deloria Jr, V. 1999, *Spirit and Reason*, Fulcrum Publishing, Wheat Ridge, Colorado.

Fanon, F. 1968, *Black Skin, White Masks*, MacGibbon and Kee, London.

Fanon, F. 1971, *The Wretched of the Earth*, Penguin Books, Harmondsworth.

Foucault, M. 1978, *The History of Sexuality, Volume 1*, Pantheon Books, New York.

Fraser, N. 2016, 'Expropriation and Exploitation in Racialized Capitalism: A Reply to Michael Dawson', *Critical Historical Studies*, Spring, pp. 163–178.

Fredrickson, G.M. 2002, *Racism: A Short History*, Scribe Publications, Melbourne.

Gilroy, P. 2000, *Against Race: Imagining Political Culture Beyond the Colour Line*, The Belknap Press of Harvard University Press, Cambridge, Massachusetts.

Goldberg, D.T. 1993, *Racist Culture: Philosophy and the Politics of Meaning*, Blackwell, Cambridge, Massachusetts.

Goldberg, D.T. 2002, *The Racial State*, Blackwell, Malden, Massachusetts.

Gossett, T.F. 1997, *Race: The History of an Idea in America*, new edn, Oxford University Press, New York and Oxford.

Gould, S.J. 1996, *The Mismeasure of Man*, revised edn, W.W. Norton, New York.

Habermas, J. 1987, *The Philosophical Discourse of Modernity: Twelve Lectures*, The MIT Press, Cambridge, Massachusetts.

Hannaford, I. 1996, *Race: The History of an Idea in the West*, Washington D.C., The Woodrow Wilson Centre Press, and The Johns Hopkins University Press, Baltimore, Maryland/London.

Hartz, L. 1964, *The Founding of New Societies: Studies in the History of the United States, Latin America, South Africa, Canada, and Australia*, Harcourt, Brace & World, New York.

Herodotus 1972, *The Histories*, revised edn, trans. A. de Sélincourt, Penguin Books, London.

Hirschman, C. 2004, 'The Origins and Demise of the Concept of Race', *Population and Development Review*, vol. 30, no. 3, pp. 385–415.

Israel, J. 2002, *Radical Enlightenment: Philosophy and the Making of Modernity 1650–1750*, Oxford University Press, Oxford.

Israel, J. 2006, *Enlightenment Contested: Philosophy, Modernity, and the Emancipation of Man 1670–1752*, Oxford University Press, Oxford.

Issar, S. 2021, 'Listening to Black Lives Matter: Racial Capitalism and the Critique of Neoliberalism', *Contemporary Political Theory*, vol. 20, no. 1, pp. 48–71.

Jefferson, T. [1785] 2016, *Notes on the State of Virginia*, 2nd edn, John Stockdale, London.

Jordan, W. 1969, *White Over Black: American Attitudes Toward the Negro, 1550–1812*, Penguin Books, Baltimore, Maryland.

Kovel, J. 1970, *White Racism: A Psychohistory*, Penguin, New York.

Kovel, J. 1995, 'On Racism and Psychoanalysis', in A. Elliott and S. Frosh (eds), *Psychoanalysis in Contexts*, Routledge, London, pp. 205–222.

Linnaeus, C. 1758, *Systema Naturae*, 10th edn, 3 vols, Salvius, Stockholm.

Linnaeus, C. 1935, *Systema Naturae*, Schouten, Amsterdam.

Lovejoy, A.O. 1971, *The Great Chain of Being: A Study of the History of an Idea*, Harvard University Press, Cambridge, Massachusetts.

Malik, K. 2008, *Strange Fruit: Why Both Sides Are Wrong in the Race Debate*, One World Publications, Oxford.

Miles, R. 1982, *Racism and Migrant Labour*, Routledge and Kegan Paul, London.

Miles, R. 1989, *Racism*, Routledge, London.

Miles, R. and Brown, M. 2003, *Racism*, 2nd edn, Routledge, London.

Mills, C.W. 1997, *The Racial Contract*, Cornell University Press, Ithaca and London.

Mills, C.W. 2007, 'Critical Race Theory: A reply to Mike Cole', *Ethnicities*, vol. 9, no. 2, pp. 270–281.

Mills, C.W. 2008, 'Racial Liberalism', *PMLA*, vol. 123, no. 5, pp. 1380–1397.

Moreton-Robinson, A. 2004, 'Whiteness, Epistemology and Indigenous Representation', in A. Moreton-Robinson (ed.), *Whitening Race: Essays in Social and Cultural Criticism*, Aboriginal Studies Press, Canberra, pp. 75–88.

Mosse, G.L. 1978, *Toward the Final Solution: A History of European Racism*, J.M. Dent and Sons, London.

Mosse, G.L. 1981, *The Crisis of German Ideology: Intellectual Origins of the Third Reich,* Schocken Books, New York.

Müller-Wille, S. 2015, 'Linnaeus and the Four Corners of the World', in K.A. Coles, R. Bauer, Z. Nunes and C.L. Peterson (eds), *The Cultural Politics of Blood, 1500–1900*, Palgrave Macmillan, Basingstoke, pp. 191–209.

Omi, M. and Winant, H. 2015, *Racial Formation in the United States*, 3rd edn, Routledge, New York.

Paradies, Y. 2020, 'Unsettling Truths: Modernity, (De-)Coloniality and Indigenous Futures', *Postcolonial Studies*, vol. 23, no. 4, pp. 438–456.

Poliakov, L. 1982, 'Racism from the Enlightenment to the Age of Imperialism', in R. Ross (ed.), *Racism and Colonialism: Essays on Ideology and Social Structure*, Martinus Nijhoff Publishers for the Leiden University Press, The Hague, pp. 55–64.

Robinson, C. [1983] 2000, *Black Marxism: The Making of the Black Radical Tradition*, The University of North Carolina Press, Chapel Hill and London.

Rubenstein, R.L. 1975, *The Cunning of History: The Holocaust and the American Future*, Harper and Row, New York.

Smedley, A. 2007, *Race in North America: Origin and Evolution of a World View*, 3rd edn, Westview Books, Boulder, Colorado.

Solomos, J. and Back, L. 1996, *Racism and Society*, Macmillan, Basingstoke.

Spencer, H. 1864, *The Principles of Biology*, vol, 1, William and Norgate, London.

Todorov, T. 1986, '"Race," Writing, and Culture', *Critical Inquiry*, vol. 13, no. 1, pp. 171–181.

Vartija, D. 2021, 'Revisiting Enlightenment Racial Classification: Time and the Question of Human Diversity', *Intellectual History Review*, vol. 31, no. 4, pp. 603–625.

Wilson, R.D. 1957, 'Justifications of Slavery, Past and Present', *The Phylon Quarterly*, vol. 18, no. 4, pp. 407–412.

Winant, H. 2000, 'Race and Race Theory', *Annual Review of Sociology*, vol. 26, no. 1, pp. 169–185.

Winant, H. 2001, *The World is a Ghetto: Race and Democracy Since World War II*, Basic Books, New York.

Wolfe, P. 2016, *Traces of History: Elementary Structures of Race*, Verso, London and New York.

# THE INTERSECTIONALITY OF RACISM, AND OTHER SYSTEMIC THEORIES OF RACISM

Racism, as will be argued in this chapter, is fundamentally systemic – it involves structure, institutions (including legal, political, economic and media) and power, and it is supported by ideology. This is the general approach of the very broad field of critical race theory, which treats race and its meanings, and the ways that race is expressed through laws and institutions, critically. This chapter engages in a broad discussion of 'intersectionality' in the context of these approaches, which have theorised the structural/institutional/systemic nature of racism.

Intersectionality, originating in black feminist thought, has become a powerful concept in the social sciences since the 1990s, sparked by Crenshaw's (1989) use of the term in her famous essay, 'Demarginalizing the Intersection of Race and Sex'. British black feminism theorists Avtar Brah and Ann Phoenix (2004, p. 76) have defined intersectionality as:

> signifying the complex, irreducible, varied, and variable effects which ensue when multiple axis of differentiation – economic, political, cultural, psychic, subjective and experiential – intersect in historically specific contexts. The concept emphasizes that different dimensions of social life cannot be separated out into discrete and pure strands.

The broad framing ideas of this emphasis, with its focus on the multiple and compounding intersecting factors/identity categories

DOI: 10.4324/9781003267690-3

affecting disadvantage and discrimination – race, gender, sexuality, class, age and ableness/disability – are fundamental to any sociology of racism, and thus it is crucial that this is discussed early in this book, as these ideas recur in later analyses, especially when we come to look closely at the intersections of race, ethnicity and nation. As Anthias and Yuval-Davis (1993, p. 2) argue, intersectionality leads to a different understanding of the nature of racisms, and the differential ways that they are experienced, and calls for an alertness to the multiplicity of factors that affect exclusion:

> In our view, the explication of racisms therefore cannot be undertaken purely with reference to ethnic or race phenomena. An adequate analysis has to consider processes of exclusion and subordination in intersection with those of the other major divisions of class and gender as well as processes of state and nation.

This chapter also addresses understandings of racism that emphasise its systemic, structural or institutional nature – as this involves an important reframing of the understanding of racism, and in particular shifts emphasis away from individualistic and psychological views of racism that focus on expressions of prejudice (Song 2014).

## THE CHALLENGE OF INTERSECTIONALITY

Prior to Crenshaw's essay, the main ideas of intersectionality had been articulated in the famous 'The Combahee River Collective Statement' from black feminists, who stated that 'we are actively committed to struggling against racial, sexual, heterosexual, and class oppression, and see as our particular task the development of integrated analysis and practice based upon the fact that the major systems of oppression are interlocking' (Combahee River Collective [1977] 2014, p. 271). Angela Davis (1981) focused on the ways that race, class and gender ('women') intersected, arguing, in a discussion of rape, that 'racism nourishes sexism' and instigates rape (Davis 1981, Ch. 11; quote at p. 177). Davis explained how racism shaped not only black women's experiences of rape, but also the particular forms of black women's rape protest, including their reluctance to fully embrace white women's political protest because of the way that black men were stereotyped as the rapists of white women and had been indiscriminately lynched on the false pretext that they had raped white women, as well as prosecuted in numbers far outweighing white male rapist prosecutions. Audre Lorde in her 1980 lecture 'Age, Race, Class, and Sex: Women Redefining Difference' (republished in Lorde 1984) critiquing white feminism, argued that:

> By and large within the women's movement today, white women focus upon their oppression as women and ignore differences of race, sexual preference, class, and age. There is a pretense to a homogeneity of experience covered by the word sisterhood that does not in fact exist.
>
> (Lorde 1984, p. 110)

From her earliest works, bell hooks also highlighted the intersections between class, racism and sexism. In *Ain't I A Woman*, hooks (1981) argued for the ways that black women are particularly oppressed, historically and in contemporary life, by racism and sexism (patriarchy), by both white men and women under white supremacist capitalist patriarchy, including within class relations organising white households where middle- and upper-class white women were the overseers of working class and, historically, of enslaved black women and domestic servants.

The intersectional approach has been theorised by Patricia Hill Collins in the US, and it also appears in the work of writers from Britain's Centre for Contemporary Cultural Studies (1982) who studied intersections of race, class and gender, most famously in *The Empire Strikes Back,* as well as in the work of Australian sociologists in the 1980s (Bottomley and de Lepervanche 1984). Arguably, intersectional ideas underpin the work of French sociologists like Pierre Bourdieu, especially the intersections of gender, culture and class theorised in works such as *Masculine Domination* (Bourdieu 2001) and *Distinction* (1984) (see Fowler 2003; Emirbayer and Desmond 2015, pp. 346–347).

In her 1989 essay, Crenshaw was mainly concerned with the double failure of white feminist theory and of black liberation, on the one hand to make sense of the centrality of race for black women (lacking emphasis in feminist theory and action) and on the other the centrality of being woman (for black liberation theory and practice). As she argued, the 'focus on the most privileged group members marginalizes those who are multiply-burdened and obscures claims that cannot be understood as resulting from discrete sources of discrimination' (Crenshaw 1989, p. 140). Crenshaw's paper was mainly concerned with discussing how societies and institutions could be reorganised to make sure that the most disadvantaged (in this case black women in the US) were given an opportunity to be equal. Crenshaw's paper focused explicitly on anti-discrimination policy and showed how it failed to deal with the intersection of race and gender by treating the two under different legal regimes, for example in employment. She made use of the metaphor of the intersection – at which black women were structurally situated. This was mainly a structural argument – about how social categories combined in particular ways to oppress people in different ways. In a subsequent paper, she used intersectionality to explore the intersection of race and gender in explaining the particularities of men's violence against black women and other women of colour, showing how this intersection shapes 'structural, political, and representational aspects of violence' (Crenshaw 1991, p. 1244).

The systemic approach is also apparent in Patricia Hill Collins's writings, who argued that 'As opposed to examining gender, race, class, and nation, as separate systems of oppression, intersectionality explores how these systems mutually construct one another' (Collins 1998, p. 63). Collins also recognises that these four systems do not exhaust all that could be included in intersectional analyses, adding that ethnicity, religion, age, and sexuality could also be examined. She explores how family rhetoric is mobilised and supports various types of hierarchies in societies. One example of an intersectional approach to racism is in Collins's argument that the authority relations that pertain to 'normal' families get overlaid and reinforce racist hierarchies:

> The logic of the traditional family ideal can be used to explain race relations. One way that this occurs is when racial inequality becomes explained using family roles. For example, racial ideologies that portray people of color as intellectually underdeveloped, uncivilized children require parallel ideas that construct Whites as intellectually mature, civilized adults. When applied to race, family rhetoric that deems adults more developed than children, and thus entitled to greater power, uses naturalized

ideas about age and authority to legitimate racial hierarchy. Combining age and gender hierarchies adds additional complexity. Whereas White men and White women enjoy shared racial privileges provided by Whiteness, within the racial boundary of Whiteness, women are expected to defer to men. People of color have not been immune from this same logic. Within the frame of race as family, women of subordinated racial groups defer to men of their groups, often to support men's struggles in dealing with racism.

(Collins 1998, p. 65)

Collins also argues that 'family operates as a privileged exemplar of intersectionality' (Collins 1998, p. 69).

Intersectionality has strong roots in resistance and critique pursued by subordinated groups and their social movements (Collins 2011). It also has strong activist roots, and involves theorising from the bottom up (e.g., initially by black feminists), providing also, as Collins argues, useful tools of resistance in pursuit of liberation and social change (Collins et al. 2021). As Collins (Collins et al. 2021) argued, the initial main focus was upon the intersection of racism and sexism, in particular focused on African American women's particular experiences. As the theory developed, the focus also expanded to incorporate other intersecting dimensions of religion, LGBTQI, ability/disability ('ableism') age, residence and so on. Collins (Collins et al. 2021, p. 694) argues that there are four guiding premises of intersectional analyses:

(1) race, class, gender, sexuality, nationality, ethnicity, ability, age, and similar markers of power are interdependent and mutually construct one another; (2) intersecting power relations produce complex, interdependent social inequalities; (3) the social location of individuals and groups within intersecting power relations shapes their experiences within and perspectives on the social world; and (4) solving social problems within a given local, regional, national, or global context requires intersectional analyses.

This powerful approach has been taken up by social movements and activists globally, including among Indigenous activists and thinkers in settler colonies such as Australia and Canada (Twine 2016).

Race formation theorists Omi and Winant, whose work is discussed further on, also recognise the transformative thinking of intersectionality. While 'race' is a master category in the US, in concrete forms of life it never operates on its own:

> It is not possible to understand the (il)logic of any form of social stratification, any practice of cultural marginalization, or any type of inequality or human variation, without appreciating the deep, complex, comingling, interpenetration of race, class, gender, and sexuality. In the cauldron of social life, these categories come together; they are profoundly transformed in the process.
>
> (Omi and Winant 2015, p. 106)

Race as an order of oppression leaks into other forms of oppression and is often a model for them. Race and racism have profoundly shaped US class relations and experiences of work, with the 'reproduction of class inequalities . . . inextricably linked to the maintenance of white supremacy' (Omi and Winant 2015, p. 107). Omi and Winant argue that racism and sexism are interlinked, and that, since slavery, 'racial parallels and racial "crossings" have shaped gender relations' (Omi and Winant 2015, p. 107). For long periods of history, women, though in different ways, depending on class, race and sexuality, have been treated in similar ways to the ways that races were treated and represented. They have been objectified and thoroughly oppressed by white men, chattelised, their labour stolen, treated as property, brutalised and given an insecure human status, and denied access to public life (Omi and Winant 2015, pp. 107). And, as black feminists have shown, black female bodies and sexualities have been represented in particular ways in racist systems, which fundamentally shape their experiences of racism and sexualised, racist violence, as explained above (see hooks 1981).

Similarly, Emirbayer and Desmond (2015, pp. 345–350) have argued that there are different social orders of domination in society, and in their book, *The Racial Order*, they have primarily focused on the racial order of domination, while recognising that in any empirical situation different social orders intersect, and influence and shape each other. Nevertheless, there can still be value in concentrating primarily on the racial order, which is a major order of social domination in many countries, and which has often been either neglected or underplayed in mainstream sociological inquiries. Thus, an intersectional approach to racism does not mean that one has to theorise all the many different orders (and their intricacies) and how they intersect in particular social situations, which can be a mammoth task. Racism can be the primary object of study, while being sensitised to the way that, in any social situation, individuals, groups and communities are subject to multiple forms of domination, and that some people are particularly and multiply affected – for example, if black, lower class, female, gay or trans, and so on through age, disability, etc. Nevertheless, black and Native American scholar France Winndance Twine (2016) has critiqued such an approach for not being intersectional enough, arguing that Emirbayer and Desmond do not thoroughly engage with gender, sexuality, the racial body and class at key points in their analysis, which she argues are central to the racial order, at their analysed levels of interactions, institutions and interstices, and when examining the social psychology/subjectivity of racial order/racism. Though they do discuss the 'racialized body' via the concept of habitus, they have neglected scholarship by race and gender theorists tackling social practices such as 'colourism' (refashioning the body by whitening or darkening, as a result of racism), and also the ways that class shapes the body in racialised habitus.

## INSTITUTIONAL, STRUCTURAL OR SYSTEMIC RACISM

Institutional or structural racism was famously defined by Carmichael and Hamilton (1967) in *Black Power* as the societal racism which allows gross racial inequalities to persist. While institutional racism was supported by 'the active and pervasive operation of anti-black attitudes and practices' (Carmichael and Hamilton 1967, p. 21), it was distinguishable from individual racial prejudices and overt, individual racism. Institutional racism included all acts, and also non-actions, that resulted in the continued reproduction of racial domination – with one white, privileged group dominating the lives of other, non-white groups in their classic formulation. Structural/institutional racism concerned the organisation of racism as a whole, whereby white society acted to systematically discriminate against people with dark skins – reflected in poorer living conditions and poorer opportunities in life. A society continues to be institutionally racist if it does nothing, or does not do enough, to rectify forms of disadvantage based on ethnicity or race.

In their discussion of 'white power', Carmichael and Hamilton (1967) argued that blacks live in a colonial state in the US, and they concluded that black power is needed to free black people from such colonial relations. Black power involves black people asserting their own position, protecting and promoting black community and black culture, establishing and having their own organisations and institutions, even their own political parties. They argued that 'liberal' institutions are 'white institutions', and these cannot be changed adequately from within, thus blacks need to create their own, challenging institutions. They were strongly critical of what they argued was the gently cooperative (with whites) approach of Booker T. Washington, head of the Tuskegee Institute, and, in particular, of his advice that blacks should stay out of direct involvement in politics, concentrating instead on building up their skills (especially trade skills) and their economic base – and that their acceptance into white society would come with this.

After a period in the late 1960s and 1970s when such understandings of the institutional/structural nature of racism had intellectual and public influence and visibility, there was a strong tendency within sociology to focus on racism as ideology. In an influential paper, Bonilla-Silva (1997) argued for a reorientation of the study of racism and proposed his own 'structural theory of racism'. Writing in the late 1990s, he argued that 'most analysts regard racism as a purely ideological phenomenon' (Bonilla-Silva 1997, p. 465), whereas it is fundamentally a structural phenomenon. The prevailing view in the social sciences at that time, he argued, was that racism is a set of beliefs, or an ideology, which results in racial prejudice that might, in turn, lead to racially discriminatory actions (Bonilla-Silva 1997, p. 466). Versions of this approach are also characteristic of Marxist theories of racism, which emphasise how race and class structure social relations, but in the end see class as primary, and racism as the ideology that, for example, divides the working class, thus serving the ruling class. Even in more sophisticated Marxist accounts, in the end, 'racial antagonisms are still regarded as byproducts of class dynamics' (Bonilla-Silva 1997, p. 466). Instead, Bonilla-Silva (1997, p. 469) argued, we needed to ground 'racism in social relations among the races', and thus the focus of studying racism should shift to 'practices' rather than 'mere ideas'.

The argument was, however, ambiguous, due to some confusion about terminology. It seems that Bonilla-Silva was actually arguing for a theory of something he terms more generally as racial phenomena or a racial system, since he himself adopted a restrictive definition of racism as ideology, as in the following quote (Bonilla-Silva 1997, p. 467):

> Although 'racism' has a definite ideological component, reducing racial phenomena to ideas limits the possibility of understanding how it shapes a race's life chances. Rather than viewing racism as an all-powerful ideology that explains all racial phenomena in a society, I use the term racism only to describe the racial ideology of a racialized social system. That is, racism is only part of a larger racial system.

Later in the article he further explains this point as follows, further limiting the concept of racism to a part of the broader ideological apparatus that helps, in some way, to reproduce a racial system or order:

> I reserve the term *racism* (racial ideology) for the segment of the ideological structure of a social system that crystallizes racial notions and stereotypes. Racism provides the rationalizations for social, political, and economic interactions between the races.
>
> (Bonilla-Silva 1997, p. 474)

In Bonilla-Silva's perspective, it is wrong to consider racist beliefs as 'irrational' – and thus something that can be corrected, for example by educating individuals away from racist beliefs. Rather, these beliefs are produced by the racial system, and therefore are functional for that system (see Bonilla-Silva 1997, p. 468).

Bonilla-Silva saw races as real collectivities. Though originally formed via the social construction process known as 'racialisation' that has a historical dimension (it was established at some point in time, for example, to justify oppressive relations), race then gets transformed in new circumstances. Once formed, the groups become 'real': 'After the process of attaching meaning to a "people" is instituted, race becomes a real category of group association and identity' (Bonilla-Silva 1997, p. 472).

Bonilla-Silva's argument also connects to an intersectional approach:

> What are the dynamics of racial issues in racialized systems? Most important, after a social formation is racialized, its 'normal' dynamics always include a racial component. Societal struggles based on class or gender contain a racial component because both of these social categories are also racialized; that is, both class and gender are constructed along racial lines.
>
> (Bonilla-Silva 1997, p. 473)

Racialised systems are systems that are fundamentally structured as hierarchies of race, with dominating and dominated races. He defines 'racialised social systems' as (Bonilla-Silva 1997, p. 474):

> societies that allocate differential economic, political, social, and even psychological rewards to groups along racial lines; lines that are socially constructed. After a society becomes racialized, a set of social relations and practices based on racial distinctions develops at all societal levels. I designate the aggregate of those relations and practices as the racial structure of a society.

More recently, Bonilla-Silva (2014) has argued that, though we might look at surveys of attitudes across time, and at anti-discrimination policies, and think that people are becoming less racist, this does not actually show that society is becoming less racist. Detailing a range of powerful statistics on racial inequality in the American context, he shows that the racial hierarchy continues to exist, and that people of colour continue to be dominated and to suffer disproportionately in many societies and are institutionally oppressed. Racism, Bonilla-Silva argues, involves a fundamental systemic antagonism between dominating whites and dominated others:

> racism forms a social system organized around practices, mechanisms, cognitions, and behaviors that reproduce racial domination. Consequently, racism has a material foundation – Whites, as the dominant race, are invested in preserving the system because they receive tangible benefits, whereas non-Whites fight to change it.

The driver of racial history then is not stupidity, ignorance, or irrationality, but the process of racial contestation.

(Bonilla-Silva 2019, p. 2)

I return again to Bonilla-Silva's theory of racism when I focus on his distinctive account of 'new racism' in Chapter 5.

As already indicated, structural racism is a term that has wide meanings. It is about the ways that society and its institutions systematically discriminate against people from different, non-white racial backgrounds, actively shaping their lives and opportunities. For some theorists of this concept, structural racism does not require privileged white participants in those institutions to necessarily consciously hold what we would think of as racist views, opinions and stereotypes of others (Anthias 1999).

This position was famously argued by Chair Sir William MacPherson in the 1999 MacPherson report in the UK. Steven Lawrence was a young, black British teenager (19 years old) who was stabbed to death in London in 1993 by a group of white racist youths. The inquiry was into the actions of the Metropolitan police force and the Crown prosecutor in responding to the boy's murder, which pointed to a series of serious institutional failures – including careless treatment of Stephen Lawrence's family, and of black witnesses, because they were black and not taken seriously – that MacPherson put down to widespread and embedded forms of discrimination in the police force and in Britain's major institutions. MacPherson, for example, highlighted the widespread and disproportionate practice of police 'stop and searches' of young black men on the street (e.g., disproportionate to street searches of whites). MacPherson defined institutional racism as:

The collective failure of an organisation to provide an appropriate and professional service to people because of their colour, culture or ethnic origin. It can be seen and detected in processes, attitudes, and behaviour which amount to discrimination through unwitting prejudice, ignorance, thoughtlessness, and racist stereotyping which disadvantage minority ethnic people.

(Sir William MacPherson, Report of the Stephen Lawrence Inquiry, 1999; cited in Garner 2004, p. 21)

Nevertheless, those who experience white privilege will, inevitably, be shaped by unconscious biases and beliefs that contribute to the reproduction of structural racism.

In settler-colonial contexts, such as the US, Canada, Australia and New Zealand, the terrible situation of many Indigenous people is fundamentally determined by ongoing institutional/structural racism. At its most general, this means that the whole society, which emerged through colonial expropriation of Indigenous land and the attempted destruction of Indigenous societies, is built on racist foundations that continue to powerfully shape relations between settlers and Indigenous people; that racism against Indigenous people is built into the whole system of society; and also that this contributes to individual racist views about Indigenous people.

Miles and Brown (2003) are critical of some versions of 'institutional racism', which they argue are examples of 'conceptual inflation', in that they include all practices that result in advantage for some groups and disadvantage for other groups (groups usually designated by colour, as white and black) (Miles and Brown 2003, pp. 66–67). Miles and Brown referenced Carmichael and Hamilton, and also sociologists such as Blauner and Wellman, who, they argued, focused on institutional processes of racism and argued for racism to be judged by its effects – the maintenance of racial dominance – rather than by the presence of prejudiced attitudes. They argued that the concept, in both the US and British contexts, is employed too often without analytical rigour, and in many cases was not defined, nor its processes explained (Miles and Brown 2003, pp. 68–69). However, they do not dismiss the usefulness of the concept outright but, instead, argue for its use in a very particular way. They argue that racism is always in a sense 'institutional' because it is a 'social creation' (Miles and Brown 2003, p. 109). They argue for the retention of racist ideology in the definition of institutional racism, which is understood as being evident in at least two ways:

> first, circumstances where exclusionary practices arise from, and therefore embody, a racist discourse but which may no longer be explicitly justified by such a discourse; and second, circumstances where an explicitly racist discourse is modified in such a way that

the explicitly racist content is eliminated, but other words carry the original meaning.

((Miles and Brown 2003, pp. 109–110)

The key requirement is that institutional racism is an 'embodiment' of racist discourse – whether hidden, or explicit, and it is the job of the analyst or critic of racism to show this in studies of institutional racism. In this way, one might, for example, examine the historical formation of a particular racially discriminatory institution, and show that it has continued with its traditional practices, which were originally shaped by racism and even justified by a racist discourse:

> Thus, in order to determine the presence or otherwise of institutional racism, one assesses not the consequences of actions but the history of discourse and its manner and moment of institutionalisation in order to demonstrate that prior to the silence (or transformation), a racist discourse was articulated.
>
> (Miles and Brown 2003, p. 110)

They provide the example of British immigration policies since 1945, which, they argue, are institutionally racist even though their explicit language is not racist and avoids mention of racism. But the hidden intention *was* racist, as indicated by the debates and rationales used to introduce the policies.

## RACIAL FORMATION AND OTHER STRUCTURAL/SYSTEMIC RACISM THEORIES

The broad ideas encapsulated by institutional or structural racism are evident in a series of important theories of racism. In initially developing 'racial formation' theory, Omi and Winant attempted to capture both the institutional and significatory dimensions of racism, as explained in a later essay by Winant:

> the theory of racial formation . . . looks at race not only as the subject of struggle and contest at the level of social structure, but also as a contested theme at the level of social signification, of the production of meanings. By the former we mean such issues as the racial dimensions of social stratification and distribution,

of institutional arrangements, political systems, laws, etc. By the latter we mean the ways in which race is culturally figured and represented, the manner in which race comes to be meaningful as a descriptor of group or individual identity, social issues, and experience. . . . ,

We argue that in any given historical context, racial significa-tion and racial structuration are ineluctably linked. To represent, interpret, or signify upon race, then, to assign meaning to it, is at least implicitly and often explicitly to locate it in social structural terms.

(Winant 1998, pp. 755–756)

Racial formation theory attempted to link '*the micro- and macro-aspects of racial signification and racialized social structure*' (Winant 2000, p. 181; italics in original). In essence, racial formation theory is a soci-ohistorical approach to the continuing creation of racial meanings, racial stratification and racial identities, and their ongoing transfor-mation and sometimes destruction (Omi and Winant 2015, p. 109). 'Racial projects' are crucial to this, as they are enacted by differ-ent racial-ethnic groups in the political contest and conflict over racial matters, including racial hierarchy and stratification, and do the work of linking structure and signification:

Racial projects do both the ideological and the practical 'work' of making these links and articulating the connection between them. *A racial project is simultaneously an interpretation, representation, or explanation of racial identities and meanings, and an effort to organ-ize and distribute resources (economic, political, cultural) along particular racial lines.* Racial projects connect what race *means* in a particu-lar discursive or ideological practice and the ways in which both social structures and everyday experiences are racially *organized*, based upon that meaning. Racial projects are attempts both to shape the ways in which social structures are racially signified and the ways that racial meanings are embedded in social structures.

(Omi and Winant 2015, p. 125; italics in original)

These include anti-racism projects that have contributed to the unfinished project of racial democracy (see my further discussion in Chapter 6). Thus, not all racial projects are 'racist' projects.

Winant argued that, even in an era since World War Two where race has been undermined as a concept, where racism and discrimination have been repudiated by many people and states, and where multiculturalism and anti-discrimination have been promoted by state elites, social theorists needed to account for why racial classification and racial stratification of societies continued. Winant (2000, p. 181) argues that race remains ubiquitous, present 'in both the smallest and the largest features of social relationships, institutions and identities'. Race in the contemporary world is an important feature of politics, in the sense that politics and political movements have been shaped by attempts to deal with the challenges of race, including attempts to overcome racism. Racial formation aims to be comprehensive in approach. It attends to the unstable meanings of race and the experiences of racial identity, forged in political contestation. It involves the contestation of different 'racial projects' that 'combine representational/discursive elements with structural/institutional ones'. Such 'intersections' are viewed 'as iterative sequences of interpretations (articulations) of the meaning of race that are open to many types of agency, from the individual to the organizational, from the local to the global' (Winant 2000, p. 181).

Joe Feagin (2006) has produced what he argues is a different, more convincing 'systemic racism' approach than that provided by racial formation theory, with a central focus on the long-standing 'white racial frame' that shapes race relations, most notably in the US, which is the main context for his analysis (Feagin and Elias 2013). 'Systemic racism' puts white racial groups at the centre of the analysis, as those who set up and benefit from racial hierarchy. It 'refers to the foundational, large-scale and inescapable hierarchical system of US racial oppression devised and maintained by whites and directed at people of color' (Feagin and Elias 2013, p. 936). Systemic racism theory aims to provide a 'materialist' account of white racism in the US, emphasising the socioeconomic and other benefits that the racial system supports for whites (established when the US was founded, and continuing relatively unchanged into the present), at the expense of all others, and the white racial frame that provides the ideological justification and ballast:

In the social history of white Americans' interrelations with Americans of colour, systemic racism has been a foundational and complex reality and included: (1) the many exploitative and discriminatory practices perpetrated by whites; (2) the unjustly gained resources and power for whites institutionalized in the still-dominant racial hierarchy; (3) the maintenance of major material and other resource inequalities by white-controlled and well-institutionalized social reproduction mechanisms; and (4) the many racial prejudices, stereotypes, images, narratives, emotions, interpretations and narratives of the dominant 'white racial frame' designed to rationalize and implement persisting racial oppression.

(Feagin and Elias 2013, p. 937)

The materialist approach, Feagin (2006, pp. 6–7) argues, distinguishes systemic racism theory from racial formation theory:

In racial formation theory there is not enough consideration of the grounding of US society today, as in the past, in the provision of large-scale wealth-generating resources for white Americans; nor is significant attention given there to the intergenerational transmission of these critical material and related social assets.

The white racial frame (Feagin 2013) is a centuries old world view, and it is deeper and more extensive than surface-level racial prejudices. It is a 'perspectival' frame that is held by all whites, who are socialised into it from birth, through their families and widening social circles and networks, and through society's white institutions (see also Feagin 2006, pp. 36–38, 43–46). It operates to understand and order interpersonal relations and also society:

This white racial frame is broad and complex . . . Over time white Americans have combined in it a beliefs aspect (racial stereotypes and ideologies), integrating cognitive elements (racial interpretations and narratives), visual and auditory elements (racialized images and language accents), a 'feelings' aspect (racialized emotions), and an inclination to action (to discriminate).

(Feagin 2013, p. 10)

It is a frame that helps to produce and reproduce racial oppression and is 'a generally destructive world view' (Feagin 2013, p. 10). It is thoroughly embedded in the US's whole set of institutions, and profoundly shapes its economy and access to resources. It has for centuries 'shaped and protected US society's extremely inegalitarian structure of resources and hierarchy of power established by and for whites, particularly elite whites' (Feagin and Elias 2013, p. 937).

In this respect, Feagin and Elias see the continuing power and hegemony of the white racial frame as a challenge to the view of Omi and Winant that such ideological framing has been substantially transformed in the post-civil rights era – it has not been weakened and shifted in a progressive way, Feagin and Elias argue. The white racial frame is also crucially enacted by whites, especially white elites, and Feagin (2006) and Feagin and Elias also see this view as a challenge to approaches that speak of societal or state racial framings (as does racial formation theory) – the systemic racism approach focuses centrally on the role of whites, including in their attempts to protect their racial privilege; there are 'actual white architects and promoters of the USA's systemic racism' (Feagin and Elias 2013, p. 938). In fact, this is one of Feagin and Elias's main claims – that systemic racism needs to be studied with a strong emphasis on the actual, sometimes conscious role, of white racial groups in dominating the racial system, as conscious 'racial rulers' (Feagin and Elias 2013, p. 941).

In a similar way to the way that white families inherit and reproduce privileges down through the generations, key institutions in fields of economics, employment, politics, education and housing, originally set up by and for white people, and excluding African Americans and other racial groupings, continue to reproduce themselves as white institutions across the generations, with white leaders actively maintaining these institutions as reproducers of white privilege (Feagin 2006, pp. 40–43):

> Because of this social reproduction of white-normed and white-controlled institutions, from the 1600s to the 1960s – about 90 percent of this society's existence – whites were the major or exclusive beneficiaries of almost all major programs of government aid and resource support, such as the homestead (land) acquisitions.
>
> (Feagin 2006, p. 41)

Feagin claims to draw much more substantially on the black radical tradition than does racial formation theory – centring the work of key black sociological thinkers who have produced a counter-narrative of racism in the US. These 'counter-system analysts' – such as Du Bois, Oliver C. Cox and bell hooks, among many others – have provided a powerful account of 'racial meanings, social-psychological dimensions of racialized relations, and the power and structural realities of racism' (Feagin and Elias 2013, p. 938). To the extent that there have been any progressive changes to the white suprema-cist racial hierarchy in the US – and, according to Feagin (2006), such changes have been relatively minimal and always powerfully resisted by dominant whites as a unified racial group, compared to the broad persisting racist system that has been in place since North America's foundation, reflecting the system of slavery – these have emerged through the critique and political agitation of radical black intellectuals and social movements. In addition, black theorists from critical race theory are centrally drawn upon, in particular draw-ing on their insights concerning '"property interest in whiteness" and "racial realism"' (Feagin and Elias 2013, p. 938). Feagin and Elias argue that systemic racism theory also adopts a strong intersec-tionalist approach, when 'examining ways that whites of different backgrounds possess different types of racialized power, as well as in examining the intersecting social inequalities/contexts/identities and diverse responses of those targeted by racial and other forms of oppression' (Feagin and Elias 2013, p. 941).

While this approach seeks to highlight the powerful racial inter-ests that stand behind the setting up and perpetuation of the racist system, there is a danger that such a system becomes like a closed circuit that, once set up, is almost impossible to transform. This is a dominant theme in *Systemic Racism*, where time and again Feagin reiterates that the basic racial structure was laid down in the 1600s, and that it has remained in place ever since, as a relatively unchanging system of white over black racial oppression: 'Once in place, racial oppression has had a strong social inertia, remaining a fundamental part of society even when modest or significant modifications are made' (Feagin 2006, p. 34). Feagin's critical approach considers any changes, especially from the civil rights era onwards, as superficial, and as repeating in a slightly different form the system of the past, including the slavery structure. Omi and Winant (2013) argue that this can lead to political defeatism, and also that it unintentionally plays down the powerful agency and impact of black radical intellectuals, activists and social movements, as well as of their white allies. In addition, whites become a homogeneous interest group with very little indication that there may be heterogeneity within a broad white racial category, and also that there may be a range of racial interests at play among whites, even including racial interests in dismantling the white supremacist racist system (Omi and Winant 2013).

Returning explicitly to the theme of intersectionality, while both racial formation theorists such as Omi and Winant and systemic racism theorists such as Feagin and Elias make explicit reference to intersectionality, Wingfield (2013) has criticised both approaches for only doing this superficially. For example, she argues that disparities of wealth need to attend to the gender-shaping of these, in combination with race, noting that black and Latina women are the worst off in terms of wealth inequalities, and also that they face particular forms of state control of reproduction (including access to family planning services, health care and subsidised child care) that significantly disrupt their capacity to accumulate wealth.

Finally, the pioneering work by Philomena Essed (1991) on 'everyday racism' is yet another approach to thinking about systemic racism, with its central focus on micro-macro relations, while retaining a strong focus on the social interactions of everyday life. Essed's work is also underpinned by the position that those who experience racism have unique insights into the often-hidden nature of racism, insights that are not available to the privileged (mainly white) racial subjects in racially dominated societies. Her theory is also intersectional, with a strong focus on 'gendered racism', highlighting how, while 'genderism' and 'racism' have distinct histories, they are also profoundly intersecting, as 'interwoven formations of race and gender' (Essed 1991, quoted in Essed 2002; see also Essed and Muhr 2018).

Essed's (1991) *Understanding Everyday Racism* focused on the reproduction of racism in everyday life, through countless mundane racist and discriminatory acts, gestures and words, and the immense suffering this caused. Essed (2002, p. 202) has referred to this as 'everyday inferiorization', accounts of which had been absent from much racism research, but abundantly outlined in the memoirs, fiction, nonfiction and poetry of black intellectuals and writers. Based on interview research conducted with black women in the US, and with black

Surinamese first-generation immigrant women in the Netherlands, Essed highlighted examples of everyday discrimination such as: the dismissive treatment of people of colour by hotel receptionists, a form of racism that may be invisible to white people (the receptionists themselves and to white bystanders); ubiquitous forms of racist street abuse and avoidance (Essed 2002); widespread use of racial put-downs, considered by perpetrators as jokes but experienced by victims of racism as abusive; the avoidance by white people of people of colour in racially mixed but white-dominated societies (what Joel Kovel (1970) called 'aversive racism'), including avoidance of physical contact in social situations; and not taking people seriously, in a range of contexts including educational and work environments, because of their colour or ethnic/racial background. Through such myriad everyday discriminatory actions, white people contribute to the reproduction of racial hierarchies through their social action, including words and gestures. At the same time, such racist actions occurred because white people grew up in racially hierarchised societies that produced behaviours that were commonsensical, and even unconscious (Essed 1991; see also Essed 2002). Essed argues that the theory of everyday racism highlights the power associated with the global racial formation created by colonialism and imperialism, that lives on in the present, but in context-specific ways, so that everyday racism will be experienced in nuanced ways, depending upon the macro-structures of the societies (Essed 2002). It helps us to see that 'racism is a process involving the continuous, often unconscious, exercise of power predicated on taking for granted the privileging of whiteness (Frankenberg, 1993), the universality of Western criteria of human progress, and the primacy of European (derived) cultures' (Essed 2002, p. 204).

Essed (1991, 2002, p. 208) highlighted three 'mutually dependent' processes by which racism operates in everyday life: 'the marginalization of racial and ethnic groups, the problematization of attributed group characteristics and culture, and the repression of (potential) counter action.' Marginalisation is already framed by the systemic racism of society, but is reproduced in myriad ways in everyday life and in specific ways according to social locations and types of activities: in classrooms, workplaces and restaurants, when shopping and house-hunting or using public transport, when staying at hotels or watching television. Whiteness is the unconscious norm that shapes these marginalising interactions. This also supports the processes by which ethnic and racial others are deemed to be problematic and to have various deficits (in language, dress, 'professionalism', competence, social skills, work ethic, etc.), which directs attention away from the unexamined assumptions and racism of cultures and institutions that frame expectations of right behaviour and evidence of skill and competence, thus also contributing to perpetuation of the gross racial inequalities in education, employment, health and housing. And finally, when people speak up about racism they are ridiculed, undermined, not taken seriously, encouraged to doubt their perceptions of situations, and told that they have been damaged by previous societal structures that are no longer present in society (Essed 2002). Thus, their capacity for resistance is undermined, and the racist status quo maintained.

The focus on the 'everyday' draws upon the concept of 'everydayness' as mundane, repetitive, regular, uniform, familiar, the realm of common sense and taken-for-grantedness, as argued by writers such as Lefebvre and Agnes Heller (Bourabain and Verhaeghe 2021). The domain of the everyday in this sense is central to social order and the reproduction of societies. Majority peoples are socialised into racial scripts and habituated into taken-for-granted racist practices: 'everyday interactions follow scripts that are influenced by society's socio-historic framework' (Bourabain and Verhaeghe 2021, p. 224). Before racism was challenged so dramatically after World War Two, racism could be much more overt and open. As racism became publicly condemned in liberal-democratic societies, which still nevertheless retained racial hierarchies and are systemically racist, racism was reproduced in different, far more subtle and hidden ways, captured by the concept of everyday racism. It is the social relations in which people are embedded that allow for and create everyday racism. In a systematic review of everyday racism research, Bourabain and Verhaeghe (2021) have emphasised the macro-account that is a central feature of Essed's theory, but which is frequently underplayed or neglected. They point out that there is an 'interdependent link between micro-interactions and macro-structures' that is central to Essed's approach (Bourabain and Verhaeghe 2021, p. 221). Essed (2002, p. 203) has explained that her concept of everyday racism 'relates day-to-day experiences of racial discrimination to the macrostructural context of group inequalities represented within and between nations as racial and ethnic hierarchies of competence, culture, and human progress'.

## CONCLUSION

This chapter began by discussing the central concept of intersectionality, which points to the multiple and compounding forms of discrimination that occur in societies of racial domination. Intersectionality sensitises us to the unique positions that people occupy, and the particular forms of discrimination that they face. As discussed in the various accounts of systemic, structural or institutional racism, including in the theories of 'racial formation' (Omi and Winant), 'structural racism' (Bonilla-Silva), 'systemic racism' (Feagin) and 'everyday racism' (Essed), intersectionality has also informed such theories (as it also has the theory of the 'racial order' (Emirbayer and Desmond), which I will discuss in more detail in Chapters 4 and 6). These theories also highlight the structural and material bases of racism as central to what racism is and means. In each of these approaches there is a strong argument about the relationship between structure and racist representation, discourses and practices. The concept of intersectionality also informs the next chapter, where I examine the complex intersections between race, racism, nation and nationalism.

## REFERENCES

Anthias, F. 1999, 'Institutional Racism, Power and Accountability', *Sociological Research Online*, vol. 4, no. 1, viewed 15 May 2023, http://www.socresonline.org.uk/4/lawrence//anthias.html.

Anthias, F. and Yuval-Davis, N. 1993, *Racialised Boundaries: Race, Nation, Gender, Colour and Class and the Anti-Racist Struggle*, Routledge, London.

Bonilla-Silva, E. 1997, 'Rethinking Racism: Toward a Structural Interpretation', *American Sociological Review*, vol. 62, no. 3, pp. 465–480.

Bonilla-Silva, E. 2014, *Racism Without Racists*, 4th edn, Rowman and Littlefield, Lanham, Maryland.

Bonilla-Silva, E. 2019, 'Feeling Race: Theorizing the Racial Economy of Emotions, 2018 Presidential Address', *American Sociological Review*, vol. 84, no. 1, pp. 1–25.

Bottomley, G. and de Lepervanche, M. (eds) 1984, *Ethnicity, Class and Gender in Australia*, Allen & Unwin, Sydney, New South Wales.

Bourabain, D. and Verhaeghe, P.-P. 2021, 'Everyday Racism in Social Science Research: A Systematic Review and Future Directions', *Du Bois Review*, vol. 18, no. 2, pp. 221–250.

Bourdieu, P. 1984, *Distinction: A Social Critique of the Judgment of Taste*, trans. R. Nice, Harvard University Press, Cambridge, Massachusetts.

Bourdieu, P. 2001, *Masculine Domination*, trans. R. Rice, Stanford University Press, Stanford, California.

Brah, A. and Phoenix, A. 2004, 'Ain't I A Woman? Revisiting Intersectionality', *Journal of International Women's Studies*, vol. 5, no. 3, pp. 75–86.

Carmichael, S. and Hamilton, C.V. 1967, *Black Power: The Politics of Liberation in America*, Penguin Books, Harmondsworth.

Centre for Contemporary Cultural Studies 1982, *The Empire Strikes Back: Race and Racism in 70s Britain*, Hutchinson, London; in association with the Centre for Contemporary Cultural Studies, University of Birmingham.

Collins, P.H. 1998, 'It's All in the Family: Intersections of Gender, Race and Nation', *Hypatia*, vol. 13, no. 3, pp. 62–82.

Collins, P.H. 2011, 'Piecing Together a Genealogical Puzzle: Intersectionality and American Pragmatism', *European Journal of Pragmatism and American Philosophy* (Online), III-2, pp. 1–27.

Collins, P.H., Gonzaga da Silva, E.C., Ergun, E., Furseth, I., Bond, K.D. and Martínez-Palacios, J. 2021, 'Intersectionality as Critical Social Theory', *Contemporary Political Theory*, vol. 20, no. 3, pp. 690–725.

Combahee River Collective [1977] 2014, 'The Combahee River Collective Statement', *Women's Studies Quarterly*, vol. 42, no. 3/4, pp. 271–280.

Crenshaw, K. 1989, 'Demarginalizing the Intersection of Race and Sex: A Black Feminist Critique of Antidiscrimination Doctrine, Feminist Theory and Antiracist Politics', *University of Chicago Legal Forum*, vol. 1989, issue 1, Article 8, pp. 139–167.

Crenshaw, K. 1991, 'Mapping the Margins: Intersectionality, Identity Politics, and Violence against Women of Color', *Stanford Law Review*, vol. 43, no. 6, pp. 1241–1299.

Davis, A.Y. 1981, *Women, Race & Class*, Vintage Books, New York.

Emirbayer, M. and Desmond, M. 2015, *The Racial Order*, University of Chicago Press, Chicago, Illinois.

Essed, P. 1991, *Understanding Everyday Racism: An Interdisciplinary Theory*, Sage, London.

Essed, P. 2002, 'Everyday Racism', in D.T. Goldberg and J. Solomos (eds), *A Companion to Racial and Ethnic Studies*, 1st edn, Blackwell Publishers, London, pp. 202–216.

Essed, P. and Muhr, S.L. 2018, 'Entitlement racism and its Intersections: An Interview with Philomena Essed, Social Justice Scholar', *Ephemera: Theory & Politics in Organization*, vol. 18, no. 1, pp. 183–201.

Feagin, J. 2006, *Systemic Racism: A Theory of Oppression*, Routledge, New York.

Feagin, J. 2013, *The White Racial Frame: Centuries of Racial Framing and Counter-Framing*, Routledge, Boca Raton, Florida.

Feagin, J. and Elias, S. 2013, 'Rethinking Racial Formation Theory: A Systemic Racism Critique', *Ethnic and Racial Studies*, vol. 36, no. 6, pp. 931–960.

Fowler, B. 2003, 'Reading Pierre Bourdieu's *Masculine Domination*: Notes Towards an Intersectional Analysis of Gender, Culture and Class', *Cultural Studies*, vol. 17, nos 3–4, pp. 468–494.

Frankenberg, R. 1993, *White Women, Race Matters: The Social Construction of Whiteness*, University of Minnesota Press, Minneapolis, MN.

Garner, S. 2004, *Racism in the Irish Experience*, Pluto, London.

hooks, b. 1981, *Ain't I A Woman: Black Women and Feminism*, Pluto Press, London.

Kovel, J. 1970, *White Racism: A Psychohistory*, Penguin, New York.

Lorde, A. 1984, *Sister Outsider: Essays and Speeches*, Crossing Press, Freedom, California.

Miles, R. and Brown, M. 2003, *Racism*, 2nd edn, Routledge, London.

Omi, M. and Winant, H. 2013, 'Resistance is Futile? A Response to Feagin and Elias', *Ethnic and Racial Studies,* vol. 36, no. 6, pp. 961–973.

Omi, M. and Winant, H. 2015, *Racial Formation in the United States*, 3rd edn, Routledge, New York.

Song, M. 2014, 'Challenging a Culture of Racial Equivalence', *The British Journal of Sociology*, vol. 65, issue 1, pp. 107–129.

Twine, F.W. 2016, 'The Racial Body is Gendered: A Comment on Emirbayer and Desmond's *The Racial Order*', *Ethnic and Racial Studies*, vol. 39, no. 13, pp. 2293–2296.

Winant, H. 1998, 'Racism Today: Continuity and Change in the Post-Civil Rights Era', *Ethnic and Racial Studies*, vol. 21, no. 4, pp. 755–766.

Winant, H. 2000, 'Race and Race Theory', *Annual Review of Sociology*, vol. 26, no. 1, pp. 169–185.

Wingfield, A.H. 2013, 'Comment on Feagin and Elias', *Ethnic and Racial Studies,* vol. 36, no. 6, pp. 989–993.

# RACE, RACISM AND NATIONALISM

For some racism scholars the connection between nationalism and racism is obvious; in their view, racism always stands behind and animates all forms of nationalism, whether such nationalisms present themselves as ethnic, racial or civic in character (Rattansi 2020; Valluvan 2019). Alana Lentin has argued that racism and nation are thoroughly intertwined: 'Racism, as we know it today, had its origins in the need for Europeans to define themselves internally as nations' (Lentin 2012, p. 30). She has argued that the modern nation-state, during its formation in Europe, was intrinsically racist, in the sense that it defined its unique identity through a racialising process involving the positing of a racial nation people ('us', viewed positively) and many negatively racialised others (them, outsiders), residing within national territory and outside. Racism, she argued, is fundamentally a state-organised process: 'Until there is a widespread realisation of the need to analyse racism from a perspective that sees the state as central to its origins, its persistence and perhaps its resolution, it will remain impossible to redress the injustices that racism has left as legacies imprinted upon society and individuals' (Lentin and Lentin 2006, p. 10). Rattansi (2020, p. 157) argues that 'the notion of "nation" is closely linked to "race", [and] that in popular discourse "race-nation-ethnicity" operates as a complex triad in which each slides repeatedly and inconsistently into the other', so that national populism and racism can never be neatly separated. Stuart Hall (2017) referred to 'race, ethnicity, nation' as the 'fateful triangle'. Nevertheless, he also argued that the 'discourse of "nation" . . . has a complex and ambivalent relationship to both race and ethnicity' (Hall 2017, p. 126).

DOI: 10.4324/9781003267690-4

Paul Gilroy (2002) in *There Ain't No Black in the Union Jack*, first published in 1987, also argued forcefully that racism and nationalism were inextricably intertwined – so much so that any leftist attempts to counteract belligerent conservative right-wing British nationalism (as evident in the period in which he was writing) with a milder, more inclusive and modern form of nationalism would inevitably fail, because nationalism, and nationalist tropes, always contained racism at the core. Discussing the British context, he argued that a political strategy of resistance less prone to racism was to invoke more local and regional identities that 'do not articulate with "race" in quite the same way as the national equivalent' (Gilroy 2002, p. 58). There was no way to engage with nationalist tropes in more inclusive ways, he argued, because they were weighed down with the baggage of racism. Any reference to 'the people' in the UK was code for reference to the 'white British race', because of the very strong articulation between race and nation in Britain, so that 'The discourses of nation and people are saturated with racial connotations' (Gilroy 2002, p. 60).

This argument has also been made by recent scholars addressing leftist nationalist attempts to counter the resurgence of right-wing, far-right and white-racist nationalisms, especially in Europe (Valluvan 2019). Bhattacharyya (2020, p. 1430) has argued that 'any attempt to expand the terms of national belonging, however well-intended, can be incorporated in a reconfigured set of exclusionary practices.' Citing Valluvan's (2019) argument that once nationalism is invoked by people on the left, it will escape any of their attempts to wind it back to a less nationalist, more inclusivist left-wing programme, Bhattacharyya (2020, p. 1432) writes that:

> The warning is to those who wish to flirt with nationalist tropes for short-term political gain, and it is well-made. We see across Europe the moving rightwards that arises from the attempts of mainstream parties to incorporate a flavour of nationalism-lite into their programmes and presentation.

There is a profound suspicion among racism scholars of state-based nationalism of any kind – in fact, of any form of nationalism or appeal to national identity (Valluvan 2019; Valluvan and

Kalra 2019). And there are historical reasons for this, including the powerful intersection between racism and nationalism in the nineteenth and early twentieth centuries, leading up to the two World Wars (see Mosse 1995); and there are contemporary reasons too, given the ways that even apparently benign and inclusive nationalism can suddenly turn and oppress racialised others within national boundaries.

On the other hand, there is not always the same suspicion of nondominant, non-state-based nationalisms, such as Indigenous nationalisms or, more generally, anti-colonial nationalisms. Stuart Hall, for example, highlighted the Janus face of nationalism but nevertheless accepted that nationalism had played a more positive role in anticolonial movements for liberation, as well as in the 'African American struggle against racial exclusion and oppression' (Hall 2017, p. 158). And Balibar, who analysed strong connections between racism, nationalism and sexism, cautioned that we should avoid equating the nationalism of the dominators with that of the dominated – though, he also warned that very often 'the nationalisms of liberation' turn into 'the nationalisms of domination', pointing to 'the oppressive potentialities contained within every nationalism' (Balibar 1991a, pp. 45–46; quotes at p. 46). Even so, these ambivalences among scholars who are otherwise very negative in their view of nationalism imply that nationalism can have more positive forms and outcomes, in certain historical and political circumstances.

Racism is not a prominent theme in the now voluminous writing on nationalism by historians, sociologists and political scientists, and indeed in the work that has become canonical in nationalism studies – with key figures and publications including Hans Kohn (1944), Elie Kedourie (1960), Anthony D. Smith (1987, 2009), Ernest Gellner (1983), Eric Hobsbawm (1990), Benedict Anderson ([1983] 2006), John Breuilly (1994), and John Hutchinson (1994), among many others. There, the concern is with the connection or not between ethnicity, ethnic groups and nations and nationalism, rather than races or racism, except where extreme forms of nationalism, like Nazism, are discussed. The connection between race and some forms of nationalism does appear in these works, sometimes under the guise of the concept of ethnic- or ethno-nationalism, but race and racism are not central to these theoretical approaches. Hans Kohn, for example, in his classic text *The Idea of Nationalism* (Kohn 1944) saw illiberal, authoritarian 'ethnic nationalism', which was obsessed with blood and belonging, and which he associated with Eastern Europe, as a derivative, reactive and romantic nationalism of the nineteenth century, that had branched off from the Enlightenment-inspired liberal, civic nationalism (see Calhoun 2007, pp. 119–120). Smith's (1987, 2009) arguments for an ethno-symbolic account of nations and nationalism makes use of a concept of ethnicity as a long-standing historical form of sociological community that has a powerful connection with modern nationalism and nations, but these forms of ethnicity are generally viewed more positively as cultural forms of belonging, unlike race and racism which have predominantly negative associations. The index of Calhoun's (2007) important and more recent contribution to mainstream nationalism studies, *Nations Matter*, has no entry for race or racism, and the book only mentions racism briefly. As we will see below, Anderson's ([1983] 2006) famous book, *Imagined Communities*, does have a chapter on the theme, but this involves an argument that racism and nationalism have different sources.

The argument of this chapter is that: (a) nationalism does not always descend into racism, and (b) the strong distinction between ethnic and civic nationalism (often associating these with countries) is untenable, and a more convincing position is that all nationalisms have within them different strands, and it depends which strands get mobilised in particular historical contexts (see Yack 1996; Calhoun 2007, Ch. 6). This also aligns with the broad approach of Miles and Brown (2003, p. 148) who argued: 'These ideologies – nationalism and racism – are not independent and autonomous forces but are generated and reproduced within a complex interplay of historically constituted economic and political relations.'

In the next sections I will consider some contrasting views of the connections between racism and nationalism, focusing especially on the classic arguments of George L. Mosse, Benedict Anderson and Étienne Balibar. I will illustrate some powerful historical connections between racism and nationalism, with extended examples of nineteenth -and early twentieth-century nationalisms in China and Australia. In the last section of the chapter, I will return to arguments about racism and nationalist populism.

## NATIONALISM AS THE HANDMAIDEN OF RACISM: HISTORICAL CONNECTIONS

One prominent argument is that nationalism has often been the handmaiden of racism, but that this is not an inherent relation; the relationship occurs in particular historical contexts, and under particular historical conditions. An incisive exemplar of the argument is George L. Mosse, the author of famous works on Nazism, the Holocaust, German nationalism and European racism, including its links with sexuality (see Mosse 1978, 1981, 1985). In his essay 'Racism and Nationalism', Mosse (1995) argues that racism and nationalism should not be equated, and that it was not always the case that racism and nationalism went together, but that it was a recent historical (rather than necessary) articulation:

> Racism and nationalism did not join because racism was ill-defined but because an integral or all-inclusive nationalism developed in such a way during the nineteenth century as to meet and to marry this world view. Indeed, without such a marriage European racism would have remained impotent. Through nationalism racism was able to transform theory into practice. Racism was dependent upon nationalism, but nationalism itself could exist without any necessary reliance on racism.
>
> (Mosse 1995, pp. 164–165)

Thus, the coupling of racism with nationalism made racism far more powerful as an ideology and practice because it could engage all that nationalism had at its disposal in terms of, for example, rallying the people behind racist tropes and obsessions and making use of territory and the state. On the other hand, nationalism could flourish, in different ways, without racism. As we will see, this is different to the argument of another prominent theorist Étienne Balibar, but in line with Benedict Anderson's distinction between the ideologies of racism and nationalism.

Mosse argued that racism and nationalism only grew close together when nations had a consistent definition of 'national character', as in the 'integral nationalism' of the last decades of the nineteenth century in Europe. He explains how this 'integral nationalism' of late nineteenth-century France, Germany and England – with a strong focus on national character, using the same kinds of images of health and beauty (classical Greek male bodies/types) that were also central to racism – meant that national type had a close fit with racial type, building on the same symbols. On the other hand, Mosse also stressed that it was not essential for nations to have the symbols of a definitive national character in order to exist and thrive, whereas 'such symbolism was central to racist ideology' (Mosse 1995, p. 167).

Another possible distinction that Mosse points to is the need for counter-types – he argues that while nationalism primarily needs these in times of 'crisis', racism *always* needs them, as a necessary foil. However, he also contends that such counter-types remain latent in most if not in all nationalisms (Mosse 1995, p. 170). Nevertheless, the unholy marriage between nationalism and racism has proved catastrophic, as in the Nazi example:

> When nationalism allies itself with racism discrimination is no longer the issue, but instead war has to be waged against the 'outsider' defined as the enemy both of nation and race. Racism was the catalyst which pushed German nationalism over the edge, from discrimination to mass extermination. German nationalism like all nationalisms had alternative traditions to that of racism, and however chauvinistic much of German nationalism turned out to be after the First World War, mass murder was not usually part of its agenda.
>
> (Mosse 1995, p. 171)

Mosse argues that, because nationalism and racism have often shared the same ideal types (superior national and racial types), and because they have also engaged with the same gender/sexual differences and separateness, it is easy to mistake them as the same phenomenon. However, Mosse notes that nationalism is a kind of 'patriotism', less concerned with the bodily appearances of ideal types: 'it can tolerate ethnic difference; it does not have to be self-assertive or preoccupied with looks and appearance.' Racism on the other hand, cannot tolerate such ethnic difference, and is obsessed with purity (Mosse 1995, p. 168). This implies that nationalisms can shift and change, with different ethnic, racial and civic strands coming to the fore, dependent on particular historical, social, economic and political conditions.

The fusing of racism and nationalism was especially inspired by the unmoorings of identity and personal securities endemic to the shift from feudal society to industrial modernity, where 'race' became a longed-for, secure foundation for burgeoning new communal forms that were coalescing as nationalism (Mosse 1978). Mosse argues that racist nationalism became such a powerful force in Germany – less so in France (even though it had strong traditions of anti-Semitism and racism) – because of Germany's experience of extreme economic, social and political crisis after World War One and a 'death atmosphere' arising from the annihilation of war, which inspired a fusing of mystical racism with nationalism in the 1920s and 1930s (Mosse 1978, pp. 193–196).

In his book *Nationalism and Sexuality*, after examining the ways that ideologies of respectability and nationalism intersected in different ways across time with sexuality, Mosse (1985) cautions against dismissing nationalism because of its abuses and stresses its role in fomenting solidarities; an argument also made by Calhoun (2007). As Mosse (1985, p. 191) concluded:

> One must not assess a system of thought and behaviour solely by its abuses. Nationalism cannot be so easily absolved [compared to 'respectability'], though even here, at least until the first World War, much of it, whether in Germany or elsewhere in England and Europe, was not aggressive but recognized the right of every nation to its existence and its own culture. Nor must we forget that society needs cohesion – without it, not only dictatorships but parliamentary governments cannot function.

Though Mosse's main focus was Europe, race and its discourses spread far beyond, becoming modular, so that racism could also support and infuse nationalism in non-Western, non-white-dominated societies. Dikötter (1992, 2008), for example, has discussed the power of race and racism in the construction of modern Chinese national identity in the nineteenth and early twentieth centuries; emphasising, at the same time, that we should adopt an 'interactionist' approach, appreciating the local ways that racist thinking has been taken up, expressed and institutionalised, not simply imbibed in already finished form delivered by Western imperial centres. We should thus recognize the importance of human agency, as historical agents around the globe interpreted, adapted, transformed and possibly even rejected racism in their own specific ways. Far from being fixed or static entities, the polyphony and adaptability of racial discourse in different historical circumstances should be recognized if their enduring appeal is to be understood. The interactive model of interpretation . . . emphasizes the worldviews constructed by local historical agents, analysing the complex cognitive, social and political dimensions behind the indigenization and appropriation of racist belief systems: put briefly, it highlights inculturation where others see acculturation.

(Dikötter 2008, p. 1482)

After defeat in war by Japan (1894–1895) Chinese nationalists, as part of the reform movement, searched for a powerful symbol to unite China as a nation and found it in race. 'Yellowness' had long been revered in China (Dikötter 2008, p. 1484). Chinese nationalists imbibed evolutionary racial theories from the UK, and, also connecting these with China's lineage theories, claimed a 'yellow race' descended from the 'Yellow Emperor', and that this was what united the nation:

Thriving on its affinity with lineage discourse, the notion of 'race' gradually emerged as the most common symbol of national cohesion, as 'race' overarched differences of rank, class, lineage and region to integrate the country conceptually into a powerful community linked by blood.

(Dikötter 2008, pp. 1488–1489)

Reformers adapted and constructed a racialised world view that pitted 'yellows' in a struggle against 'whites', on a level above the more 'degenerate' 'browns', 'blacks' and 'reds' (Dikötter 2008, p. 1488). The 'yellow race' included all people living in the middle kingdom, including the Manchus (signifying the ruling elite). The 'yellow race' became less attractive not long after, with revolutionaries wanting to overthrow the Qing Dynasty, adopting a notion of the Han race rather than the yellow race, thus excluding the Manchu elite, who became an 'inferior race' (Dikötter 2008, p. 1489). The revolutionaries excluded a range of groups from the 'Han' race: not only the 'reviled' Manchus, but also Mongols, Tibetans and other populations. In the early decades of the twentieth century, the new term for the Han 'race' was 'Minzu', 'a new composite term meaning literally "people-lineage", and was often used to translate the term "nation" and "nationality"', based on imagined shared blood and descent that established symbolic boundaries, such that '"nationalities" as political units were equated with "races" as biological units'. This fusion of nation and race 'promoted unity against foreign aggressors and suppressed internal divisions'. It uplifted 'the "peasants with weather-beaten faces and mudcaked hands and feet"', who 'could be represented as the "descendants of the Yellow Emperor"' (Dikötter 2008, p. 1489).

The close intermeshing of racism and nationalism can also be seen in the example of Australian settler-nationalism. It is well known that racism played a special role in colonial contexts (Anderson [1983] 2006) and was central to imperialism (Arendt 1986), and this is true of settler-colonial societies such as in Australia, where the marriage between race, racism and nationalism was intense, especially in the first part of the twentieth century. 'White Australia' emerged as a nationalist, race ideology in the late nineteenth century, stimulated by the history of dispossession of Australia's Indigenous people, and by Australia's positioning as a 'white outpost' in Asia and its predominantly white British immigrant population's desire to prevent Asian and other 'coloured' migration.

In the early nineteenth century, the British settlers brought with them to Australia a sense of national identity that had been forged over the two preceding centuries (Greenfeld 1992; Helgerson 1992). Thus, Australian nationalism had its initial grounding in British nationalism. The myth of Anglo-Saxondom was attractive in the Australian colonies because of its direct association with Britain. Though the idea of a pure Anglo-Saxondom did not take a racial form until the nineteenth century, the myth itself had a long history, dating back to sixteenth- and seventeenth-century English beliefs about the purity of the Anglo-Saxon church and the secular myth of the free nature of Anglo-Saxon political institutions. It had for long been important as a source of communal pride and self-esteem. The writing of history in the eighteenth century had paved the way for transforming the idea of the success of Anglo-Saxon institutions, into one that took Anglo-Saxon blood as being the main reason for that success. The development of the Aryan myth, in the middle of the nineteenth century, transformed the Anglo-Saxon myth: freedom-loving Anglo-Saxons became the racially powerful and destined Aryan people. German philologists, through studies of the linguistic roots of English and German languages, claimed that both peoples stemmed from a common root. The argument was that the Aryans of India – the 'forebears' of the Anglo-Saxons –impelled by an irresistible force, began to migrate westward. They brought with them qualities of self-reliance and independence as a direct result of the migration, and these qualities became the key features of the German and English peoples. Thus, institutional superiority as well as revolutionary and expansionary success were given a perceived biological basis, and became racial superiority (see Horsman 1981, pp. 1–24, and Gossett 1997, Ch. XIII for a discussion of the history of the Anglo-Saxon myth).

The racial theory of de Gobineau and Robert Knox (Mosse 1978) inspired claims in Australia that the world was divided between competing civilisations, and that this justified exclusive white colonisation. White British settlers were in conflict with 'Negroid', 'Coloured', 'Oriental' or 'Asiatic' peoples for the world's land and other resources. Prominent nineteenth-century liberal Charles Pearson (1894) in his book, *National Life and Character: A Forecast* claimed that Australia was needed for the 'white race' to continue to develop as a civilisation, and his book and ideas were discussed by prominent parliamentarians during debates about Australia's Immigration Restriction Act in 1901, the foundation of the White Australia Policy. In a text written to celebrate the centenary of European settlement, published in 1888, the historian Alexander Sutherland, reflecting upon the ethical questions raised by colonisation, wrote of an Anglo-Saxon race that, in accordance with a mixture of divine and natural laws, had supplanted Australia's natives:

> the fact is that mankind, as a race, cannot choose to act solely as moral beings. They are governed by animal laws which urge them blindly forward upon tracks they scarce can choose for themselves. If it is a divine law that the Anglo-Saxon people must double

themselves every half-century, it must be a divine law that they are to emigrate and form for themselves new homes in waste lands. But every spot suitable for man's sustenance is held by some sort of human occupant; and, therefore, the Anglo-Saxon cannot choose but intrude upon the haunts of other races . . . In obedience to natural laws over which they had no control, seeing that they would not and could not brain their infants as the Australians did, the Anglo-Saxons sought these lands, and settled side by side with the natives.

> (extracted and quoted in Reynolds 1989, pp. 10–11)

Population pressures in England, therefore, justified the settling of lands and forests where 'savages' merely wandered and hunted. Sutherland argued that, even if it meant the complete disappearance of Aboriginal blood, settlement was justified by the alleviation of the sufferings of Anglo-Saxons in the crowded cities of England, and, in any case, simply conformed to 'a law above that which man makes for himself', exhibiting a mix of pseudoscientific notions of 'the survival of the fittest' and religious notions of the divine plan (extracted and quoted in Reynolds 1989, pp. 10–11).

The Australian nation moved towards its political consolidation (it federated in 1901) at exactly the time, in the late nineteenth century, when racism as an ideology was flourishing in Europe, and infusing important nationalist movements. Maintaining the physical and cultural integrity of a postulated 'white race' took on an aspect of world historical importance for white intellectuals in Europe and America, and in the smaller colonial societies such as Australia (Lake and Reynolds 2008). The great achievements of British or European civilisation were considered proof of the superiority of a white race that stood at the head of world civilization.

However, white racism was not simply imported into Australia as an intellectual movement deriving from Europe and its racial thinkers and scientists. In many respects its specific Australian form derived from conditions inherent in colonial imperialism, emerging out of a system that sanctioned the removal of Indigenous people from their lands in the name of colonial enterprise. Arendt (1986, p. 160) argued that racism was 'the main ideological weapon of imperialistic politics'.

Racism was important for European imperialism in Australia because it served to justify the exploitation of Indigenous peoples and their lands, and even their eventual 'extinction'. Despite movements within Britain and the Colonial Office to protect Australia's Indigenous peoples – especially evident from the 1830s to the 1850s – the sporadic measures adopted were not allowed to stand in the way of the development of the land for capitalist purposes. Settler-colonialism, because it is based on the expropriation of land, is inseparable from racism (see Wolfe 1999, 2016). The act of expropriation is, in itself, racist because it refuses to recognise the rights to land of entire categories of people. The settler-colonial situation is thus an inherently racialised one; it is a powerfully lived relation between settler and native. Race theories, largely formulated in European colonial centres, thrived in this atmosphere.

Conceptions of race, whether based on commonsense beliefs, 'experience', folklore, science, or a combination of all, were central in organising the clear demarcation between settler and Indigenous communities from the days of early contact. These conceptions changed over time and under the influence of different pressures and forces. More articulate notions of race were operative from at least the early part of the nineteenth century with regard to Indigenous people, though they did not gain scientific sanction – they were also transformed and hardened by science – until later in the century. White racial ideology justified the process of dispossessing Indigenous peoples as it was happening, as evident from the 1840s onwards in public comments in parliaments, newspapers and journals, where it was sometimes claimed that Indigenous people were being replaced by a 'finer' white race (see many examples in Woolmington 1973).

Anglo-Saxondom or Britishness – the two terms could be used interchangeably – represented an overarching civilisation within which white Australians could stake out their own specific national claim. Settler-Australians in the process of forming their nation needed, nevertheless, to articulate their own symbols of unity in order to convince themselves that they formed a distinct society: British-derived but not simply British – a society and a culture, a nation of their own. The myth of Australian nationhood could rely in part on the myths invigorating the British nation, but these could not serve the purpose of distinguishing the Australian nation as a new entity in the world. Towards the end of the nineteenth century, as nationalism became more culturally and politically articulate, the symbol 'white Australia' was used to embrace the new continentally unified people.

White Australia united otherwise disparate and competing interests (English, Scots, Welsh and Irish, capitalists and workers, free traders and protectionists). In this respect it was a powerful nationalist symbol and ideology. Through white Australia, these different interests could unite as if they were all guided by the same purpose, while they could believe, at the same time, that they were pursuing their independent aims. The role of the labour movement is illustrative. On the whole it supported white Australia and could, at the same time, see itself as defeating the agents of capitalism who, in importing cheap non-white labour, would have reduced white workers to the level of the despised Asiatic indentured labourers (Gollan 1967, Ch. 11; Kellaway 1953). A white Australia also enhanced its sense of pride: even workers were members of the white race, superior to all other peoples. As David Roediger has argued for America, making use of Du Bois' (1966) famous argument in *Black Reconstruction in America* about the 'public and psychological wage' of whiteness, in Australia's often harsh working-class conditions the 'pleasures of whiteness' functioned as a 'wage for white workers', beyond economic benefits (Roediger 1991). The 'dignity of labour' (Birrell 1995, p. 253) was perhaps the most important meaning of white Australia for the working classes; such dignity had to be defined against indignity. The hard-working indentured labourers were slaves; the Chinese were servile labourers who worked too diligently and lived in degraded conditions. Their servile nature was exemplified by their capacity and willingness to live in appalling conditions, which no 'decent' white worker would tolerate. Indigenous people, where they were used for labour, were rarely paid at all. The freedom of Indigenous life, potentially desired by workers, could be denigrated by strictly separating white workers from them. Indigenous people were seen as lazy, destitute, immoral, as against white workers who looked after each other, and who worked hard. The formation of this consciousness had a long historical development, dating back to the convict days.

After federation in 1901, Australia became a nation-state that defined itself explicitly in white racial terms. According to its racial ideology, Australia secured itself as a democratic society by maintaining 'racial unity', which for many meant racial purity. Racial impurity, and allowing in to the country non-white 'races', many claimed, would lead to inevitable racial conflict and potentially national disintegration.

## BENEDICT ANDERSON: RACISM AS EMERGING FROM IDEOLOGIES OF CLASS, NOT NATIONALISM

Benedict Anderson's famous argument in *Imagined Communities* (Anderson [1983] 2006) about the origins and global spread of nationalism explicitly disassociates the ideologies of racism and nationalism. He saw the two phenomena as emerging from different sources as well as expressing different emotional structures, with nationalism more inspired by love of people and country, and racism inspired by hate and disgust.

Print cultures and vernacular languages, he argued, are central to nationalism, rather than the 'blood' mythology that animates racism. Anderson argues that language looms out of the past (a bit like nations), and is nevertheless embedded in historical time, unlike races, which are timeless: 'If nationalness has about it an aura of fatality, it is nonetheless a fatality embedded in *history*', unlike races (Anderson [1983] 2006, p. 145). Nations can be joined, whereas races cannot – and that is because joining a nation can be like joining a language: 'from the start the nation was conceived in language, not in blood, and . . . one could be "invited into" the imagined community' (Anderson [1983] 2006, p. 145). Nations are both inclusive and exclusive: 'Seen as both a historical fatality and as a community imagined through language, the nation presents itself as simultaneously open and closed' (Anderson [1983] 2006, p. 146). Anderson's argument was aimed partly at Tom Nairn who claimed in *The Break Up of Britain* (Nairn 1981) that racism and anti-Semitism derive from nationalism; this, Anderson argues, is wrong:

The fact of the matter is that nationalism thinks in terms of historical destinies, while racism dreams of eternal contamination, transmitted from the origins of time through an endless sequence of loathesome copulations: outside history . . . The dreams of racism actually have their origin in the ideologies of *class*, rather than in those of nation: above all in claims to divinity among rulers and to 'blue' or 'white' blood and 'breeding' among aristocracies.

(Anderson [1983] 2006, p. 149)

Anderson sees the connection between racism and nationalism mainly in the form of 'official nationalism', which always arose from the challenge of 'popular, vernacular nationalisms'. Official nationalisms were promoted by the upper classes – 'dynastic and aristocratic groups' – and these emerged especially in colonial situations: 'Colonial racism was a major element in that conception of "Empire" which attempted to weld dynastic legitimacy and national community' (Anderson [1983] 2006, p. 150). Colonial racism's 'aristocratic or pseudo-aristocratic derivation' was also apparent in 'the typical "solidarity among whites," which linked colonial rulers from different national metropoles, whatever their internal rivalries and conflicts'. These trans-state solidarities were similar to the 'class solidarity of Europe's nineteenth century aristocracies . . .' (Anderson [1983] 2006, p. 153).

Anderson devoted a chapter of *Imagined Communities* to 'official nationalism' which he sees as the nationalism promoted by dynasts in Europe and elsewhere to homogenise their populations, from above – 'Russification' is an example. As the 'willed merger of nation and dynastic empire', it is a phenomenon of the second half of the nineteenth century, following on from the popular national movements in Europe from the 1820s onwards (Anderson, [1983] 2006, p. 86). Thus, he sees 'official nationalism' as a response to popular nationalism. He provides an example from Thailand where, in the early twentieth century, Monarch Wachirawut pursued official nationalism in reaction to local worker unrest: 'Here is a fine example of the character of official nationalism – an anticipatory strategy adopted by dominant groups which are threatened with marginalization or exclusion from an emerging nationally-imagined community'

(Anderson [1983] 2006, p. 101). The target of his official nationalism was the large, imported Chinese male working class, who were racialised as 'The Jews of the Orient', which was the title of one of his pamphlets (Anderson [1983] 2006, p. 100).

Anderson's distinction between nationalism and the class origins of racism is, however, too neat and clear-cut. Writing of the British experience, Gilroy argued against Anderson's claims about nationalism emerging from language/print cultures rather than images of 'blood' or biology – the references to Britain as an island race and the 'bulldog breed', he argued, indicated the racial basis of British nationalism (Gilroy 2002, p. 44). Miles (1987) also emphasised the strong foundation of race in English/British nationalism, and thus argued against Anderson's clear distinction between the ideologies of racism and nationalism. Acknowledging that the ideologies are analytically distinguishable, they are nevertheless frequently articulated together in empirical situations, and share the quality of inclusion/exclusion in terms of human populations, even if they do this in different ways (nation typically relying on culture/language, race relying on biology). He provides the example of nineteenth-century racial scientists such as Robert Knox and de Gobineau, who claimed that races were foundational to nations and to civilisational development (though the claim was also disputed), to show that '"race" and "nation" are not necessarily antipathetic and can be ordered in a hierarchical interdependence in which "race" determines "nation"' (Miles 1987, p. 31), as he also showed in his empirical example of English nationalism. He also argued that this was evident in 'certain varieties of fascist ideology' that, while incorporating 'a racist theory of history', have at the same time 'advanced a nationalist project which utilizes an idea of "race" to project a positive "historical destiny" as well as "eternal contaminations"' (Miles 1987, p. 41). In this respect, he notes that 'Anderson's error is to assume that the category of "race" is always used as a method of negatively-evaluated exclusion', whereas nationalism is more positive. 'In reality', he argues, 'the "race" category is also liable to be used first as a positively-evaluated means of inclusion which thereby excludes' (Miles 1987, p. 27); and, again, English nationalism is a case in point. This was also the case in Nazi Germany where 'a theory of race was first used to define the criterion of positive inclusion':

The imagined community of the German 'nation' was therefore identified by a positively evaluated signification of supposed
'racial' characteristics. In this instance, 'race' was not an 'eternal
contamination' grounded in negative emotion but was used to
generate a positive sense of 'nation', from which emerged a process of exclusion which led finally to the physical extermination
of those considered not to belong to the imagined community.

(Miles 1987, p. 41)

Nevertheless, the ideologies have one important point of distinction. While nationalism has a clear political objective – that the
nation would be a political unit in a particular territory, that has the
right to govern itself, racism has no such distinct political ideology
(Miles 1987, p. 32).

## INTERSECTIONS

The arguments above about relationships between nationalism and
racism remind us also to think intersectionally about racism. This
means not assuming that racism and nationalism are the same thing,
but that they condition each other in particular historical situations.
And they also intersect with gender, sexuality and class (already
implied in several discussions above). As Peter Wade (2001) reminds
us, Foucault's writing on sexuality stressed how the control of sexuality was closely linked to nations and nationalism, with sexual health
seen as vital to the reproduction of the nation, and to racial health.
European bourgeoisies in the nineteenth century were concerned
with racially purifying the national population (Wade 2001, p. 846).
As noted above, Mosse also focused on the interrelations of race, sexuality and nation. Wade argues that it is not surprising that sexuality,
as a form of human behavior, is such a concern for both racism and
nationalism, and thus vitally intersects with both, because it is concerned with reproduction of peoples (designated as races, ethnicities
and nations) through the generations, via procreation (Wade 2001,
p. 852). Nations (including when imagined as expressing races) have
visions of ideal typical males and females and their heteronormative
sexualities. Hall (2017, p. 140) argued that in the example of British
nationalism,

national identity has been consistently constructed through the virtues said to be characteristic of certain kinds of men who become, for this very reason, the bearers of the national story. Constructed around 'manly' virtues of self-discipline and self-restraint, stories of national valor and heroism in the narratives of Britishness are deeply caught up with the stiff-upper-lipped, understated, emotionally armor-plated, and buttoned-up values of certain kinds of English masculinity, which thus become representative of a certain generation and class. This gendering of national identity is, in turn, intimately related to the forging of the British nation as it is constitutively related to its imperial 'others.'

As noted in Chapter 2, Patricia Hill Collins argued that the family was a key institutional form for thinking about intersectionality, and she made this point about family, nation and race: 'Overall, by relying on the belief that families have assigned places where they truly belong, images of place, space, and territory link gendered notions of family with constructs of race and nation' (Collins 1998, p. 69).

Étienne Balibar, in a series of essays (Balibar 1991a, 1991b, 1991c; 2011) has argued that there are intersections between racism, sexuality and nationalism. The following statement explains the nationalism and racism connection:

> racism is not an 'expression' of nationalism, but *a supplement of nationalism* or more precisely *a supplement internal to nationalism*, always in excess of it, but always indispensable to its constitution and yet always still insufficient to achieve its project, just as nationalism is both indispensable and always insufficient to achieve the formation of the *nation* or the project of a 'nationalization' of society.
>
> (Balibar 1991a, p 54; italics in original)

There is not a simple 'juxtaposition of merely analogous behaviours and discourses applied to a potentially indefinite series of objects independent of each other, but *a historical system of complementary exclusions and dominations which are mutually interconnected*'. There are not separate 'ethnic racisms' and 'sexual racism', but a systematic combination of racism and sexism, such that '*racism always presupposes sexism*' (Balibar 1991a, p. 54; italics in original). Balibar (1991a, p. 53) argues that we need to recognise

> the necessary polymorphism of racism, its overarching function, its connections with the whole set of practices of social normali-zation and exclusion, as we might demonstrate by reference to neo-racism whose preferred target is not the 'Arab' or the 'Black', but the 'Arab (as) junky' or 'delinquent' or 'rapist' and so on, or equally, rapists and delinquents as 'Arabs' and 'Blacks'.

The connection between racism and nationalism relates also to this 'broad structure of racism'. Because nationalism requires the creation of a 'fictive ethnicity' – the national people – this ultimately falls back on racism as a major contributor to producing this fiction. Thus, racism and nationalism are not the same thing, but there is a 'necessary relation' between them (Balibar 1991a, p. 54). Racism is not a perversion of nationalism, and nor are nationalism and racism formally the same; rather there is a 'historical articulation'. There is a

> cycle of historical reciprocity of nationalism and racism, which is the temporal figure of the progressive domination of the system of nation-states over other social formations. Racism is constantly emerging out of nationalism, not only towards the exterior but towards the interior.
>
> (Balibar 1991a, p. 58)

It is a subtle argument, always denying an easy slippage that would claim that nationalism is simply racism (even if disguised). There is a '*gap . . . between the representations and practices of nationalism and racism*' (Balibar 1991a, p. 59; italics in original).

In a later essay Balibar (2011, p. 2) returned to this theme and clar-ified that racism as a supplement intrinsic to nationalism meant that:

> when the nation-form becomes challenged and undergoes a crisis (which happens throughout its history), the development of racist ideologies and practices appears as a natural 'solution' (solution which, indeed, essentially aggravates the crisis), not only at an

intellectual or strategic level controlled by the state, but also at a popular and social level.

## RACISM AND THE RISE OF POPULIST NATIONALISM

There has been renewed attention to the connections between racism and nationalism stimulated by the prominence of right-wing populist nationalism in many countries, spanning Europe, the Americas, Asia and Australasia. Rattansi (2020, Ch. 7) argues that the resurgence of right-wing populism (as a form of nationalism) since the 1990s, and especially after the global financial crisis of 2008, involves an intensification of racism and racialisation, evident in 'nativist' backlashes against refugees, asylum-seekers and undocumented workers.

The Trump presidency (2017–2021), in a context of this resurgence of right-wing nationalist, populist and authoritarian governments in Europe and Asia (Brubaker 2017), also indicated the spectre of the close connection between racism and nationalism, especially as white nationalism flourished in the US, contributed to by Trump's political style and rhetoric, with his direct appeal to whites, his playing down of the extremism of white nationalists and neo-Nazis, his disparaging of and policies against Muslim and Mexican immigrants, and his negative commentaries on blacks and urban crime. White nationalism had already been resurgent in Europe, characterised by Chetan Bhatt (2012) as a 'xenologie' that gathered together a range of ideological concerns with non-white migrants, Muslims, sharia law, desecularisation, and a reinvigoration of the old ideology of European civilisation degeneration and decline. This white nationalism brought together in a loose, contradictory coalition a newly formed 'counter-jihad movement' and a resurgent, but much older, European New Right. Brubaker (2017) has emphasised that the obsessions with opposing Islam and asserting Europe's Christian civilisational roots are what unify resurgent national-populism across northern and western Europe, now in an 'identarian Christianism' mode, since the early 2000s. Brexit, the decision of Britain to leave the EU after a referendum in 2016 is widely seen as illustrative of the rise of backward-looking nationalism infused with racism expressed as anti-immigration and anti-asylum-seeker politics, against migrants, asylum-seekers and refugees from the EU, especially eastern Europe, and from underdeveloped and politically unstable regions, most of whom are non-white (Valluvan and Kalra 2019; Virdee and McGeever 2018).

Some right-wing governments in Europe engaged in blatant racist tropes, such as Hungary's president Viktor Orbán using anti-Semitic imagery when attacking billionaire philanthropist George Soros. In the 2017 Hungarian parliamentary election Orbán pointed to a world conspiracy of Jewish financiers, and Soros was attacked in posters that many saw as having anti-Semitic messages. Orbán and his Fidesz party have also had a strong anti-immigrant message, couched in nationalism, and particularly directed at Muslims (Echikson 2019; Brubaker 2017).

The right-wing populist former President of Brazil, Jair Bolsonaro, claimed on the one hand that Brazil was largely free of racism while on the other hand he openly and publicly denigrated Indigenous and black Brazilians and dismissed anti-racism policies such as affirmative action and racial quotas aimed at improving the situation of Brazil's racially oppressed (Alfonso 2019).

During the global coronavirus pandemic (beginning in early 2020), not only was there a spike in racism (as often occurs during crises, including natural disasters like pandemics, as racist scapegoating proliferates, exacerbated by existential fear), but this was arguably stimulated by, or articulated with, rising nationalist sentiment and the closing of borders, showing yet again, for some, how racism is in lockstep with nationalism (see Elias et al. 2021).

Though the racism of national populists is easier to notice, critics argue that there are undercurrents of racism also among more apparently 'civic' nationalists, some of whom have tried to counter nationalist populism with their own versions of nationalism, and defence of sections of populations. In the British and US contexts it is argued that there is on the communitarian and liberal left this undercurrent of racism, underpinned by nationalism, inspiring them to speak of the 'left behind' white working class whose identities, including their experiences of white and national identity, should be vigorously attended to by progressive politics (Bhambra 2017). Leading figures who advocate this view are David Goodhart, on the political left, who has argued that too much diversity disrupts the solidarity that supports social welfare (Goodhart 2004), that the liberal left support for multiculturalism and high levels of immigration alienates the white majority in the UK, and that governments should pay more heed to national populist sentiments of the majority population, especially those outside London in rural and coastal villages and towns (Goodhart 2017; 2019). Eric Kaufmann (2019), in his popular and controversial book *Whiteshift*, has argued that white majority nations (many of whom are trending towards becoming non-white majority countries, demographically) have legitimate identity concerns about the way that immigration may transform their national cultures. Arlie Hochschild (2016) in her book, *Strangers in Their Own Land*, seeks to understand the white supporters who felt 'left behind' in the wake of racial minorities and others after the civil rights movement and ended up aligning with the conservative, populist, pro-market and anti-immigration Tea Party movement (that emerged in the Republican Party in early 2009) and later with Trump. Apart from the unthinking racial exclusion by such critics of the many non-whites who make up the working class left behind by neoliberal austerity policies and the retreat of the welfare state, with the focus always on the left behind 'white working class,' and arguments that their identity experiences and economic situation is of special concern in class politics (Bhambra 2017, Lentin 2017; Valluvan 2019, p. 10), it is argued that this left and centrist dalliance with nationalism is dangerous in that it always reinvigorates racial hierarchies and racialisation of ethnic and immigrant minorities, and institutes racial exclusions from the nation (Bhattacharyya 2020; Valluvan 2019; Valluvan 2022).

As already noted, there are good contemporary reasons for the suspicion that in every nationalism lurks the danger, or spectre, of racism. However, at the same time, and not only conceptually, it is also important to consider the distinctions between race/racism, nation/nationalism and ethnicity. They are frequently enmeshed and intersecting, but nationalism can, at the very least, involve an anti-racist agenda, and nationalists can challenge racist strands of nationalism within their own nation, making use of alternative nationalist arguments and discourses that are not, as Valluvan (2019) claims, inevitably and ultimately racist. Right-wing nationalist populism and white nationalism do not represent the true essence of nationalism that other forms of nationalism conceal. Nationalism can be universalistic and internationally oriented and focused (Calhoun 2007, p. 146), and inclusive of a range of differences that racism never is. There are strongly ethnic and racial/racist forms of nationalism, just as there are less ethnic and racial/racist forms of nationalism; but this distinction is more about time periods, and the influence of nationalist tendencies and particular movements within countries, rather than representing clear distinctions between countries.

At the beginning of this chapter, I suggested that, in terms of thinking through the connections between race, racism and nationalism, it was useful to think about the different strands existing within nationalisms that get mobilised in particular economic, political and social conditions. Returning briefly to the Australian example, even the old white Australia involved a fusion of ethnic/racial with civic elements (it was not only about race) – the latter to do with citizenship and its obligations and entitlements, commitment to homeland, feelings of connection with territory and landscape, and a commitment to equality (egalitarianism and 'mateship' in the Australian context) (McGregor 2006) at least among white Australians, though this excluded non-white others, including demonised 'Asians' and Australia's Indigenous peoples. The civic elements came more to the fore and became more predominant from the late 1960s onwards, and gradually became more inclusive and detached from ethnic/racial elements, inspired by a range of historical changes including the decline of the British empire and Britain's turn towards Europe, Australia's need to engage with Asia, the gradual, hesitant recognition that Australia needed to include its Indigenous peoples in the nation, stimulated by protest movements and including movements for Aboriginal land and citizenship rights from the late 1960s onwards, a broader anti-racist movement, the impact of mass, multi-ethnic immigration that transformed the population from the end of World War Two onwards, and the writing of revisionist histories that critiqued colonialism and racism (McGregor 2006). Arguably, in the period from the early 1970s onwards, as Australia declared itself to be a multicultural nation, the racial underpinning of Australian nationalism declined in influence (Moran 2017), even if it never completely disappeared and may, still, remain as a dominating core around which multiculturalism and the settler-Australian relations with Indigenous people are organised (Hage 1998, 2003). This is not to claim that

Australia is a racial democracy without racial hierarchy. That would be wrong and naïve, given the experiences of Indigenous people and the ongoing colonisation and structural racism that oppressively shapes their lives (with unresolved questions and demands of treaty, sovereignty and land rights). In addition, more recent immigrant groups and their descendants from Africa, many parts of Asia and the Middle East have experienced serious racism and systemic exclusion (including a serious problem with Islamophobia, as discussed in Chapter 5). Despite multiculturalism, the Australian national identity remains closely associated with whiteness (on recent African immigrant experiences of exclusion from national belonging and racism see Mapedzahama and Kwansah-Aidoo 2017; Clarke, Magan and Yussuf 2019). Nevertheless, the ideological and symbolic support for multiculturalism as an ethic for the nation, and as characterising the contemporary Australian national identity, allows some room for racist exclusion to be challenged publicly, even if Australian governments have been less than proactive with anti-racism strategies.

## CONCLUSION

If nationalism is conceived too narrowly and in the abstract, without reference to historical and political context, then it is too easy to slip into seeing nationalism as the same as racism and that racism is always central to its operations. The arguments about nationalism always stimulating and underpinning racism need to be tempered by the historical variation of nationalism's forms. Such arguments also miss the other features of nationalism, such as the contribution that it can make to forms of internal solidarity – in resistance, for example, to the darker aspects of globalisation, to supporting cultures of democracy, and to supporting key institutions such as welfare states and the development of services for the 'national people' (see Calhoun, 2007, especially Ch. 7). And even that nationalism can be internationalist and universalist in ways that racism is not and cannot be, as Calhoun argues that the theorist of nationalism Hans Kohn showed (Calhoun 2007, p. 146). Nevertheless, as argued in this chapter, there have been many circumstances where racism and nationalism are deeply enmeshed, and where nationalism stimulates racism and its exclusions; not least of all in the contemporary phenomenon of right-wing populist nationalism.

## REFERENCES

Alfonso, D.A. 2019, 'Bolsonaro's take on the "absence of racism" in Brazil', *Race & Class*, vol. 61, no. 3, pp. 33–49.

Anderson, B. [1983] 2006, *Imagined Communities: Reflections on the Origins and Spread of Nationalism*, 2nd edn, Verso, London.

Arendt, H. 1986, *The Origins of Totalitarianism*, André Deutsch, London.

Balibar, E. 1991a, 'Racism and Nationalism', in E. Balibar and I. Wallerstein, *Race, Nation and Class: Ambiguous Identities*, Verso, London, pp. 37–67.

Balibar, E. 1991b, 'Is There a "neo-racism"?', in E. Balibar and I. Wallerstein, *Race, Nation and Class: Ambiguous Identities*, Verso, London, pp. 17–28.

Balibar, E. 1991c, 'The Nation Form: History and Ideology', in E. Balibar and I. Wallerstein, *Race, Nation and Class: Ambiguous Identities*, Verso, London, pp. 86–106.

Balibar, E. 2011, 'The Genealogical Scheme: Race or Culture?', *Trans-Scripts*, vol. 1, pp. 1–9.

Bhambra, G.K. 2017, 'Brexit, Trump, and "methodological whiteness": On the Misrecognition of Race and Class', *The British Journal of Sociology*, vol. 68, issue S1, pp. 214–232.

Bhatt, C. 2012, 'The New Xenologies of Europe: Civil Tensions and Mythic Pasts', *Journal of Civil Society*, vol. 8, no. 3, pp. 307–326.

Bhattacharyya, G. 2020, 'Nationalism – A Hard Habit to Break', *Ethnic and Racial Studies*, vol. 43, no. 8, pp. 1428–1435.

Birrell, R. 1995, *A Nation of Our Own: Citizenship and Nation-building in Federation Australia*, Longman, Melbourne, Victoria.

Breuilly, J. 1994, *Nationalism and the State*, 2nd edn, University of Chicago Press, Chicago, Illinois.

Brubaker, R. 2017, 'Between Nationalism and Civilizationism: The European Populist Moment in Comparative Perspective', *Ethnic and Racial Studies*, vol. 40, no. 8, pp. 1191–1226.

Calhoun, C. 2007, *Nations Matter: Culture, History and the Cosmopolitan Dream*, Routledge, Abingdon.

Clarke, M.B., Magan, M. and Yussuf, A. (eds) 2019, *Growing Up African in Australia*, Black Inc., Melbourne, Victoria.

Collins, P.H. 1998, 'It's All in the Family: Intersections of Gender, Race and Nation', *Hypatia*, vol. 13, no. 3, pp. 62–82.

Dikötter, F. 1992, *The Discourse of Race in Modern China*, Stanford University Press, Stanford, California.

Dikötter, F. 2008, 'The Racialization of the Globe: An Interactive Interpretation', *Ethnic and Racial Studies*, vol. 38, no. 8, pp. 1478–1496.

Du Bois, W.E.B. 1966, *Black Reconstruction in America*, Russell & Russell, New York.

Echikson, W. 2019, 'Viktor Orbán's Anti-Semitism Problem', *Politico*, 13 May, viewed 15 May 2023, https://www.politico.eu/article/viktor-orban-anti-semitism-problem-hungary-jews/

Elias, A., Ben, J., Mansouri, F. and Paradies, Y. 2021, 'Racism and Nationalism During and Beyond the Covid-19 Pandemic', *Ethnic and Racial Studies*, vol. 44, no. 5, pp. 783–793.

Gellner, E. 1983, *Nations and Nationalism*, Cornell University Press, Ithaca, New York.

Gilroy, P. 2002, *There Ain't No Black in the Union Jack: The Cultural Politics of Race and Nation*, 2nd edn, Routledge, London.

Gollan, R. 1967, *Radical and Working Class Politics: A Study of Eastern Australia, 1850–1910*, Melbourne University Press, Melbourne, Victoria.

Goodhart, D. 2004, 'Too Diverse?', *Prospect Magazine*, 20 February 2004.

Goodhart, D. 2017, *The Road to Somewhere: The New Tribes Shaping British Politics*, Penguin, London.

Goodhart, D. 2019, 'Wishful Thinking and Unresolved Tensions', *Ethnicities*, vol. 19, no. 6, pp. 983–990.

Gossett, T.F. 1997, *Race: The History of an Idea in America*, new edn, Oxford University Press, New York and Oxford.

Greenfeld, L. 1992, *Nationalism: Five Roads to Modernity*, Harvard University Press, Cambridge, Massachusetts.

Hage, G. 1998, *White Nation: Fantasies of the Supremacy in a Multicultural Society*, Pluto Press, Sydney.

Hage, G. 2003, *Against Paranoid Nationalism: Searching for Hope in a Shrinking Society*, Pluto Press, Sydney, New South Wales.

Hall, S. 2017, *The Fateful Triangle: Race, Ethnicity, Nation*, edited by K. Mercer, Harvard University Press, Cambridge, Massachusetts, and London.

Helgerson, R. 1992, *Forms of Nationhood: The Elizabethan Writing of England*, University of Chicago Press, Chicago, Illinois, and London.

Hobsbawm, E.J. 1990, *Nations and Nationalism Since 1780: Programme, Myth, Reality*, Cambridge University Press, Cambridge, and New York.

Hochschild, A.R. 2016, *Strangers in Their Own Land: Anger and Mourning on the American Right*, The New Press, New York and London.

Horsman, R. 1981, *Race and Manifest Destiny: The Origins of American Racial Anglo-Saxonism*, Harvard University Press, Cambridge, Massachusetts, and London.

Hutchinson, J. 1994, *Modern Nationalism*, Fontana Press/Harper Collins, London.

Kaufmann, E. 2019, *Whiteshift: Populism, Immigration, and the Future of White Majorities*, Abrams Press, New York.

Kedourie, E. 1960, *Nationalism*, Hutchinson, London.

Kellaway, C. 1953, '"White Australia" – How Political Reality Became National Myth', *Australian Quarterly*, June, pp. 7–17.

Kohn, H. 1944, *The Idea of Nationalism: A Study of Its Origin and Background*, Macmillan, New York.

Lake, M. and Reynolds, H. 2008, *Drawing the Global Colour Line: White Men's Countries and the Question of Racial Equality*, Melbourne University Press, Carlton, Victoria.

Lentin, A. 2012, *Racism: A Beginner's Guide*, Oneworld Publications, London.

Lentin, A. 2017, 'On Class and Identity Politics', *Inference Review*, vol. 3, no. 2, viewed 15 May 2023, https://inference-review.com/letter/on-class-and-identity-politics.

Lentin, A. and Lentin, R. 2006, 'Introduction', in A. Lentin and R. Lentin (eds), *Race and State*, Cambridge Scholars Publishing, Cambridge, pp. 1–14.

Mapedzahama, V. and Kwansah-Aidoo, K. 2017, 'Blackness as Burden? The Lived Experience of Black Africans in Australia', *Sage Open*, July–September, pp. 1–13.

McGregor, R. 2006, 'The Necessity of Britishness: Ethno-Cultural Roots of Australian Nationalism', *Nations and Nationalism*, vol. 12, no. 3, pp. 493–511.

Miles, R. 1987, 'Recent Marxist Theories of Nationalism and the Issue of Racism', *The British Journal of Sociology*, vol. 38, no. 1, pp. 24–43.

Miles, R. and Brown, M. 2003, *Racism*, 2nd edn, Routledge, London.

Moran, A. 2017, *The Public Life of Australian Multiculturalism: Building a Diverse Nation*, Palgrave Macmillan, Basingstoke.

Mosse, G.L. 1978, *Toward the Final Solution: A History of European Racism*, J.M. Dent and Sons, London.

Mosse, G.L. 1981, *The Crisis of German Ideology: Intellectual Origins of the Third Reich*, Schocken Books, New York.

Mosse, G.L. 1985, *Nationalism and Sexuality: Respectability and Abnormal Sexuality in Modern Europe*, H. Fertig, New York.

Mosse, G.L. 1995, 'Racism and nationalism', *Nations and Nationalism*, vol. 1, no. 2, pp. 163–73.

Nairn, T. 1981, *The Break-up of Britain: Crisis and Neonationalism*, Verso, London.

Pearson, C.H. 1894, *National Life and Character: A Forecast*, 2nd edn, Macmillan, London.

Rattansi, A. 2020, *Racism: A Very Short Introduction*, 2nd edn, Oxford University Press, Oxford.

Reynolds, H. (compiler) 1989, *Dispossession: Black Australians and White Invaders*, Allen and Unwin, Sydney, New South Wales.

Roediger, D.R. 1991, *The Wages of Whiteness: Race and the Making of the American Working Class*, Verso, London.

Smith, A.D. 1987, *The Ethnic Origins of Nations*, Basil Blackwell, Oxford and New York.

Smith, A.D. 2009, *Ethno-Symbolism and Nationalism: A Cultural Approach*, Routledge, London and New York.

Valluvan, S. 2019, *The Clamour of Nationalism: Race and Nation in Twenty-First-Century Britain*, Manchester University Press, Manchester.

Valluvan, S. 2022, 'Racist Apologism and the Refuge of Nation', *Ethnic and Racial Studies*, vol. 45, no. 3, pp. 466–477.

Valluvan, S. and Kalra, V.S. 2019, 'Racial Nationalisms: Brexit, Borders and Little Englander Contradictions', *Ethnic and Racial Studies,* vol. 42, no. 14, pp. 2393–2412.

Virdee, S. and McGeever, B. 2018, 'Racism, Crisis, Brexit', *Ethnic and Racial Studies*, vol. 41, no. 10, pp. 1802–1819.

Wade, P. 2001, 'Racial Identity and Nationalism: A Theoretical View from Latin America', *Ethnic and Racial Studies,* vol. 24, no. 5, pp. 845–865.

Wolfe, P. 1999, *Settler Colonialism and the Transformation of Anthropology: The Politics and Poetics of an Ethnographic Event*, Cassell, London and New York.

Wolfe, P. 2016, *Traces of History: Elementary Structures of Race*, Verso, London and New York.

Woolmington, J. (ed.) 1973, *Aborigines in Colonial Society: 1788–1850. From 'Noble Savage' to 'Rural Pest'*, Cassell Australia, Melbourne, Victoria.

Yack, B .1996, 'The Myth of the Civic Nation', *Critical Review*, vol. 10, no. 2, pp. 193–211.

# THE SUBJECTIVITIES OF RACE AND RACISM

Racism, as a system, produces racist subjectivities, as well as racialised subjectivities (we can think of this as a continuum) – these in turn help to reproduce racism – to oil the racism machine and keep it moving. As Emirbayer and Desmond (2015, p. 243) have argued, 'No discussion of the racial order is possible without racialized selves'. In his earlier work Bonilla-Silva (1997) challenged sociologists to adopt and develop a materialist account of racism as systemic, and argued for the focus to be upon that structure and the practices that support that system of domination, rather than the attitudes and beliefs of individuals. However, in recent work Bonilla-Silva (2019) has addressed the theme of racist subjectivities more directly, via the concept of 'racialized emotions', arguing that it is important for sociologists of racism to understand how these contribute to the reproduction of the racist system.

Though implicit accounts of race subjectivities are often present, explicit attention to subjectivities is frequently neglected in sociological accounts of racism (and it has instead been left to disciplines like social psychology, with its focus on group emotions, processes of creating insiders and outsiders, prejudice and stereotyping; for a classic statement, see Allport 1954). There have nevertheless been important engagements between social science and psychoanalysis exploring this theme, especially within the Frankfurt school of critical theory, as well as later authors inspired by them, who attempted to explain the deep, complex interconnections between inner and external worlds (which were in fact always intermeshed). Stephen Frosh (1989, p. 210) has argued that a complete theory of racism

DOI: 10.4324/9781003267690-5

requires an account of the processes of its reproduction – and it is at the level of reproduction, and ongoing processes of racism, rather than as an explanation for the generation of racism and its systemic features, that psychoanalysis makes its contribution. Racism, he emphasises, 'is indubitably a social phenomenon' (Frosh 1989, p. 209), produced by economic and political oppression, including, most importantly, Western imperialism, serving particular dominant groups, and infused throughout society's institutions. Thus, as a large-scale, systemic phenomenon, it requires a sociohistorical explanation. Once historically formed, racism, as 'the most vicious and danger-ous form of social oppression', achieves its power in part by being 'inscribed deeply in individual psychology' (Frosh 1989, p. 210). The psychoanalytic understanding of racist subjectivity involves showing the processes by which society's ideologies and structures are internalised by individuals in racist societies. In addition, it helps explain how certain inhospitable features of modernity – including major inequalities and oppressions, fears and uncertainties related to identities in constant flux, and other destructive and frightening fea-tures of social life, including fragmentation– reverberate with and give shape to internal psychological life, exacerbating fears and anxie-ties that are a central part of psychological functioning, and resulting in various defensive mechanisms that feed directly into racist beliefs, feelings and actions (Frosh 1989, pp. 226–27).

There have also been important examples of sociological accounts of racist and racial subjectivities, drawing upon arguments about dis-courses and social positioning (often broadly influenced by Foucault) that will be discussed in this chapter. There have been various approaches to understanding racial and racist subjectivities, from the accounts of black subjectivities contained in famous works such as Frantz Fanon's (1968) *Black Skin, White Masks* (which also drew upon phenomenology and psychoanalysis), to the accounts of whiteness that have burgeoned into 'whiteness studies' since the late 1980s. Not all whiteness research is focused on the specificities of white identities; some is more of a broad critique of symbolic and violent 'whiteness', as a general world view and system through which people who are 'not-white' move and are oppressed – the notion of 'white spaces' has been an important source of investigation (see, for example, Ahmed 2007; Anderson 2015). I will also discuss Emirbayer and Desmond's (2015) account of racist and racialised subjectivities, which draws heavily on Bourdieu, in particular on the concept of racialised habitus – a concept that I will also illustrate through a brief discussion of the ethnographic work of Bourgois and Schonberg (2009).

## PSYCHOANALYTIC APPROACHES TO RACISM AND RACIST SUBJECTIVITIES

Intellectuals associated with the Frankfurt school, or critical theory, such as Wilhelm Reich ([1933] 1970), Erich Fromm (1960), and Theodore Adorno (Adorno et al. [1950]1969), especially in their direct engagement with Nazism, Fascism and anti-Semitism, provided historically situated, psychoanalytically informed accounts of racist subjectivities. And, since then, other theorists have followed this engagement with psychoanalysis to understand racism, including Fanon (1968), Kovel (1970), Sherwood (1980), Theweleit (1987), Rustin (1991, ch. 3), Frosh (1989), Clarke (2003), and Hook (2004, 2008, 2018), among many others.

That said, a perennial problem of psychoanalytic understandings of racism has been a tendency to reduce racism, racist expressions and racist social relations to psychological states or particular workings out of 'universal' libidinal (instinctual) conflicts and fantasies as ultimate causes or explanations (Cohen 2002; Goldberg 1993; Hook 2018). Such reductionism is hard to avoid when trying to explain connections between psychology and broad social phenomena such as racism. In addition, psychoanalysis, like most brands of Western thinking, has also been shaped by Eurocentrism (for example, assuming 'universal' unconscious processes unaffected by culture, but drawn from European experiences and cultures), colonialism and racism, as can be seen in some of its fundamental assumptions about the distinctions between 'civilisation' and 'primitive', and also in the ways that it characterised so called primitive cultures as 'childlike', or assigning them to the pre-history of modern, enlightened humanity (Frosh 2013).

Despite the weaknesses and flaws of the approach, an understanding of complex subjectivity (with an account of the unconscious) seems necessary in order to provide a convincing explanation of at least some aspects of racism and how it works, especially at the level of interpersonal relations and imaginings of the 'racial other', including its ferocity and 'excess'. This includes understanding the tenacious hold that racist beliefs have, even when rational arguments are used to challenge such beliefs (Adorno et al. [1950] 1969; Rustin 1991; Frosh 1989; Hook 2004). In the absence of alternatives, these accounts are perhaps the best that we have in terms of explaining the excess of many violent racist acts, including sexually violent ones.

Wilhelm Reich in *Mass Psychology of Fascism,* first published in the early 1930s, theorised authoritarian family relations, with harsh, patriarchal, disciplinarian and punishing fathers, that repressed sexuality and helped produce the 'character armour' that, in turn, resulted in a mass of people prone to Fascism. Like other critics, he highlighted the propensity of the lower middle class (petite bourgeoisie) to support Fascist ideologies and political parties and to be attracted to racism (such as anti-Semitism), pointing out that this arose because of their particular powerlessness in the economic and social structure and the prevalence of an authoritarian family structure that reflected that social location (Reich [1933] 1970, pp. 40–62). Reich argued that the Fascist youth and labour clubs allowed some diverted expression of homosexual sexual desire, including the intense adoration of authoritarian leaders. Sadistic impulses were expressed through socially sanctioned targets, including, most importantly, the Jews, as the 'race enemy' of the German people. His theme of character armour was taken up in new ways by other critical theorists (Fromm 1960; Adorno et al. [1950] 1969) and influenced later thinkers such as Klaus Theweleit (1987), author of the two-volume *Male Fantasies,* who studied the 'male armour' of the *Freikorps* (via letters and other writing) in Germany in the 1920s, as well as Fascist writers of that period, whose subjectivities were fundamentally organised around misogyny and anti-Semitism, driven by a repulsion and phobic reaction to fluidity, which the feminine, among other things (the figure of the 'Jew' among them), represented, in a chain of signification.

Erich Fromm (1960), in works such as *Fear of Freedom*, sought to explain the appeal and success of Fascism in Europe by arguing in a related way for a particular form of sado–masochistic character structure that involved sadistic destructiveness, violence and aggression aimed at socially sanctioned outgroups, and masochistic relations with authoritarian leaders. Fromm linked this modern character structure with the shift from feudalism to modernity (and the tumult of capitalism) that, echoing Marx's 'all that is solid melts into air', meant that people were faced with unprecedented experiences of freedom, and with identity uncertainty that resulted in characteristic psychological propensities to flee from freedom. Fromm adopted a broad Freudian theory of the instincts, seeing (like Reich) the appeal of Fascism as being related to forms of repression of more positive sexual instincts, and playing down the propensity for destructiveness that Freud emphasised in his later account of the 'death instinct' in *Civilization and its Discontents*. In Fromm's view, the kinds of destructiveness that led to Fascism (and by extension to racism) were socially produced, and related to the ways that societies, and especially the class-based societies of capitalism, thwarted individual expansiveness, spontaneity and expressiveness.

Adorno et al.'s ([1950] 1969) *Authoritarian Personality* involved a direct engagement with psychoanalysis in order to understand the psychic structure (or, as these authors termed it, the authoritarian personality) that was most amenable to extreme forms of prejudice such as racism and anti-Semitism and political formations such as Fascism. They developed their famous F-scale survey instrument to measure the authoritarian personality. Emerging out of the particular economic and social condition of the petite bourgeoisie and its family structures (but also reflecting a broader mass experience), with authoritarian, affection-withholding fathers and distant mothers, wide-scale development of a sado-masochistic personality prone to aggressive stereotyping, black-and-white thinking, slavish obedience to authoritarian leaders, the inability to tolerate difference and complexity in the world (which such personalities desired to wipe out) and aggression against others, significantly produced and supported racist prejudices and racist societies. Adorno and colleagues used a range of psychoanalytic concepts, ideas and theories – such as the structure of mind (unconscious and conscious, ego, id and superego), the Oedipus complex, repressed urges, wish fulfilment, symptom, neurosis and psychosis, aggressiveness and destructiveness, displacement, projection, 'omnipotent' and other fantasies, defence mechanisms, and rationalisation – to explain the nature and tenacity of prejudice. Adorno's use of extended essays (see especially Ch XVI) specifically explaining anti-Semitism was in many ways a tour de force, full of insight, including about the nature of alienating bureaucratic, mass society and culture, destructive ideological structures, and the particularity of myths about Jews that made them such targets for psychological projection and scapegoating.

Sociologists such as David Wellman and Zygmunt Bauman have critiqued the focus on personality types in understanding the ways that racism works and reproduces itself. In *Portraits of White Racism*, Wellman (1993) argued for an approach more focused upon the relations between economic, status, and political interests on the one hand and ideological racism on the other, and the ways that this shapes racial domination enacted by whites as rational and normal from their particular racial locations, and does not require 'abnormal', destructive and hateful psychologies or personalities, arguing that:

> . . . racial consciousness is still most fruitfully analysed in rela-
> tion to the organisation of advantage rather than the structure of
> personality. Thus, racism continues to be a defence of racial priv-
> ilege, not a psychological abnormality or the product of psycho-
> logical manipulation. And the racial consciousness of European
> Americans is still profitably interpreted as culturally acceptable
> responses to struggles over scarce resources, not ill will or the
> deviant expressions of intolerant, unsocialized bigots. Put differ-
> ently, racial consciousness still needs to be located at the socio-
> logical intersection between structural and cultural constructions.
> (Wellman 1993, pp. 24–25)

Similarly, in *Modernity and the Holocaust*, Bauman (1989) critiqued the 'authoritarian personality' approach to understanding extreme forms of racism, like the racist anti-Semitism leading up to the Holocaust, arguing that racism organised on a societal level, as in Nazi Germany, did not require a mass of 'authoritarian personali-ties', nor did it even require the production of mass racist conscious-ness. Instead, it could rely upon the workings of bureaucracy and gradual processes and policies that enacted moral distancing between 'Germans' and Jews, supported by the existence of a much older European pre-racist (pre-modern) anti-Semitism of a less genocidal character, but one that stimulated moral indifference to the plight of Jews under Nazism.

Even more specifically focused on racism (rather than generalised prejudice and character structure accounts of propensity for stereo-typing, for destructiveness and for Fascism), in his extended empirical example of the historical formation of white supremacy in the US, Joel Kovel (1970) explained how colonialism and slavery resulted in the association of certain primitive (unconscious) fantasies and symbols with symbols and fantasies of race. This also links back directly to the arguments about the powerful link between Western modernity and racism (see Chapter 1) – with Kovel's (1995) critique of the way that puritan Western modernity and capitalism created white selves that renounced sexuality and the enjoyment of a more polymorphous and open psychic experience of the world, that then contributed to projecting fantasies of the licentious black self that was an object of both intense desire and revulsion. Kovel provided compelling accounts of the fantastical imaginings of white racist subjects in their relations with black subjects in the US, including the sexual fantasies, obsessions and repressions that were involved. However, there was a reductive tendency in this work, to take the very basic, primitive fantasies of all human subjectivity and to see these as working their way, in a disastrous fashion, through white Western history, so that the whole of modernity became a kind of repressed fleeing and avoidance of dirt (derived from universal anal fantasies associated with the very beginnings of subjectivity). Kovel (1970) made a distinction between dominative and aversive racism in North America and argued that the former derived from and was associated with Oedipal fantasies, while the latter was derived from and associated with even earlier defecation fantasies, dating back to the symbolisation involved in early processes of the infant's separation of self from the mother and world. In this account, in the context of a racist social formation, including a distinctive system of slavery, black African Americans were made the repositories for fantasies about expelled faeces and dirt.

Frantz Fanon (1968) in *Black Skin, White Masks*, produced a classic, visceral, autobiographical account of the experience of black subjectivity in a white-dominated, colonialist society. This account of black subjectivity has been the focus for much of the taking up of Fanon since then, especially by scholars of colour and decolonizing theorists, with the 'Fact of Blackness' chapter being the centrepiece. Fanon is rightly famous for the way that he explained the damage that racism did to black subjectivities, drawing upon Lacanian concepts, including the 'mirror stage', to argue that the black person is inhibited in their sense of unified subjectivity by seeing him- or herself always negatively fragmented in a white mirror; a racialised version of the argument that Lacan made in his famous essay 'The mirror stage as formative of the function of the I as revealed in the psychoanalytic experience' (Lacan 1977 [1949]; see also Frosh 2013). Where the white person looks into the metaphoric mirror and sees an illusory image of white unity (though, see my qualification below), the black person only sees the negative white reflection of the black self. The black person growing up in a white supremacist, colonial culture and society seeks an ideal of 'whiteness' that they can never achieve and will always be barred from due to the 'fact of blackness' and the damaging, eviscerating colonial white gaze. The brutalised and frightening image of blackness and of 'the Negro' also haunts the black imagination, including dream life.

However, at the same time, given that productions of self and other are intersubjective (they form a dialectic of self and other), and drawing upon his therapeutic psychiatric work with a range of white and black patients, his deep knowledge and reading of French and other Western history and literature, and popular culture (including children's literature and folk stories), Fanon also produced a vivid portrayal of white subjectivities. The colonial encounter is central to this account, as is the development of white Western modernity. One of Fanon's key insights in this respect was that, within a racist society, the black body becomes a 'phobic' object for whites. There was a long history through which that occurred, including developing accounts of 'blackness' and associating it with all that was 'evil' and hidden, but also secretly desired, and, in Fanon's view, an extensive form of instinctual, including sexual, renouncement, through puritan, white Western culture, which shaped particular imaginings of the body and of the white person's relation to their own body.

Fanon provides a fascinating, phenomenological and psycho-analytically informed account of the ways that images, imaginings and hallucinatory visions of blackness, black bodies and their sexual potency, violence and power, structured white subjectivities, at their core, arguing for example that the phobia of the black body is so intense that it disrupts white subjectivity and experiences of the white body. Returning to Lacan's mirror stage, where the subject 'misrecognises' itself as a unitary 'I', he argues that once the image of the 'Negro' enters the white imagination, as it does early in the psychic life organised by the colonised world, this disrupts the feeling of imaginary unity and bodily integrity: 'the real other for the white man is and will continue to be the black man. And conversely. Only for the white man The Other is perceived on the level of the body image, absolutely as the not-self – that is, the unidentifiable, the unassimilable' (Fanon 1968, p. 161). The 'imago' of the black body, which involves the fear of the biological for the white, is central to the reproduction of racist relations, and guides white people in all their relations with black 'Others' (Fanon 1968, p. 169).

Writers on racism influenced by the work of psychoanalyst Melanie Klein tend to focus on the impact of pre-Oedipal object relations, and in particular on what she termed paranoid-schizoid and depressive positions of mental functioning (that are never completely overcome in the psyche), and mechanisms of defence against unconscious anxiety and instinctual conflicts, such as splitting and projection/projective-identification, that then map onto racist objects/others in the external world, linking up in continuous ways with the psychic inner-worlds (in other words, in people's racist subjectivities) (see Sherwood 1980; Frosh 1989). In these accounts, the important contribution of psychoanalysis to the explanation of racist subjectivity might be in helping to explain what is going on in more extreme racist movements and acts of racist violence, and in explaining the hatreds and extreme stereotyping involved in some forms of racism. According to Rustin (1991), this understanding of the deeper psychic dimensions of racism is also vital in understanding the possibilities of successful anti-racism. He argues that anti-racism strategies that mainly attend to trying to undo 'false' racist beliefs and ideas may not actually engage with the deeper, more unconscious workings of race, including their powerful hold as sources of threatened identity, and the uses of hated racist objects to protect the self. These Kleinian psychoanalytic accounts may also contribute to understanding how emotionally wounding racism is, in that it gets deeply into people's psyches, especially the victims of racism. Simon Clarke (2003), for example, saw 'projective identification' as a central concept that helped explain intersubjective relations in racist systems, in particular focusing on the way that the recipients of projective identification take into themselves (internalise) harmful projective identifications (for example, victims of racism). He argued that projective identification shed light on Fanon's experience of abject blackness in *Black Skin, White Masks* (see Clarke 2003, pp. 162–63).

Derek Hook, writing about post-apartheid South Africa and drawing upon the work of Zizek, Lacan, Kristeva and others, has argued that attention to psychic life, using concepts like *jouissance* ('theft of enjoyment', as in Zizek's account of what psychically animates and drives racism) (see Hook 2018), and abjection (the powerful fears and anxieties around bodies, death and pollution, as in Mary Douglas and Julia Kristeva) (see Hook 2004), is needed to truly confront racism. He argues that these psychoanalytic approaches, with their deep understanding of the psychic complexity of racist subjectivity and affective life, add to the explanation of the tenacity of racism – historical, everyday, structural – in changed political circumstances in places like South Africa. This would be one element of the answer to the question:

> why is it that one could (theoretically) change the concerned social constructions of race and racism, transform the terms of public discourse, change even the material and structural conditions of society such that there is no longer any palpable reward for being racist and that racism would conceivably nevertheless persist?
>
> (Hook 2004, p. 678)

## SOCIOLOGICAL APPROACHES TO RACIAL AND RACIST SUBJECTIVITIES

I will turn now to other more sociological accounts of racial and racist subjectivities. As a way of opening, I introduce Appiah's general approach to thinking about racial identities. Appiah (1994) while arguing against the existence of 'races' – a meaningless biological category, if thought of as signifying distinct biological groups – nevertheless argued that racial identifications existed, and that these could be thought of as emerging from a sociocultural history of racism. He characterised racial identities as follows:

> a label, *R*,
>     associated with *ascriptions* by most people (where ascription involves descriptive criteria for applying the label); and

*identifications* by those that fall under it (where identification implies a shaping role for the label in the intentional acts of the possessors, so that they sometimes act *as an* R);

where there is a history of associating possessors of the label with an inherited racial essence (even if some who use the label no longer believe in racial essences).

(Appiah 1994, p. 110)

In this formulation, 'racial identities could persist even if nobody believed in racial essences, provided both ascription and identification continue' (Appiah 1994, p. 110). Appiah makes clear in further discussion that racism is centrally involved here, in terms of the history of the race ascriptions, which often have racist effects, such that inhabiting racial identity has more positive consequences for some (e.g. whites) and more negative consequences for others (e.g., blacks), though for the latter racial identity can be embraced as a source of resistance:

It is obvious, I think, that the persistence of racism means that racial ascriptions have negative consequences for some and positive consequences for others – creating, in particular, the white skin privilege that it is so easy for people who have it to forget; and it is clear, too, that for those who suffer from the negative consequences, racial identification is a predictable response, especially where the project it suggests is that the victims of racism should join together to resist it

(Appiah 1994, p. 111)

What Appiah is getting at is not just the cognitive but also the affective experience of race. The study of 'racialized emotions' indicates how different emotional repertoires are produced for different racialised subjectivities in racist systems, which, Bonilla-Silva argues, contributes to our understanding of how racism works and is reproduced, and also of its immense psychic costs, especially for non-whites:

Although racial affairs cannot be properly understood without a structural perspective on racism, I no longer regard racial domination as just a matter of presumably objective practices and mechanisms driven by the socioeconomic material interests of actors. Racial actors, both dominant and subordinate, simply cannot transact their lives without RE [racialized emotions]. While Whites believe the system is fair . . . , the racially subordinate experience the unfairness of the system, leading each group to develop emotions that match their 'perceptual segregation' . . . Accordingly, races fashion an emotional subjectivity generally fitting of their location in the racial order.

(Bonilla-Silva 2019, p. 2)

As Bonilla-Silva argued, he had been *feeling* race his whole life, without attempting to theorise it. Having previously neglected this dimension, he now argued that understanding racialised emotion was crucial to developing an *affective* politics of anti-racism. 'Eradicating racism' he argued, 'will require a radical process to uproot its visible, "objective" components as well as demolish its emotional skeleton' (Bonilla-Silva 2019, p. 2). Distinctive racial emotional repertoires shape both orientation to society and how people with different racial subjectivities read each other, interact in social situations, and apprehend social realities, typically in divergent ways depending on their racial position. Racialised subjects do not simply learn to be so by learning through interactions and experience 'how to interpret racialized relationships', but they also learn this emotionally (Bonilla-Silva 2019, p. 4).

Bonilla-Silva (2019, p. 2) has argued that

whether consciously or not, we all feel race because the category is produced not just 'objectively' but subjectively. Much like class and gender, race cannot come to life without being infused with emotions, thus, racialized actors feel the emotional weight of their categorical location.

Racialised emotions are not emotions in general, but the 'socially engendered' emotions specifically generated by racial situations. These include not only interactions, but also engagement with images, news items, locations and so on that people encounter (Bonilla-Silva 2019, p. 3). They are relational, as can be seen in the binary of 'whiteness' and 'blackness', which means that whites fear blacks in social encounters (because of constructions of blacks as savage, dangerous, violent, etc.), while blacks experience anxiety, fear and discomfort in 'white spaces'. Even white resistance to racism – for example, challenging family members' racist utterances – can be suppressed, and the racist order thus continually reproduced because of being constrained by white social relations, group belonging and historically shaped emotional scripts and 'emotional group norms' (Bonilla-Silva 2019, p. 4).

bell hooks provides a vivid account of such lived experiences of race, in her many books and essays including *Ain't I A Woman* (hooks 1981) and in *Black Looks* (hooks 1992), where she highlights the everyday terrorisation of black women (and men) by white people and by 'whiteness' as a system of norms, assumptions and stereotypes and social positioning of power, under patriarchal, capitalist white supremacy. Such research and writing, often deeply autobiographical but at the same time sociologically and historically grounded in the effects of political and economic structures, slavery and its ongoing structuring of social interaction between whites and blacks, racist policy frameworks and social movements, provides vivid portraits of intersectional black subjectivities.

Bonilla-Silva also argues that in the racist system there is a hierarchy dictating which emotions are taken seriously – for example, the 'hurt feelings' of whites in difficult racial encounters are treated as more worthy and legitimate than the anger and rage or hurt of blacks and other people of colour. Such emotions are often treated as irrational, as overreactions, as misreadings of social situations (Bonilla-Silva 2019, p. 6). The raw feelings related to publicised acts of racial terror when expressed by people of colour can be downplayed, or not understood by whites, who can experience more emotional distance from such acts against people who they do not personally know (Bonilla-Silva 2019, p. 7). Dominant whites gain not only material but emotional well-being from their dominant position, and therefore there are powerful reactions when such 'well-being' is disrupted – for example, when they perceive that racially 'inferior' others are gaining ground, including gaining status, which directly affects their emotional well-being. He sees, for example, Trump's appeal in the way that he connected with whites' sense of emotional well-being, by claiming that he would control and deal with various non-white (including Muslim) others, who are considered as less worthy, less hard-working and more dangerous ('black urban crime', 'Muslim terrorists').

### Racial discourses and subjective positionings

One prominent focus of sociological approaches to understanding racist subjectivities is on the ways that racist and racial discourses that circulate and predominate in society position people into particular subjectivities that then help to reproduce racist systems and societies. This is the general approach of Miles (Miles 1989; Miles and Brown 2003) when he focuses upon signification and representations and the intersubjective nature of racist/racialised identities formed out of such historical and transforming (through time) processes of distinguishing between self and others, which are also associated with racist group identities. There is often a general Foucauldian understanding of discursive formations underpinning such theories.

Goldberg (1993) made this argument in *Racist Culture*, where he addressed racist subjectivity as a direct product of the possible positionings within racist social formations, making use of Althusser's notion of 'interpellation', 'calling' different individuals to specific ideological, racial subject positions as made available through the symbolic order of a racial formation:

> By converging with related discourses and interiorized by the individual, the discourse underlying racism comes to codefine not only subjectivity but otherness also. It molds subjects' relations with others. Subjects' actions are rendered meaningful to themselves and others in light of the values that this discourse, among others, makes available or articulates to the parties involved. In this way, racialized discourse – reproduced, redefined perhaps, and acted upon – reconstitutes the relations of power that produced them.
>
> (Goldberg 1993, p. 57)

Althusser's (1971) notion of interpellation concerned the ways that subjects were 'called' or 'hailed' to subject positions in ideology, which direct thought, emotion and action, and the involvement of these in relation to others, co-defined in the discourse, along certain lines. These forms of interpellation can forestall, for example, the extension of human solidarity to certain groups of people defined as outgroups, or racial antagonists or enemies. In Goldberg's account, individuals can move between these subject positions responding to the power of prevailing or emergent ideologies. Goldberg writes of 'discursive fields' in which racial subjects interact:

> racialized discourse does not consist simply in descriptive representations of others, it includes a set of hypothetical premisses about human kinds . . . and about the differences between them (both mental and physical). It involves a class of ethical choices (e.g., domination and subjugation, entitlement and restriction, disrespect and abuse). And it incorporates a set of institutional regulations, directions, and pedagogic models.
>
> (Goldberg 1993, p. 47)

Thus racist ideologies can shape relations so that negatively constructed racialised others can only enter designated spheres of social life under certain conditions and in a certain manner – for example, via forms of deference – or may be completely excluded and kept at a distance. Or, in extreme cases, other 'races' find no place in one's universe of moral obligation.

The potential dynamism of such an approach to theorising subjectivity is evident in Nigerian-British scholar Amina Mama's (1995) *Beyond the Masks*, based on interview/focus group research and participant observation in groups and meetings in the early 1980s, and focused on the subjectivities of black women in Britain. Her title was addressed to Fanon's argument that black people wore 'white masks', which she sought to challenge and go beyond. She combined a Foucauldian/post-structuralist approach to discourse with a psychodynamic understanding of the psychosocial in order to capture both the fluid positionings that women moved through – because of being positioned and influenced by multiple and competing discourses on race and identity – and also the rigidity of subject positions because of the powerful psychodynamics, including unconscious processes, that kept people tied to particular subject positions, as well as the support that hegemonic discourses (including of racial types, characters, emotional life, etc.) gained through societies' political and social structures. The complex of discourses that women negotiated were historical, cultural productions, and included both dominant racial and resisting discourses, the former tied to key institutions, formal knowledges, assumptions, etc., and thus hegemonic, powerfully supported and difficult to resist and overcome within subjectivity; the latter emerging through the resistance activities of social movements and collectivities. Mama also focused on activist black feminist transformation and consciousness raising and highlighted the creativeness, openness to change, and active challenging by these women of the negative racist constructions and assumptions about racial psychologies that oppressed them. Such challenges and subjective transformations, she argued, were collective achievements brought about through social movement mobilisation and active, black feminist consciousness raising. The challenges and transformations also came about because of discursive contradictions and oppressions faced by black women, meaning that the 'anxieties and discomforts of being black and female' made these women 'seek and take up new positions' (Mama 1995, p. 164).

One of Mama's powerful critiques was of images of black pathology, and of the tendency (including among some black theorists – for example, Fanon) to homogenise black subjectivities as completely damaged by colonialist racism, and in fundamentally the same ways. She aimed to highlight the complexity and dynamism of black subjectivities, which were never simply related to blackness and which were transformed over time in relation to different social and political contexts and conditions, including the world brought about by anti-colonial movements, black nationalism and black feminism, that had challenged the West. As she wrote (Mama 1995, p. 142):

> people are not simply either black or white but rather complex, multilayered beings, with a capacity to move between positions, create new ones, and constantly negotiate and renegotiate their identities as they struggle to make sense of a world in which fixed categories are constantly subverted and changed.

Examining white women's subjectivities, Ruth Frankenberg's (1993) *White Women, Race Matters* was also an interview-based research project, exploring the subjectivities of progressive, mainly anti-racist, white women from different ages and backgrounds in the US, and making a significant contribution, alongside earlier pioneering work by Du Bois ('The Souls of White Folk', Du Bois 1975), the above-mentioned Fanon, bell hooks and Toni Morrison, to what has become known as whiteness studies. The book analyses the social geography of race, across different locations, making the point that in all the women's narratives 'landscape and the experience of it were racially structured – whether these narratives seemed to be marked predominantly by the presence or the absence of people of color' (Frankenberg 1993, p. 69). Her point was that, in racially defined societies, race affects everyone – but in distinctive ways; racism also powerfully structures whites' experience and sense of self and others.

Frankenberg highlights what has been a major point made by whiteness theories about the ways that white subjectivity is so taken for granted, so much considered the norm, that it is not even imagined as a racial identity. Instead, all non-white others are considered as raced. This is one reason why the white women she spoke to were so inarticulate about race matters, which she needed to approach in very round-about ways through lengthy interview discussions interspersed with the telling of her own provocative stories about her experiences as a white woman. By contrast, one could not envisage many people who were non-white *not* thinking at some point every day about the nature of their difference, their markedness as raced, in white dominant or white supremacist societies. bell hooks (2013) gives a powerful account of this experience of always being racially defined, and perceiving oneself as belonging to a black race, in her essay 'Writing Beyond Race' (from her book with the same title), where she speaks of staying in her home so that she can avoid the constant daily assaults of 'the culture of imperialist white supremacist capitalist patriarchy' (hooks 2013, p. 185) that forever remind her of being black. The essay begins with the sentence, 'Home is the only place where there is no race' (hooks 2013, p. 184), and she writes that '[a]s soon as I walk out the door, race is waiting, like a watchful stalker ready to grab me and keep me in place, ready to remind me that slavery is not just in the past but here right now ready to entrap, to hold and bind' (hooks 2013, p. 185).

Frankenberg highlights the uneasiness that underpins the efforts to maintain a stance of being 'color blind' – the claim that colour is not really relevant, or that the white women who she interviewed, many liberal and feminist, do not really see it or think of it. The underside of colour-blindness is that an individual can feel (even if unconsciously or semi-consciously) that non-whiteness (colour) is bad in and of itself and should not be mentioned, or even noticed:

> people of color are 'good' only insofar as their 'coloredness' can be bracketed and ignored, and this bracketing is contingent on the ability or the decision – in fact, the virtue – of a 'noncolored' – or white – self. Colorblindness, despite the best intentions of its adherents, in this sense preserves the power structure inherent in essentialist racism.
>
> (Frankenberg 1993, p. 147)

This also intersects with liberal humanist discourse, setting up something like two levels of identity and then dismissing one of them – an essential, under-the-skin self, and a coloured racial allocation, the relevance of which is dismissed (Frankenberg 1993, pp. 147–148). This evasive discourse also implicitly denies the relevance of the social aggregates related to race and skin colour, and thus is useful politically for those seeking to preserve the racial hierarchy. The white women who Frankenberg interviewed, who often refused to talk about race at all, defensively claimed that they never noticed race or colour, and in their discourses about their life experiences in American society used strategies of 'essentialisation', 'colour evasion' and 'power evasion' to explain away racial difference, division and racial discomfort (Frankenberg 1993).

In more recent work, Steve Garner has explored the nature of white subjectivities by examining 'the racialisation of white identities' in the UK, via a psychosocially informed interview project with about 400 white (English) participants in six UK cities (Garner 2015, p. 14), in the mid to late 2000s, 'focusing on community, national and local identity, home and entitlement' (Garner 2015, p. 157). He explores these identities via the concept of 'frames', which he adapts from Goffman's 'frame analysis' as 'interpretive structures that allow people to inject meaning into things that happen, and thus organize people's experiences and guide them in their actions' (Garner 2015, p. 13). There are four such main frames: (i) 'Unfairness', which concerns perceptions of the unfair distribution of society's key resources, underpinning ideas and feelings that whites have become disadvantaged and ignored by the state in key areas; (ii) 'Political Correctness Gone Mad' (PSGM), which refers to the commonly held belief that the world is constrained by unprecedented 'political correctness' on issues of race, that white people cannot speak freely, importantly about what they perceive as discrimination against whites; (iii) 'From repressed Englishness to the (un)finished business of Empire', which reflects a set of thoughts about Englishness being more meaningful and important than abstract Britishness, as well as a diverse set of feelings and reflections on Empire ranging from renewed pride, to some recognition that bad things were done but a prevailing feeling that this period is over and that people should move on; and (iv) '(Im)possible integration', which is a way of thinking that sets the conditions for adequate and inadequate integration of migrants/non-English people, using a set of criteria including language, dress, sexual relations, religiosity and degree of ethnic/racial segregation (assumed to be self-segregation), and having an underpinning doubt about the capacities of some cultures to integrate and the problems that this presents to Englishness, where too many different values are allowed to circulate in the national space (Garner 2015, pp. 15–16).

These frames form what he terms a 'moral economy of whiteness' as a 'discursive cultural fabric out of which identities appear to be wrought'. This moral economy of whiteness involves the 'micro-level establishment of a "we" enabling talk of a "they" to have resonance as an expression referring to the non-economic elements of whiteness, and how they are ordered through ideas of fairness' (Garner 2015, p. 163). This is like a kind of 'neoliberal common sense', practical knowledge available to ordinary people, not requiring deep thought and reading of complex texts, but rather providing everyday cognitive and emotional tools for imagining one's place in the world and in relation to the local community, the nation and Others.

These white identities are class-shaped, embattled identities (a trait shared by middle-class and working-class whites), dealing with a context that they feel has become hostile, unsupportive and discriminatory to its white majority. At the same time, it involves a 'post-racial' world view in the sense that race is not meant to affect the lives of many racialised non-white people, while at the same time feeling that they are the victims of a new era of race-based political correctness where, as an increasingly embattled white English identity, they are losing ground to a multitude of racial others who the state actively helps. This belief is, of course, not borne out by the statistics, which indicate that, in the UK (as in many other white majority countries), people from minority ethnic backgrounds are in fact the ones losing ground (Garner 2015, p. 159).

### Racial habitus

Another powerful way to theorise racial/racist subjectivities, while avoiding the pitfall of individual psychologising (as critiqued in the above discussion of some psychoanalytic approaches), is to make use of the concept of 'habitus' – in this case, racial or racialised habitus. Habitus, as theorised by Pierre Bourdieu (1977), is a concept that seeks to overcome the agency-structure dualism, showing how agency is always structured, and is also related to key concepts including capitals and fields. Habitus is generated (in particular class and other social circumstances) but it is also generative; it gives us the (unconscious) tools (dispositions) to act, to create our actions, and to engage in fields that are always structured by power, where we also utilise the capitals that we have available (capitals are themselves related to our habitus) – economic, social, cultural and symbolic. Habitus is not simply agency or subjectivity; it combines structure and agency, objectivity and subjectivity. It refers to habituated dispositions in its theory of action. Habitus is deeply expressed through the body (see also Wacquant 2016).

In *The Racial Order*, Emirbayer and Desmond (2015) argue for the importance of thinking through the various forms of racial habitus, adapting this concept from Bourdieu and, before him, Durkheim. Bourdieu analysed and discussed habitus mainly through culture, class and gender, but others, such as the ethnographers Bourgois and Schonberg (2009), made extensive use of the concept of racial or ethnicised habitus in their powerful study of drug-injecting homeless people in San Francisco, whose subjectivities involved forms of racialised habitus formed through childhood and adult lives immersed in the deep structures of racialised society, and which both enabled them to operate in distinctive ways in their racially mixed milieu, resulting in forms of camaraderie, conflict and betrayal, across racial lines, and also constrained them and contributed to their suffering (see further discussion below).

Reflecting on racial habitus, Emirbayer and Desmond (2015, p. 237) describe it as follows: 'A product of history, both collective (phylogenesis) and individual (ontogenesis), the racial actor incorporates race into her very bones and inhabits the racial order not only cognitively but also through her moral dispositions and expressive styles.' The most decisive shift in their analysis is from a focus on prejudiced beliefs and attitudes to the study of deep, practical and unconscious dispositions, that are fundamentally racialised, and 'the racialized body in all its cognitive, moral, and expressive dimensions' (Emirbayer and Desmond 2015, p. 280).

In their characterisation of white habitus, they state:

> Above all, the white habitus is characterized by a mode of being that (mis)represents itself as unraced and universal, even as it marks other collective habitus in the space (the habitus of people of color) as raced and particular. In its refusal or, more to the point, its dispositional disinclination to speak its own name, it presents itself as normal.
>
> (Emirbayer and Desmond 2015, p. 251)

Their characterisation is relatively brief, and its main outlined elements would be very familiar to those writing about whiteness and white spaces – including notions like being an 'absent core', the race that does not think it is raced, the race that feels unnerved when its assumptions of free access to all public spaces, including 'black social spaces', is thwarted (Anderson 2015), the race that cannot bear being characterised by someone else in race terms (because white people never think of themselves that way).

White habitus is the dominant habitus in the racialised field. Non-white or black habitus is explored through the concept of symbolic violence (Bourdieu 1991) – so, therefore, in terms of the ways that it is drawn into a dominating field, and to some extent accepts its 'naturalised' position within that field. As Emirbayer and Desmond argue:

> Racial domination persists because the dominants are able to impose (on fields in which they enjoy privilege) certain categories, classifications, and structures of affect that ensure their continued ascendancy; they are able to produce (in these fields) subordinate actors predisposed to think, perceive, feel and act in ways that consolidate the relations of domination.
>
> (Emirbayer and Desmond 2015, p. 255)

In such systems, black people and others subordinated by dominant whiteness are affected by 'subtle, insidious, invisible mechanisms of internalized oppression' (Emirbayer and Desmond 2015, p. 256).

The ethnographic work of Bourgois and Schonberg (2009) provides deeper insight into the nature of racialised habitus. They spent over ten years engaged with a group of racially diverse, homeless, street-based heroin users in San Francisco during the 1990s and early 2000s. Their book, *Righteous Dopefiend*, contains detailed portraits of many individuals and discusses how racialised habitus works and what it does, how it shapes and directs the lives of the book's protagonists. Racialised habitus is not only general (it can be characterised in general terms), but also particular, tied to the intricacies of individual biographies, gender, racial mixture, sexuality and specific social fields where individuals grew up. They also emphasise the embodied character of habitus, for example in different injecting practices that generally distinguish white from African American heroin injectors, with subsequent different bodily scarring and experiences of health and disease. Habitus shapes different drugs consumption practices, and different ways of carrying the body. They distinguish broadly between the 'outlaw' habitus of African American homeless drug addicts, and the 'outcast' habitus of white, homeless heroin addicts.

Outlaw habitus involves certain upright and proud ways of carrying the body, proud styles of dress and hygiene, distinctive styles of street begging (active, even aggressive), ways of moving about the city (African Americans in their cohort were hyper-mobile), relations with employment (and relations with employers shaped by the history of slavery), savvy ways of getting the cash needed for the daily heroin supply to ward off dope sickness, ways of experiencing drugs (generally displaying hyper-enjoyment, ecstasy, and persistently searching for veins in order to ensure the best 'high'), patterns of sexual expression (also profoundly shaped by gender and sexuality, with males openly bragging about their sexual prowess and activities, and using sexually violent speech), and forms of family connection (remaining connected to families despite living on the street).

The white racial 'outcast' habitus reflects the ways that these homeless white men and women are placed in the racial hierarchy, where they feel that their position should be above that of the many other non-white people that they encounter, but where they also feel that they are immense failures as whites (in ways that the African Americans do not feel that they have failed in the system of white racism), and therefore 'outcasts' in their own eyes and in the eyes of their families (that they tend to have little connection to, unlike African Americans with their families). They carry their bodies in downcast ways, they have given up as sexual beings, they beg on the street in postures of submission (eliciting pity in ways that African Americans could never elicit pity), they are less ecstatic than African Americans in their drug use, giving up on collapsed veins and shooting into their skin instead (thus contributing to the greater propensity to suffer from abscesses). Nevertheless, despite their abject position and intense feelings of failure, they assert their racial superiority as whites through racist expressions and insults, in an effort to convince themselves and others of their racial superiority.

These habituses are formed in the crucible of the system of racism. As a general point, Bourgois and Schonberg (2009) refer to the deeply generative nature of historical interactions with the criminal justice system, with all the African Americans having experienced juvenile incarceration before they were adults (for example, because of involvement in gangs) and before they were taking drugs, and the whites only experiencing imprisonment later in life, as a result of drugs consumption leading to crime as their habits spiralled out of control. These early experiences had a profound shaping effect on the 'outlaw' habitus of African Americans:

> This historical, institutionalized ethnic pattern from the 1970s was a crucial generative force shaping the contrasting dopefiend habituses of outlaw versus outcast that became visibly racialized on Edgewater Boulevarde [the fictive name for the San Francisco neighbourhood] in the 2000s.
>
> (Bourgois and Schonberg 2009, p. 133)

As they further point out:

> What we call the ethnic components of habitus have emerged in the United States out of a history of slavery, racism and socioeconomic inequality. They manifest themselves through everyday practices that enforce social hierarchies and constrain the life choices of large categories of vulnerable people, who become identified in an essentialised manner as 'races' or 'cultural groups'. Ethnic components of habitus thereby become a strategic cog in

the logic of symbolic violence that legitimizes and administers ethnic hierarchy, fuels racism and obscures economic inequality.
(Bourgois and Schonberg 2009, p. 42)

The different techniques of the body – a crucial part of habitus – also contribute to the reproduction of perceptions of racial/ethnic difference. They are 'complex, historically grounded sets of innumerable cultural practices that contribute to the perception of radical ethnic [or racial] difference' (Bourgois and Schonberg 2009, p. 91), with myriad negative social and psychological effects.

Unlike many theories of racism, Emirbayer and Desmond raise the possibilities of subjectivities moving beyond those that support damaging racial hierarchy. They explore this through the concept of 'intelligent racial habitus' or 'racial democratic habitus' (Emirbayer and Desmond 2015, p. 269), hard-won habituses achieved in part through intense critical self-reflection, given expression through social structures, that need to be thoroughly transformed, and in some cases dismantled. Thus, to go back to a theme discussed in Chapter 1, this is an argument firmly within the Enlightenment tradition, rather than seeing that tradition as inherently white racist. They describe this as a conjoining of Bourdieusian socio-analysis and Freudian psychoanalysis, to 'undo the mechanisms of, both primary and secondary socialization (in the family, schools, churches, workplace)' (Emirbayer and Desmond 2015, p. 268). Anger and other emotions like rage are not dismissed as racially unintelligent in favour of 'balance' – sometimes anger and rage are the most reasonable and balanced responses to terrible, racist and racially dominant situations; and emotions, like 'righteous indignation', also help to effect change (Emirbayer and Desmond 2015, pp. 269–274). In discussing these possibilities, they also discuss different forms of racial intelligence, including that of the 'old head' in the black ghetto, who exhibits practical wisdom in guiding the young in racially homogeneous communities, but who can offer less help in more racially mixed worlds and environments; or, the 'multiracial habitus' in racially mixed environments that, while still rooted in racialised worlds and consciousness (in its mixing of relatively unified 'races'), represents some kind of brokerage between racial identities; and 'cosmopolitan habitus' that, like the others, indicates possibilities such as 'kindness to strangers', which helps to negate white privilege and limitations in terms of overcoming racialised habitus and racial domination (Emirbayer and Desmond 2015, pp. 275–280).

## ABOLISHING WHITENESS?

The main thrust of whiteness studies literature characterises the negative and dominative aspects of 'whiteness' as it developed historically, and as it is experienced and lived in contemporary societies. It is a dominating subjectivity, inextricably tied to white supremacy, which it is an expression of and which it fundamentally supports, whose main features have been explained above. In his book, *Towards the Abolition of Whiteness*, whiteness historian David Roediger (1994) argues that the only way for white people to be anti-racist is to shed their whiteness, to flee it. There is, he argues, no such thing as 'white' culture that people could justifiably feel attached to, unlike other racialised cultures, which are organised around resistance and creativeness. Drawing inspiration from a brief essay by James Baldwin, he writes that 'It is not merely that whiteness is oppressive and false; it is that whiteness is *nothing but* oppressive and false . . . It is the empty and therefore terrifying attempt to build an identity based on what one isn't and on whom one can hold back' (Roediger 1994, p. 13).

Similarly, in his account of white 'allies' who joined with Native Americans in support of their treaty-based fishing rights in the lakes of northern Wisconsin, and against an organised white supremacist coalition challenging those rights, Lipsitz (2008, pp. 101–102) characterises whiteness in such a way that the only way to overcome it is to leave it:

Whiteness recruits white people to be defenders of white group position and privilege rather than opponents of exploitation and injustice. It directs their fears toward the gains that might be made at their expense by subordinated racialized groups, while deflecting their attention away from the grossly unequal and unjust distribution of resources and power in society in general. It is nearly impossible to create a subject position that is both white and anti-racist, for whiteness is not so much an embodied identity as a structured advantage tied to the racial subjugation of others.

Thus, the white allies – environmentalists, workers, other local rural people, pacifists, and entrepreneurs – who were encouraged and prepared to join, were encouraged by Native American leaders to 'imagine and enact anti-racist identities that would not unwittingly reify and strengthen the forms of white privilege they seek to oppose', which are basically negative, anti-white identities, described as 'subject positions' and 'roles' rather than identities:

> This struggle entailed the creation of new subject positions and social roles *for* whites but not necessarily *as* whites. Instead, whites were invited to become witnesses to white supremacist violence and nonviolent interveners against it, advocates for local self-determination and opponents of corporate greed and proponents of ecologically sound and sustainable economic development.
>
> (Lipsitz 2008, pp. 109–110)

Labour historian Arnesen (2001), focusing in particular on Roediger's arguments, has argued that this kind of approach – of seeing 'whiteness' as simply something to get rid of – as naïve and potentially dangerous politics, built only on abnegation of identity.

Omi and Winant (2013) make a similar argument in their racial formation approach, which distinguishes race from racism, and also allows for a range of 'racial identities', white, black and other designations, which are more or less hierarchically organised and related to racism and racist domination. They raise the prospect of racial democracy where people might still experience themselves as having racial identities but that some white identities within such a democracy would not necessarily be simply negative, racist identities. For example, they argue that there are white anti-racists who do not necessarily completely disavow their embodied white identities. In a rejoinder to Feagin and Elias's (2013) critique of their racial formation theory, they ask the question 'whether there are any "positive" dimensions of white identity or whether it is a purely "negative" quality, signifying only the absence of "colour"' (Omi and Winant 2013, p. 964).

Linda Alcoff (2015) also takes an alternative view to whiteness as simply absence and domination in her semi-autobiographical exploration of whiteness, *The Future of Whiteness*. Her starting point is that in white-dominated societies such as the US, demographic shifts mean that 'whites' will, in the next 50 years, become a large minority rather than a numerical majority. Such demographic shifts do not inevitably, of themselves, lead to a diminishing of white supremacy. However, Alcoff sees in such changes the opening of other possibilities, including for other, less racist experiences and expressions of whiteness. Re-examining the history of whiteness, she notes that it has developed in complex forms, tied always to particular contexts. Though it has been always closely connected to racism and white supremacy, she suggests that there are possibilities for the experience of 'whiteness' and white identity to move beyond racism and supremacy: 'The truth is that whiteness is not an illusion but a historically evolving identity-formation that is produced in diverse locations, while constantly undergoing reinterpretation and contestation' (Alcoff 2015, p. 21).

She reflects upon her own particular location of whiteness, as a white-skinned Panamanian, growing up in a poor family, favoured by her white grandparents because of her lighter skin, unlike her darker-skinned, older sister who had a far different experience in both family and society. Hers is an argument against eliminationist approaches to white identities. White people who inhabit such subjectivities cannot just escape their identities, even if they choose to, or try to. These are 'social ontologies' that are lived, are historical and have internal diversities. There is, she argues, an overwhelming need for the transformation of such identities, and anti-racism is central to this, including the thorough dismantling of white racial privileges; but she argues that, as well, more positive identity agendas are needed. Thinking of a perhaps utopian future, she argues that a white identity could just become a particular among particulars. She argues that there is a crisis of white identity that opens up such possibilities – it is no longer experienced by most whites in a triumphal way; it is also shaped by the experience of living with non-white views and perspectives; and by the experience of no longer being the 'vanguard' race or identity. There have been different responses to this of course – and we could point in particular to the fierce and large-scale white nationalist reactions represented by many of Trump's supporters. But there are other, more reparative responses.

## CONCLUSION

I have discussed several attempts to theorise and categorise racist and racialised subjectivities. The psychoanalytic-inspired attempts to understand some of the extreme modes of thinking and feeling underpinning racism also provide insight into the emotional power and the 'madness' of racism, including its infusing with fear and hatred, its eroticisation of bodies, its sexual and other forms of violence. These accounts also provide insight into the sheer tenacity of racist thought and feeling, and racism's resistance to rational argument about the 'illusions' of race and the unreasonableness and incoherence of racist stereotypes of racialised others. Empirical and theoretical investigations of what might be thought of as 'ordinary' racial and racist subjectivities, either through accounts based on discursive formations and the way that they position subjectivities in racist discourses, that provide them with the resources and repertoires to act and think in racist systems, or the idea of racialised habitus, all show that race is thus a 'lived reality', and that as a lived reality it contributes to the reproduction of racism. At the same time, there are possibilities for resistance inherent in subjectivity, including within the conception of subjectivity inspired by psychoanalysis, and also by ideological positioning in discourses (for example, Mama's accounts of transforming black women's identities), and in the arguments about non-racist white subjectivities, or white habituses, in racial democracy. There are possible future non-racist but nevertheless racial identities, as suggested here by Alcoff with her reflections on white subjectivities.

## REFERENCES

Adorno, T., Frenkel-Brunswick, E., Levinson, D.J. and Nevitt Stanford, R. [1950] 1969, *The Authoritarian Personality*, Norton, New York.

Ahmed, S. 2007, 'A Phenomenology of Whiteness', *Feminist Theory*, vol. 8, no. 2, pp. 149–168.

Alcoff, L. 2015, *The Future of Whiteness*, Polity Press, Cambridge.

Allport, G. 1954, *The Nature of Prejudice*, Addison-Wesley, Cambridge, Massachusetts.

Althusser, L. 1971, 'Ideology and Ideological State Apparatuses', in *Lenin and Philosophy*, Monthly Review Press, New York and London, pp. 127–186.

Anderson, E. 2015, '"The White Space"', *Sociology of Race and Ethnicity*, vol. 1, no. 1, pp. 10–21.

Appiah, K.A. 1994, *Race, Culture, Identity: Misunderstood Connections, The Tanner Lectures on Human Values*, University of California at San Diego, California.

Arnesen, E. 2001, 'Whiteness and the Historian's Imagination', *International Labor and Working-Class History*, no. 60, Fall, pp. 3–32.

Bauman, Z. 1989, *Modernity and the Holocaust*, Cornell University Press, New York.

Bonilla-Silva, E. 1997, 'Rethinking Racism: Toward a Structural Interpretation', *American Sociological Review*, vol. 62, no. 3, pp. 465–480.

Bonilla-Silva, E. 2019, 'Feeling Race: Theorizing the Racial Economy of Emotions, 2018 Presidential Address', *American Sociological Review*, vol. 84, no. 1, pp. 1–25.

Bourdieu, P. 1977, *Outline of a Theory of Practice*, trans. R. Nice, Cambridge University Press, Cambridge.

Bourdieu, P. 1991, *Language and Symbolic Power*, Polity Press, Cambridge.

Bourgois, P. and Schonberg, J. 2009, *Righteous Dopefiend*, University of California Press, Berkeley, California.

Clarke, S. 2003, *Social Theory, Psychoanalysis and Racism*, Palgrave Macmillan, Basingstoke.

Cohen, P. 2002, 'Psychoanalysis and Racism: Reading the Other Scene', in D.T. Goldberg and J. Solomos (eds), *A Companion to Racial and Ethnic Studies*, Blackwell Publishers, London, pp. 170–201.

Du Bois, W.E.B. 1975, *Darkwater: Voices from Within the Veil,* Kraus-Thomson, Millwood, New York.

Emirbayer, M. and Desmond, M. 2015, *The Racial Order*, University of Chicago Press, Chicago, Illinois.

Fanon, F., 1968, *Black Skin, White Masks*, MacGibbon and Kee, London.

Feagin, J. and Elias, S. 2013, 'Rethinking Racial Formation Theory: A Systemic Racism Critique', *Ethnic and Racial Studies*, vol. 36, no. 6, pp. 931–960.

Frankenberg, R. 1993, *White Women, Race Matters: The Social Construction of Whiteness*, University of Minnesota Press, Minneapolis, Minnesota.

Fromm, E. 1960, *Fear of Freedom*, Routledge and Kegan Paul, London.

Frosh, S. 1989, *Psychoanalysis and Psychology: Minding the Gap*, Macmillan Education, London.

Frosh, S. 2013, 'Psychoanalysis, Colonialism, Racism', *Journal of Theoretical and Philosophical Psychology*, vol. 33, no. 3, pp. 141–154.

Garner, S. 2015, *A Moral Economy of Whiteness: Four Frames of Racializing Discourse*, Routledge, London.

Goldberg, D.T. 1993, *Racist Culture: Philosophy and the Politics of Meaning*, Blackwell, Cambridge, Massachusetts.

Hook, D. 2004, 'Racism as Abjection: A Psychoanalytic Conceptualisation for a Post-Apartheid South Africa', *South African Journal of Psychology*, vol. 34, no. 4, pp. 672–703.

Hook, D. 2008, 'The "Real" of Racializing Embodiment', *Journal of Community & Applied Social Psychology*, *18*, pp. 140–152.

Hook, D. 2018, 'Racism and *Jouissance*: Evaluating the "Racism as (the Theft of) Enjoyment" Hypothesis', *Psychoanalysis, Culture & Society*, vol. 23, no. 3, pp. 244–266.

hooks, b. 1981, *Ain't I A Woman: Black Women and Feminism*, Pluto Press, London.

hooks, b. 1992, *Black Looks: Race and Representation*, South End Press, Boston, Massachusetts.

hooks, b. 2013, *Writing Beyond Race: Living Theory and Practice*, Routledge, New York.

Kovel, J. 1970, *White Racism: A Psychohistory*, Penguin, New York.

Kovel, J. 1995, 'On Racism and Psychoanalysis', in A. Elliott and S. Frosh (eds), *Psychoanalysis in Contexts*, Routledge, London, pp. 205–222.

Lacan, J. 1977 [1949], 'The Mirror Stage as Formative of the Function on the I as Revealed in the Psychoanalytic Experience', in J. Lacan, *Écrits: A Selection*, Tavistock, London.

Lipsitz, G. 2008, 'Walleye Warriors and White Identities: Native Americans' Treaty Rights, Composite Identities and Social Movements', *Ethnic and Racial Studies*, vol. 31, no. 1, pp. 101–122.

Mama, A. 1995, *Beyond the Masks: Race, Gender and Subjectivity*, Routledge, London.

Miles, R. 1989, *Racism*, Routledge, London.

Miles, R. and Brown, M. 2003, *Racism,* 2nd edn, Routledge, London.

Omi, M. and Winant, H. 2013, 'Resistance is futile? A Response to Feagin and Elias', *Ethnic and Racial Studies*, vol. 36, no. 6, pp. 961–973.

Reich, W. [1933] 1970, *The Mass Psychology of Fascism*, 3rd edn, trans. V.R. Carfagno, Farrar, Straus and Giroux, New York.

Roediger, D. 1994, *Towards the Abolition of Whiteness: Essays on Race, Politics, and Working Class History*, Verso, London and New York.

Rustin, J. 1991, *The Good Society and the Inner World: Psychoanalysis, Politics and Culture*, Verso, London.

Sherwood, R. 1980, *The Psychodynamics of Race*, Harvester Press, Hassocks.

Theweleit, K. 1987, *Male Fantasies*, Polity Press, Cambridge.

Wellman, D.T. 1993, *Portraits of White Racism*, 2nd edn, Cambridge University Press, New York.

Wacquant, L. 2016, 'A Concise Genealogy and Anatomy of Habitus', *The Sociological Review*, vol. 64, issue 1, pp. 64–72.

# NEW RACISMS?

This chapter is concerned with a discussion of expression and practices of racism in the post-1960s context – broadly speaking, in a world where racism had been strongly challenged by global anti-colonisation movements, and the introduction of a range of UN international human rights documents directly aimed at overcoming racism globally, such as *The Universal Declaration of Human Rights* (UN General Assembly 1948), and *The International Convention on the Elimination of All Forms of Racial Discrimination* (UN General Assembly 1965). What sorts of shifts in racism occurred in this period? Were there new forms of racism, or was this simply a case of old wine in new bottles? The chapter discusses the original argument about 'new racism' as enunciated by Martin Barker, and also the way that this has been explored in contexts outside Britain, such as France, the US, Singapore and Japan. In discussing racism in Singapore and Japan, the focus is upon non-colour-coded forms of racism, addressing what is seen as a neglect by racism scholars of forms of racism that are not captured by the white/black binary. The chapter includes a discussion of 'colour-blind' racism and related claims that we have entered a 'post-racial' age, which is strongly challenged and critiqued. The chapter ends with a discussion of Islamophobia, which, it will be argued, has existed in some form for a long period of history, but which has intensified in more recent decades, stimulated and transformed by new global political contexts.

DOI: 10.4324/9781003267690-6

## THE CLASSIC ACCOUNTS OF 'THE NEW RACISM'

Martin Barker (1981) famously argued that, in response to the rise of anti-racism in 1960s and 1970s Britain, the global undermining of the concept of biological races, and in the context of the aftermath of the large-scale migration of people from Britain's former colonies in the Caribbean and the Indian subcontinent (post-colonial migration from peripheries to metropole), the expression of racism shifted from mainly biological concerns to concerns with 'culture' – and he termed this the 'new racism'. Racism of this kind increasingly asserted the 'incommensurability of cultures' – that some cultures could not be assimilated into a British cultural way of life. This form of racism was centrally concerned with national identity and had been especially articulated by a movement within the British Conservative Party and associated intellectuals. New racism did not rely upon or even concern itself with claims about racial superiority and inferiority, did not rely on negative racial stereotyping, nor did it primarily concern itself with claims about the impact of immigration on social and economic problems. Rather, it expressed a concern with the capacity of a distinctive British culture-nation to preserve itself as a bounded cultural community. The new racism claimed that a people's desire for such cultural survival and boundary protecting was a natural impulse. The new racism did, however, essentialise and reify cultures.

The new racism argument became very popular over the following decades, sometimes being referred to as 'cultural racism' in order to distinguish it from what was seen as the older, 'biological' racism. When Islamophobia became more prominent in the 1990s, many argued that it was a form of this new racism, with its emphasis on religion and culture rather than biology (see later discussion in this chapter). Certainly, the dominant anti-Muslim immigration arguments that developed in Europe often had strong claims about the cultural 'incompatibility' of a homogenised, simplified and caricatured 'Islamic civilisation' with European culture, political traditions and civilisation, centred on claims about the separation of church and state, upon the treatment of women, and on liberal conceptions of the individual and freedoms (Foner 2015; Halliday 1999).

By referring to it as new racism, Barker and others who followed in his use of the concept, argued for a sequence from the old to the new, from biology to culture, and the impression was for some that this replaced the 'old racism'. Many critics have argued, however, that this chronological approach is mistaken, and that these more cultural forms of racism have always been there in 'older' racism, and that cultural images and tropes have always been a feature of racism (Rattansi 2020; Garner 2010). Others, such as Stuart Hall, argued that the biological trace always lurked behind the new racism:

> Even within the language of the new racism . . . the 'grosser physical differences' continue to function discursively, through the metonymic sliding of the signifier, so as to fix the meaning of cultural differences beyond the contingencies of history and culture.
>
> (Hall 2017, p. 154)

Obviously, the strong articulation of racism with national identity was hardly new either; and, as Miles (1987) argued, race had been central to the imagining of the English nation for more than two centuries.

In addition, it is not as if the biological arguments about racism ever went away. Such conceptions continued to underpin the racism of right-wing extremist and neo-Nazi movements. Also, outside intellectual circles, the everyday (or 'folk') concepts of race frequently still have biological or pseudo-biological assumptions about the sources and meanings of racial differences (Morning 2009). As Ann Morning's work has shown, this is not only evident in folk concepts among ordinary people, but it is also evident among natural scientists (in particular biologists), who often operate with biological conceptions of race (Morning 2011; see also Dikötter 2008); and some sociologists have interpreted geneticists' recent claims about genetic clusters or classes as somehow mapping onto 'races'. Such claims are often made in the public sphere, where 'the (re-)biologisation of race is proceeding apace' – for example, 'through medical practices, pharmaceutical drugs, forensic practices, genetic genealogy tests, textbooks and the media' (Morning 2014, p. 1683). Gilroy (2000, Ch.1) argued in the early 2000s that there were, at that time, emergent new forms of thinking among scientists about biological race, associated with the discoveries of DNA and the genome.

While racism and multiculturalism scholar Tariq Modood (1997) acknowledged that racism had always mixed biological and cultural tropes, he also argued that the culture arguments needed to be taken seriously and challenged on their own merits, and should not just be seen as super-structural overlays on biological tropes. In British racism, from the late 1970s the arguments about culture had been foregrounded, even as they ultimately rested on a bedrock of biological markers that allowed the more important and influential ideas about cultural clash to be set in motion. Thus, while culture was being reified in new racism, it was not simply the same as older notions of biological race, so there was something in fact 'new' in the new racism; and anti-racism would need to challenge it on these grounds. Anti-racists were making a mistake if they simply read the cultural claims of the new racism as camouflaged biological concerns without giving full allowance to more salient arguments about cultural distinctiveness and the inability of some cultures to assimilate into British culture. While arguing against this phenomenon as new *racism*, and instead characterising it as a form of cultural fundamentalism, the anthropologist Stolcke (1995) made a similar point about taking the specific cultural arguments seriously, and challenging them, in order to challenge effectively the anti-immigration rhetoric and politics that animated the phenomenon.

The idea of new racism gained different inflections in different societal contexts. In the French context, it has been most powerfully conceptualised by Pierre-André Taguieff as 'differentialist racism' when explaining the racism characteristic of the French new right. This was political ideology among the new right largely replacing the previous 'inegalitarian racism' of the old right. It involved a 'praise of difference' that, at least superficially, seemed to adopt concurrent multicultural logic, and thus did not seem like racism at all. Differentialist racism was heterophile rather than heterophobic, emphasising the distance between cultural communities, even their incommensurability. This new racism was mixophobic, 'haunted by the threat of the destruction of identities through inter-breeding, physical and cultural cross-breeding' (Taguieff 1990; Taguieff 1993–1994, p. 101 for quote).

Writing in the 1990s, Alain de Benoist, one of the most influential Nouvelle Droite thinkers (a group of intellectuals and think-tanks of the European New Right, see François 2014), argued that he completely repudiated racism, sought solidarity with immigrants living in France (and therefore repudiated much of Jean-Marie Le Pen's and the Front National's stance on immigration and the causes of the French malaise), and was pursuing simply the revival of European culture and 'man' against the (supposed) degradation resulting from egalitarianism, globalising capitalism, imperialist American mass culture, liberal democracy and decadent Christianity (see de Benoist 1993–1994; for critique see Griffin 2000). De Benoist claimed to embrace radical difference (quoted in Griffin 1995, pp. 346–347):

What is the greatest threat today? It is the progressive disappearance of diversity from the world. The levelling-down of people, the reduction of all cultures to a world civilization made up of what is the most common. It can be seen already how from one side of the planet to the other the same types of construction are being put up and the same mental habits are being engrained . . . The joy which is experienced during a journey derives from seeing differentiated ways of living which are still well rooted, in seeing different people living according to their own rhythm, with a different skin colour, another culture, another mentality and that they are proud of their difference. I believe that this diversity is the wealth of the world, and that egalitarianism is killing it.

Immigration, according to de Benoist, is a 'tragedy' caused by capitalism. The governments of the wealthier countries of the West, he argued, should ensure that conditions improve in the poorer countries in order to remove the desire for economic and social improvement through immigration (de Benoist 1993–1994, pp. 175–176).

Balibar (1991, pp. 17–18), writing about new forms of racist expression in France, began with the formulation that:

Racism – a true 'total social phenomenon' – inscribes itself in practices (forms of violence, contempt, intolerance, humiliation and exploitation), in discourses and representations which are so many intellectual elaborations of the phantasm of prophylaxis or segregation (the need to purify the social body, to preserve 'one's own' or 'our' identity from all forms of mixing, interbreeding or invasion) and which are articulated around stigmata of otherness (name, skin colour, religious practices).

From this perspective, what was new about the new racism was mainly at the ideological or discursive level, rather than at the level of racist acts or the formation of racist communities (a central feature also of racism). Crucially, from the position of racism's victims, the ideological or discursive articulation of racism was less important than its ongoing effects through acts and even policies. Though words were violent, and racist acts in themselves, whether they were expressed in biological or other terms was less important than their power and intention to exclude and dominate, 'the violence of words in so far as they are acts of contempt and aggression' (Balibar 1991, p. 18).

The shift in racist language and, to some extent, the object – the 'immigrant' – are, Balibar argued, reflective of the global transformation resulting from decolonisation and the movements of people from the Third World colonies to the metropole of France (Balibar 1991, p. 21). This represents a different phenomenon to the racism experienced by migrant workers, including Jews, in Europe during the interwar period, where a biological rather than sociological or cultural signifier was predominant. Here all of humanity occupies the same political space, in a context where biological concepts of separate races have been undermined. Balibar, like Taguieff, notes the significance of the shift in language to 'differentialism', and away from hierarchy, and that an older form of anti-racism is powerfully undermined when the new racism concedes that there is a universal humanity, that is nevertheless expressed through discrete cultural and civilisational forms. Balibar notes that there is a strong reification of culture involved in these arguments – for the need for cultural separation to preserve cultural diversities – that *'culture can also function like a nature*, and it can in particular function as a way of locking individuals and groups a priori into a genealogy, into a determination that is immutable and intangible in origin' (Balibar 1991, p. 22; italics in original). The differentialist doctrines then make a crucial second move, which is to argue that cultural and identity protectiveness is a natural impulse, and thus preventing the immigration of 'alien' cultures will *prevent* racism by removing inevitable cultural antagonisms between groups (Balibar 1991, p. 22), and that national frontiers become the logical cultural frontiers separating cultures (Balibar 1991, p. 23). This also leads to the absurd political claim among new racists that anti-racism and policy frameworks, such as anti-discrimination and affirmative action, and positive discrimination, are the main causes of racism, because they stimulate counter-responses from cultural groups wanting, quite naturally, to preserve their own cultures (Balibar 1991, p. 23).

Balibar makes the claim that there is in fact something very old in the new racism. He sees as the model for culturalist, differentialist racism, anti-Semitism, which, while it made use of 'bodily stigmata', these were mainly 'signs of a deep psychology, as signs of a spiritual inheritance rather than a biological heredity' (Balibar 1991, p. 24). From a 'formal point of view', he argues, 'differentialist racism may be considered . . . *as a generalized anti-Semitism*' (Balibar 1991, p. 24; italics in original). In the same way that Jews have been 'the Other' for a version of European culture, 'Third World Others' are seen as having cultures that are ultimately incompatible with modern, open European culture and civilisation. Even if demands are made for such others to 'assimilate', the conditions for assimilation are in fact impossible to meet. Groups and individuals are ranked according to the degree with which they show capacity to assimilate to what is deemed to be a superior culture – which also shows that beneath differentialist ideology about non-hierarchy lurks a deep sense of cultural hierarchy, with Europeanness at the top, as the representative of universalistic and progressive culture against primitive, closed culture (Balibar 1991, p. 24).

## NEW RACISM IN SINGAPORE AND JAPAN

The concept of new racism has been used by Sylvia Ang (2018, 2021) to explore the phenomenon of non-colour-coded forms of racism – for example, the racism of ethnically Chinese, Singapore-born majority citizens in Singapore against new immigrants from Mainland China, imported primarily for unskilled labour and domestic work. Ang (2018, p. 1177) has argued that racism studies remain locked in the 'colour paradigm', typically focused on the racism of whites against a range of non-white others, black or Asian, and has ignored the 'racism by Asians and among Asians' as well as 'issues of racism in non-white settings'. Velayutham (2017) also writing about racism in

Singapore, but focused on the racial hierarchies separating Chinese from Malay and Indian Singaporeans, has also stressed the need for contemporary racism studies to move beyond the white supremacy paradigm. While recognising the fundamental importance of colonial structures and racism as formative for contemporary race relations and racism in Singapore, he argues that the new political and social contexts of postcolonial societies are also productive of their forms of non-Western racisms. In the Singaporean postcolonial island-nation, the Chinese majority is the dominant ethnic group (designated in policy as a race) and engages in forms of racial discrimination towards non-Chinese others, in particular Malays and Indians, drawing upon old, inherited colonial stereotypes in institutional and everyday practices of racialisation and racial discrimination.

Ang finds the concept of new racism to be valuable for exploring racism in these other settings because of the ways that it focuses on issues of culture, religion and class, rather than biological markers that, in her case study, cannot be used to distinguish Singaporean Chinese from mainland Chinese recent immigrants. In fact, biological similarity in a context of the intersection of global capital and migration flows with local modernity results in a new form of boundary construction, where anxieties relating to self and other are heightened by proximity between 'self' and 'migrant other', such that Singaporean Chinese nationals need to fight against fears of 'similarity' and 'substitutability' (Ang 2018, p. 1181).

Ang (2018, p. 1178) argues that 'Singaporean-Chinese enact new racism against newly arrived Chinese migrants' through focusing on cultural and other related differences, such as seeing themselves as more 'refined' (Ang 2018, p. 1185), culturally developed and sophisticated (similar tropes used by the British colonisers against native others), compared to more culturally 'backward' mainland Chinese, who spit in the street, are loud and unkempt (men with bellies hanging out, staying up all night, walking the streets and loudly chattering), whose women are prone to vice and prostitution, and who, as migrants, are largely unassimilable and form a kind of 'underclass' (thus the class dimension to racialisation that she relates to new racism).

In addition, she argues that there are parallels between 'the racialization of Chinese migrants in Singapore, and colonial racism' (Ang 2018, p. 1178), and that the current racism exhibited towards

Chinese migrants is stimulated by the hangover of Singapore's colonialist past, in the sense that the modern Singaporean state has continued with racialising habits and tropes, inherited from the British colonisers – for example, it retained the British racial population distinction between Chinese, Malay, Indians and others (Ang 2018, p. 1180). Thus, the above-mentioned stereotypes are a hangover from colonialism:

> In the same way that the state appropriated the European imaginary for its own agenda, the Singaporean-Chinese have reappropriated the European imaginary to differentiate themselves from newly arrived Chinese migrants.
>
> (Ang 2018, p. 1186)

However, she argues that this is not only a 'hangover' but that it is also stimulated by the intersection between global capital and Singapore's 'local modernity'. This last point is especially important, because she argues that the racialising of mainland Chinese migrants is a recent phenomenon in Singapore (Ang 2018, p. 1179). It is related to global migration flows and imported labour in global circuits, intersecting with the nation-state form, and stimulating the racialisation of migrant workers from a similar ethnic background. Thus, as much as it is a form of colonial hangover, it is 'the collision of global capitalism with the political circuits of the state that has created the new racism – a political circuit where labour is imported with racialized, classed, and gendered logics' (Ang 2018, p. 1188; see also Ang 2021).

Anthropologist Takeyuki (Gaku) Tsuda (2022) has explored processes of new racism in Japan, focusing upon the experiences of Nikkeijin return migrants from the Japanese diaspora who had been scattered in the Americas (the majority of the returnees being Japanese Brazilian, with a much smaller minority from the US), who face racial discrimination in racially hierarchised Japanese society. Tsuda refers to this as co-ethnic racism where colour or other biological features are not the sources of perceived racial difference. Instead, migrant status and cultural differences, and Japanese language competency, are mobilised to produce a hierarchy of racial and national belongingness. The large numbers of Japanese Brazilians, many of whom belonged to the middle-class in Brazil, returned to Japan in the late

1980s during the economic crisis in Brazil, and provided unskilled factory labour in a booming Japanese economy. In Japan, 'they are differentiated by nationality and hierarchically ordered in a discriminatory class structure . . ., producing a type of "racism" among co-ethnics without racial difference' (Tsuda 2022, p. 598). Tsuda argues that this is racism and not simply an example of ethnic discrimination, 'because the national differences of ethnic return migrants are essentialized as immutable and inferior and produce socioeconomic inequities and hierarchies that are difficult to overcome' (Tsuda 2022, p. 598). These perceived racialised national differences emerge from entrenched global inequalities between developed and developing countries, and, as in the example for Singapore, relate to global circuits of labour and capital. There is also a hierarchy within this hierarchy, with native-born Japanese at the top, Japanese Americans at the next level, often working in much more skilled fields, with higher socioeconomic/class status and treated with much more respect than Japanese Brazilians, who sit below them, facing much more discrimination and cultural stigma.

Tsuda notes that there was an initial racialisation process involved when the Japanese government allowed Japanese migrants to migrate to Japan in the late 1980s, assuming that their racial Japanese-ness meant that they would be culturally similar to native-born Japanese, and thus not disrupt the 'country's cherished ethnic homogeneity', an assumption also shared by local Japanese residents (Tsuda 2022, p. 600). When this assumption was undermined by experiences with the Japanese return migrants, who were culturally different and did not speak Japanese proficiently, they were racialised as backward, culturally inferior and poorly educated, and they were associated with images of the Third World and underdevelopment, including problems with poverty, drugs and crime (Tsuda 2022, p. 606).

Tsuda, however, distinguishes this phenomenon of co-ethnic racism from 'cultural racism' which, in its mainly US and European contexts, he argues is still mainly associated with people who look somehow biologically different, and has still predominantly focused on white supremacy and racialised non-white others, and thus on 'white/nonwhite binaries' (Tsuda 2022, p. 602). He instead uses the term 'ethnoracism' as the broad form of racism that co-ethnic racism falls within and, as noted above, this is not just ethnic discrimination because 'the victims' stigmatized cultural traits are naturalized as intrinsic and unchangeable, resulting in insurmountable inequalities and hierarchies'. Thus, even highly educated and language-proficient Japanese Brazilian migrants found themselves blocked from higher-status, higher-skilled employment, because of who they were (Tsuda 2022, p. 611).

Tsuda also sees ethno-racism as standing behind the Hutu genocide of Tutsis in Rwanda and the Bosnian Serbian genocide of Bosnian Muslims in the former Yugoslavia (Tsuda 2022, p. 603). Ethno-racism can be between different ethnic groups that look very similar, whereas the sub-form co-ethnic racism occurs within the same ethnic group; of the same perceived 'ancestry and racial descent' (Tsuda 2022, p. 603). One final, important feature of co-ethnic racism is that, for the Japanese Brazilian cohort, the children of migrants could eventually disappear and become indistinguishable from native-born Japanese – as long as they hid their Brazilian ancestry. Thus, unlike with other forms of racism, and because they cannot be distinguished by appearance, 'they may find it easier to overcome discriminatory barriers to mainstream social acceptance and upward mobility' (Tsuda 2022, p. 612).

## THE CRITIQUE OF 'COLOUR-BLIND RACISM'

There are other ways to argue about new racism. Arguments about 'colour-blind racism' originated in the US context, with a claim that a new form of racism emerged in the post-civil rights era (after the major achievements of the civil rights movement in the 1960s), one that involves the continuation and even deepening of racial inequality, expressed through institutional or systemic racism, while overt expressions of racism (for example, as can be deduced from attitudes surveys) seem to be in decline (Doane 2007; Burke 2016). One of the most significant proponents has been Eduardo Bonilla-Silva (2014), who argues that new racism, which involves key denialism strategies, is pervasive and difficult to confront. Bonilla-Silva's argument about new racism shares some attributes with, but is not the same as, the arguments made by Barker or Tagieuff in Europe. As discussed in Chapter 2, the emphasis is much more on systemic/structural features rather than ideological features of new racism: 'that is, as a network of social relations at social, political, economic, and ideological levels that shapes the life chances of the various races' (Bonilla-Silva 2014, p. 32).

Bonilla-Silva argues that this new racism 'reproduces racial domination mostly through subtle and covert practices that are often institutionalised, defended with coded language ("*those* urban people"), and bonded by the racial ideology of color-blind racism' (Bonilla-Silva 2014, p. 204; italics in original). He argues that 'most whites endorse the ideology of color blindness and that this ideology is central to the maintenance of white privilege' (Bonilla-Silva 2014, p. 23). Garner (2015, p. 44) has usefully characterised colour-blind racism as a form of neoliberal governance, capturing both the imposition of 'race' onto some, to explain 'failure', while denying the general significance of race:

> Colour-blind governance is underpinned by a racialised assumption: only people of colour have a racial identity that is available as a resource for collective failure, and this is explicable by culture. Whiteness is never deployed to explain collective deviancy, inadequacy, violence or degeneracy (although this role may sometimes be, as we are talking about neoliberalism, 'outsourced' to social class) in the same way as blackness, Muslim-ness or Asianness more generally can be.

Bonilla-Silva (2014, Ch. 2) highlights five key aspects of the new racial structure that characterises the period of colour-blind racism: (1) 'the increasingly *covert* nature of racial discourse and racial practices' (thus, the hiddenness of racism); (2) 'the avoidance of explicit race terminology', and a strong tendency among whites to claim 'reverse racism' – that they are in fact the current victims of racism in the post-civil rights era; (3) 'the elaboration of a racial agenda over political matters', but that avoids explicit use of race language, speaking the language instead of state intervention, and individual rights and responsibility; (4) 'the invisibility of most mechanisms' that produce racial inequality – but that racial inequality, as Bonilla-Silva shows through the use of available statistics, runs deep in key areas of wealth, housing, criminal justice and incarceration, education and political participation (where he recognises some improvements, but where there remain many barriers especially for black political leaders – and blacks are still grossly underrepresented in political leadership roles, compared to population statistics – and for black voting); and (5) 'the rearticulation of some racial practices from the Jim Crow era of race relations' – the examples that he gives are new forms of black-white racial segregation and racial separation in everyday social interaction, but produced in ways that are not guided by specific racial or racist Jim Crow-like laws, but covertly by other white residents and by, for example, widespread discriminatory actions of real estate agents and lending institutions (banks and other agencies); also, de facto segregation in education persists, contributing to continuing education inequality, and blacks and other minorities face discriminatory practices in schools that are more racially mixed and 'integrated' (Bonilla Silva 2014, Ch 2; quotes at p. 32).

The role of incarceration, and the actions of police and the judicial system as a whole, in the ongoing social control and racial oppression of black and other minorities in the US is perhaps the most profound example of continuing white racial domination (Bonilla-Silva 2014, Ch. 2). The state is a major enforcer of the racial social order, especially since the 1960s, and police violence has become a major issue for African Americans (for example, by 1975, 46 per cent of those killed by police were black, with little change in the statistics since then) (Bonilla-Silva 2014, Ch. 2). The 'war on drugs', and the more general crackdown on crime, has resulted in massive incarceration of African Americans, from early youth into adult life, so much so that prison becomes a normalised feature of the African American experience (particularly male) (see Bourgois and Schonberg 2009). As Bonilla-Silva (2014, Ch. 2) points out, one in three black males born in the contemporary US can expect to experience time in prison, and eight to nine per cent of blacks are arrested each year. More than half the people executed since the 1930s in the US have been black. The statistics are astounding, and the racial social control function has been highlighted as a major feature of neoliberal state action, most notably by Loïc Wacquant (Wacquant 2009).

Drawing on survey and interview research with white college students and a Detroit Area Study (surveying and interviewing white and black participants), Bonilla-Silva (2014, Ch. 3) also highlights that there are four central frames of colour-blind racism, that are used by dominating whites to justify ongoing racial inequalities: (1) *abstract liberalism* (which he sees as the most important, and as the foundation of this new racism), which assumes that simple forms of liberal equality can deal with the issues faced by individuals and groups in racialised and racist societies; (2) *naturalization* of observed racial differences, including experiences of inequality (for example, claiming that racial segregation comes about through the 'natural' inclination of people of the same type and background to want to live together; (3) *cultural racism,* '**a frame that relies on culturally based arguments such as "Mexicans do not put much emphasis on education" or "blacks have too many babies" to explain the standing of minorities in society**' (Bonilla Silva 2014, p. 71; bold in original); and (4) *minimisation of racism* – '**a frame that suggests discrimination is no longer a central factor affecting minorities' life chances ("It's better now than in the past" or "There is discrimination, but there are plenty of jobs out there")**' (Bonilla Silva 2014, p. 71; bold in original), and that if admitting racism at all, only names as racist the most extreme acts, while denying the racism involved in most other situations and institutional arrangements.

As noted, abstract liberalism, which draws upon the Western liberal tradition, is the main frame, using '**ideas associated with political liberalism (e.g., "equal opportunity," the idea that force should not be used to achieve social policy) and economic liberalism (e.g., choice, individualism) in an abstract manner to explain racial matters**' (Bonilla-Silva 2014, p. 70; bold in original). This frame allows whites to seem reasonable as they oppose all policy efforts to rectify racial disadvantage, so that, for example, equal opportunity and affirmative action laws and policies are deemed to be 'preferential treatment' (Bonilla-Silva 2014, p. 70).

Ashley Doane (2017) has sounded a cautionary note about the influence of and sociological work on colour-blind racism. It should not be misunderstood, he argues, as meaning that people actually do not 'see' race or colour. It should also not be used as a claim that there is anything wrong with aspiring to create a society that is free of racial inequality. Nor should it be seen as a free-floating set of ideas. Colour-blind racism, to emphasise Bonilla-Silva's argument, is an ideology that emerges from systemic racism, which it then supports.

This is a materialist (Marxist-influenced) argument about ideology (Doane 2017, p. 977):

> It is also important to assert that racial ideologies have no unique causal role: They cannot exist outside of a racialized structure – a social system where power and valued resources are distributed unequally across (socially constructed) "racial" lines. In the absence of racial inequality and race-based domination or competition, racial ideologies would have no staying power as there would be nothing to explain, justify, or challenge.

Where many sociologists have set about mapping the contours of colour-blind racism in various different contexts, there is a danger, Doane (2017, p. 980) argues, in seeing it as a fixed phenomenon, rather than as a flexible and changeable ideology that mutates according to political contest and conflict, as it continues to attempt to shore up white supremacy. One innovation of colour blindness is the growing adoption in societies over the last 30 years of the concept of 'diversity' and practices of 'diversity training', including by corporations and other institutions. These have been incorporated 'within the overall framework of color-blind racial ideology' (Doane 2017, p. 982). 'Diversity' is individualised, rather than seen as something that is experienced within a racially dominative social structure; and showing that an institution is positive about 'diversity' is a badge of honour, indicative of being post-racial. The underlying logic of white supremacy is not directly challenged by these approaches. 'Diversity' is too often 'color-blind diversity' (Doane 2017, p. 982). Doane has also noted that recent surveys of whites indicate that significant proportions are not 'color-blind' and even recognise the significance of systemic, racial barriers. This phenomenon is important to think through, in terms of transformation of the role of colour-blind racism – for people can acknowledge systemic issues and yet continue to benefit from a racist system, adopting, for example, an ideology that the system is so entrenched and difficult to understand that there is little that can be done to overcome it.

In addition, Doane noted that study of colour-blind racism also needed to come to terms with the phenomenon of a return to explicit racist messaging associated with the 2016 Trump election. Philomena Essed has also discussed this phenomenon of the freeing-up of speech and the return to explicitly racist language, where it has become normalised for people to 'speak about other people in racist, sexist, homophobic or Islamophobic terms' in her account of 'entitlement racism' –a much more widespread phenomenon beyond the US evident in many European countries, where people assert the right to humiliate and offend, which has become a key feature of contemporary Islamophobia, and has also freed people up to use the 'N' word, and to comment on skin colour (Essed and Muhr 2018; quote from the interviewer at p. 184).

Meghan Burke (2016) has emphasised that the materialist approach to colour-blind racism suggested by theorists including Bonilla-Silva must become even more materialist, and also intersectional, examining the complexities and shaping influences of social position and social location, and the embeddedness of racism in people's everyday and institutional lives. While there is a place for abstract generalising about key frames of colour-blindness, sociologists need to get in much closer, and look for the subtle variations of ideology as these arise in particular circumstances and social locations, seeing how this ideology emerges from whole lives and whole social relations:

> It is arguably more important for sociologists to interrogate such frames relative to the tangible social relations, experiences, locations, and contexts within which they reside or manifest. Doing so will reveal more about the intersectional social relations and inequalities that surround us, how and in what ways they are reified, and how they might best be challenged.
>
> (Burke 2016, p. 108)

## ARE WE POST-RACIAL YET?

Working a similar vein, David Theo Goldberg (2013) and Alana Lentin (2011, 2012, 2014) have discussed the more recent iteration of the 'post-racial' period of racism that was inaugurated in the US by the election of Barack Obama in 2008, amidst a flurry of commentary that the US was now post-race, and a 'debate' with critics who challenged the claim. Even to suggest that the US is post-racial, Goldberg (2013) argues, denies the salient facts of mass African American imprisonment, the reinvention in the last 30 years of school and housing segregation, and the spiralling wealth gap between white and non-white (African American and Latino) families. The post-race era has also been proclaimed in countries such as post-apartheid South-Africa, and in Europe, again despite the extensive evidence to the contrary – for example, massive structural disparities between black and white in South Africa, major levels of racial discrimination in policing and in immigration control against blacks and Muslims in Europe, and many instances of explicit racism voiced by political leaders, especially from the right.

Goldberg traces the post-racial back to the colour-blind racism of the 1960s onwards, and he also argues that it 'resonates conceptually and temporally, culturally and politically, with neoliberalism' (Goldberg 2013, p. 17), through its individualising of responsibility, thus deflecting attention from the workings of racist hierarchies. Perversely, the post-racial era – by claiming to have already removed all racial barriers, so that it is only individuals now competing on equal terms for society's resources – opens up new avenues for white people to express and get away with racist expressions that are then denied to be racist, or that are dismissed as accidental or unintended (Goldberg 2013, p. 19). Goldberg points to some key processes, including *deflection* from attention to racial disparities, and deflection of any responsibility for what a non-white person might feel was racism, with white perpetrators of racism expressing, for example, their sorrow that a victim might feel that way, rather than being explicitly sorry for their words or action. This, he argues, amounts to not simply 'racism without racists', as Bonilla-Silva has argued, but 'racism without racism', since there is no way (for victims) of naming, or even comprehending meaningfully, this racism (Goldberg 2013, p. 20). The post-racial is not the end of racism, but rather 'the afterlife, the ghostly haunting by the racial of the social supposedly rid of the racial' (Goldberg 2013, p. 21). Like colour-blind racism, post-racial racism engages in widespread claims of reverse racism – with the powerful claiming that the powerless are the true racists (Goldberg 2013, p. 23). Like colour-blind racism as argued by Bonilla-Silva, 'Structurally, postraciality keeps in place prevailing conditions of historically produced racial arrangement and power, but domestically and globally, now stripped of their historically inherited terms of recognition' (Goldberg 2013, pp. 28–29).

Lentin's (2014) argument is similar to Goldberg's, though she is explicit that it is adhered to, but in slightly different ways, by those on the political right and the left in the US and Europe. She argues that 'the notion that we are post-racial is in fact the dominant mode in which racism finds discursive expression across a variety of contexts' (Lentin 2014, p. 1270). Lentin also links the phenomenon to anti-multiculturalism, which makes claims about the creation or support of unassimilable cultures within nation-states, where culture stands for race:

> The debate on multiculturalism can be understood as being inscribed in a post-racial logic because those who oppose multiculturalism see it as having been imposed by racial and ethnic minorities whose demands for recognition were prioritized over all other concerns.
>
> (Lentin 2014, pp. 1270–1271)

Lentin (2011) has argued, adopting a distinction made by Goldberg, that in the post-war period there are two distinguishable strands of action and thought in relation to racism: anti-racism and anti-racialism. Anti-racism, in its most convincing sense for Lentin, is a form of thought, protest and action premised on the recognition of the foundational nature of race and racism for contemporary societies – rather than as something that is either a cancer to be excised from an otherwise healthy body, or as something that has invaded society from outside, like Nazism. Therefore, anti-racism tries to radically transform the whole social system and its institutions, rooting out the impact of racism and race thinking in all of society's crevices. Anti-racialism is, by comparison, a more superficial approach, that addresses the fallacy of race thinking, and tries to show that racial categories are meaningless. Anti-racialism tends to crowd out true anti-racism and presents itself as a form of coalition-building, non-alienating and constructive anti-racism, with some protagonists, such as leaders of *SOS-Racisme* in France, arguing against 'the foregrounding of race as a tool for making sense of the persistence of racism, seeing it instead as a source of further division' (Lentin 2011, p. 162). Because of the way that anti-racialism was the antecedent to what Lentin terms the cosy, relatively non-conflictual and non-challenging 'politics of diversity', she also sees it as one of the contributing sources for the emergence of 'post-racialism'. The politics of diversity plays down the distinctiveness of racial experience and racism, tending to equalise a range of different identity experiences, in the cosy language and practices of inclusion, that governments have readily adopted:

> Anti-racialism can usefully be read as a precursor to the post-racial agenda which can be said to characterise mainstream approaches to race and racism in western societies with significant levels of immigration. The relativisation of the experience of racism which characterises post-racialism is accompanied by a focus on diversity that blurs the specificity of a variety of marginalised experiences by collectively labelling them 'diverse'.
>
> (Lentin 2011, p. 163)

This then slides relatively easily into the post-race politics that Lentin sees as predominating in contemporary societies.

In the Australian context there have been critiques of multiculturalism activities, organised by various levels of government, that focus on positive celebrations of diversity and community cohesiveness and social harmony – for example, at the national level Australia celebrates 'Harmony Day' to mark the United Nations International Day for the Elimination of Racial Discrimination. These approaches are seen as directing attention away from the real work of anti-racism struggle. Jacqueline Nelson has argued that there has been an active move away from explicit anti-racism approaches at the level of local governments in Australia. Partly, this is about not wanting to stigmatise local areas with the taint of racism in the public eye by emphasising it publicly and dealing with it explicitly in local policies and agendas (Nelson 2014). Nelson reports on comments from local councillors, council officers, and other local actors (in her interview research) preferring to use the language of social inclusion and promoting harmony than of racism and discrimination – positive language about local efforts to include people from culturally and linguistically diverse backgrounds. Nelson (2015, p. 353) argued that '[t]he preference for positive terminology left participants' in her study of local actors 'without the language to contemplate interethnic disharmony or conflict, yet acknowledging negative orientations is an important part of creating space for difference'. But Nelson has also acknowledged funding pressures from higher levels of government that require local people, who may as individuals and teams want to do more explicit anti-racism work, to couch their language and explanation of programmes in language that avoids talk of race and racism (Nelson and Dunn 2017).

## ISLAMOPHOBIA

Contemporary forms of Islamophobia, as mentioned in the introduction to this chapter, have been closely associated with Barker's concept of new racism. When does anti-Muslim or anti-Islam sentiment, which could be defined sociologically as forms of religious prejudice and discrimination – prejudice on the part of Christians towards a different and rival world religion (Fredrickson 2002) – or even as ethnocentrism (one's own ethnic group's centrality and cultural superiority) and xenophobia (fear or hatred of foreigners), become a form of racism? Anti-Muslim prejudices have a very long history in the West (Taras 2013). As Deepa Kumar (2020) has argued, Islamophobia needs to be understood as anti-Muslim racism that emerges from colonialism and imperialism. In its current form, Islamophobia is created by the very structures of Western dominance – European and US domination – of the contemporary world. It is systemic, and thus there are conservative forms of Islamophobia, but also liberal forms of Islamophobia that are tied to the 'War on Terror', and to, ultimately, defending Western imperialism (Kumar 2021; see also Cainkar and Selod 2018). Focusing on current widespread expressions of Islamophobia in Europe (including Eastern Europe), Salman Sayyid has argued that this is 'not a set of problematic prejudices' but, rather, that it is 'an attempt to construct European identity within a postcolonial conjuncture in which the West is decentred', which has produced a 'crisis of European/white identity'. It is thus closely tied to the current 'reconfiguration of contemporary Europeanness' (Sayyid 2018, p. 422). This is related to what Brubaker (2017) referred to as identarian Christianism of an embattled Europeanism and the arguments of Chetan Bhatt (2012) about a composite white nationalism with a strong opposition to Islam as discussed in Chapter 3.

Drawing on Edward Said's (1979) orientalism thesis, scholars have argued that reactions to and negative constructions of Oriental, Arab others and Islam, were central to the construction of the 'Occident' (the countries of the West) and Occidental thinking in the last 500 years. Said, among others (Lentin 2020; Taras 2013), has argued that there was in fact a close connection, a 'conjuncture', between Islamophobia and anti-Semitism:

> hostility to Islam in the modern Christian West has historically gone hand in hand with, has stemmed from the same source, has been nourished at the same stream as anti-Semitism, and . . . a critique of the orthodoxies, dogmas, and disciplinary procedures of Orientalism contribute to an enlargement of our understanding of the cultural mechanisms of anti-Semitism.
>
> (Said 1985, p. 99)

Grosfoguel and Mielants (2006, pp. 1–2) argue that any discussion of Islamophobia today must situate it within a world system that is not simply 'a global inter-state system organized solely in terms of an international division of labour' (as, for example, Marxists might characterise it) but as a world system that

> includes, not as additive elements but as constitutive of the capitalist accumulation on a world-scale, a global racial/ethnic hierarchy (Europeans/ Euro-Americans vs. non-European peoples), a global patriarchal hierarchy (global gender system and a global sexual system), a global religious hierarchy, a global linguistic hierarchy, a global epistemic hierarchy, etc.

Viewing the world system in this way, they argue that 'Islamophobia as a form of racism against Muslim people is not an epiphenomenon, but constitutive of the international division of labor' (Grosfoguel and Mielants 2006, p. 2). They make a similar argument to arguments situating white supremacist racism as emerging through colonial systems, with the important added emphasis on the role of Christianity's opposition to Islam as part of the West's historical formation since the early 1500s. Thus, they argue, 'Islamophobia would be the subalternization and inferiorization of Islam produced by the Christian-centric religious hierarchy of the world-system since the end of the 15th century' (Grosfoguel and Mielants 2006, p. 2). In their argument, the older Islamophobia became biological once the Christian-dominated West shifted, in the nineteenth century, from the view of Muslims and Jews as people with the wrong, inferior religion, to a people with an inferior civilisation, within a discourse of 'scientific evolutionary hierarchical civilization' (alongside those deemed to be without religion, like Indigenous peoples in the Americas and colonised Africans), and that such inferiorisation had a basis in biological race (Grosfoguel and Mielants 2006, p. 4).

Grosfoguel and Mielants argue that the shift to 'cultural racism' in the last 60 years, inspired by the trend in world history to reject biological concepts of race after World War Two, has meant that the racism towards Muslims has had an increased focus on Islam as a religion and culture, and in this way Western racists can also avoid the accusation of racism. The contemporary tropes about being uncivilised, violent, authoritarian, terrorists, savage and primitive, are now closely associated with Islamic religious beliefs and practices, though the tropes draw on the much older tropes of biological racism. The link with colonial racism remains, though it is hidden. Contemporary Islamophobia and its hatred and fear cannot be separated from the racial hatred and fear of other non-European people, and Grosfugel and Mielants argue that it is linked 'to an old colonial racism that is still alive today, especially in the metropolitan centres' (Grosfoguel and Mielants 2006, p. 4).

Though the term 'Islamophobia' was first used as early as 1918 in France (Taras 2013) and in the French colonial context in the 1920s (Sayyid 2014), it has become a much more widely used term, including in racism studies, since the Runnymede Trust in Britain released its report, *Islamophobia: A Challenge for Us All*, in 1997, which defined Islamophobia as 'unfounded hostility towards Islam, and therefore fear or dislike of all or most Muslims' (quoted in Meer and Modood 2008, p. 34; see also Taras 2013, p. 418). Taras has pointed out that when the Runnymede Trust put 'Islamophobia' onto the agenda in its 1997 report, its list of eight main stigmatising features of Islamophobia were a mix of religious and cultural attributes and did not contain an explicitly racist or racial component. However, Taras nevertheless argues, though it draws upon a long history of 'anti-Muslimism' and 'anti-Islamism' and has been couched in the language of a clash of civilisations and fears about 'Islamicization' of Western societies, Islamophobia *is* a form a racism that has fused the former with racist ideologies in the twentieth century (Taras 2013, p. 419). In Taras's view, and referencing Taguieff, in the twenty-first century Islamophobia joins with the primary white supremacist older racist ideologies of anti-Semitism and anti-Negritude, as 'Arabism, frequently fused with anti-Islamism, in other words, Islamophobia' (Taras 2013, p. 420). Again drawing on Taguieff, he argues that there are three 'cognitive' processes involved: an essentialised category of individuals and groups is created, reducing people's identity to their common community origin; the designated groups are then symbolically excluded by extreme stigmatisation that allows their exclusion to be imagined as an absolute necessity; and these groups are racialised as barbarous and incapable of the required civilisation of normal (e.g. Western, white, liberal) society/nation, and thus are incapable of education into required norms and habits, to become civilised, and to be assimilated (Taras 2013, pp. 420–421). He concludes that Islamophobia has become endemic in Europe, and that the form it takes is relatively new: 'Racialization, race and differential racism have all become more endemic to Islamophobic stigmatizing of Muslims today than was the case in the past' (Taras 2013, p. 431). The racialising process fuses race, religion, ethnicity and culture together in contemporary Islamophobia.

Sayyid (2014, p. 11) makes the important point that the concept of Islamophobia is needed because the category of racism in itself was not able to do the work of explaining the specificity of the phenomena that the term is naming and addressing, and which theories of Islamophobia seek to explain. Islamophobia has been closely associated with the response to multi-ethnic, multinational Muslim migration into Europe, and then, later, the response to acts of Islamist terror carried out by some in the name of their interpreted version of Islam. In this period prejudices against Muslims have taken an increasingly racial form, so that, despite the claim of racism scholars such as Fredrickson (2002) 'religious prejudice' or even a form of religious ethnocentrism cannot capture its primary motivations and manifestations. For many commentators and publics, Islamophobia is definitely a form of racism, whether you describe it simply as racism, or as new or cultural racism.

Fred Halliday (1999) noted that there were many instances in Western Europe of anti-Muslim prejudice (e.g. prejudice and discrimination against Muslims as people) amounting to Islamophobia. He also noted that there were telling examples of Islamophobia in non-Western countries, citing the example of the Bharatiya Janata Party (BJP) campaigning in the 1997 election in India on three key anti-Muslim issues. He argued that it was not the religion 'Islam' that these prejudices and actions were aimed at, but rather at Muslims as people. For this reason, he argued that the more accurate term would be 'anti-Muslimism' rather than Islamophobia (Halliday 1999, p. 898). However, several authors have subsequently critiqued this position, especially the claim that Islamophobia is not really concerned with the religion of Islam as such (see Meer and Modood 2008; Sayyid 2018). The attacks on Islam as a religion also became an increasingly important feature of Islamophobia as Islamist terror groups became more prominent after the September 11 attacks on the Twin Towers in New York (2001), and subsequent acts of Islamist-inspired terror in Europe as well as in many other parts of the world, and, much later, the spectacular rise of the Islamic State of Iraq and Syria (ISIS; also known as ISIL or Daesh), with the major military takeover of territory in Syria and Iraq in 2014.

Using discourse analysis, Cheng (2015) carefully examined forms of discrimination and hostility to Muslims and Islam in Switzerland and referred to a mixed phenomenon involving hostility to Islam as a religion (which involved attacks on both religion and people, and also associating non-whiteness with Muslim religion), Muslimophobia (directed at Muslims as people) and anti-immigrant racism in her research on Swiss parliamentary debates about the banning of the construction of minarets. Moosavi's (2015) research on 'white' Muslim converts in Britain is also revealing of the strong racialising of religion involved in Islamophobia, as the white converts become 'not-quite-white' once they have converted to Islam and become the victims of subtle and not so-subtle forms of racial denigration.

Islamophobia in Australia, which is a widespread and serious racial problem (Poynting 2020) despite its relatively small, ethnically and nationally diverse Muslim population (only about 2 per cent according to the 2021 Australian census), also has a strong focus on negative stereotyping of Islam as a religion. Islamophobia is embedded in mainstream media, among some civil society groups and political parties, including some that would not be considered far right or extreme white supremacists, and is also expressed in the mainstream institutions and parties of Australian politics, including the Federal parliament. In the Scanlon Foundation's *Mapping Social Cohesion Report* of its 2017 national surveys, 25 per cent of respondents felt 'very negative', or 'somewhat negative' towards

Muslims, with 28.3 per cent feeling 'positive' towards Muslims, and 44.3 per cent feeling 'neutral'. Similar survey results have been found across 10 years of these reports, between 2010 and 2017. The 2019 report showed negative-Muslim sentiment at 21–25 per cent in interviewer-administered surveys with much higher results, at 39–41 per cent, for self-completion surveys; the most recent report, from 2022, had anti-Muslim sentiment lower than in 2019 (Scanlon Foundation 2022). This is in a context where about 85 per cent of those surveyed express general support for multiculturalism, and where Australia's large immigration programme has also received general support. Australia's multiculturalism has not prevented prejudice and discrimination against Muslims becoming a major problem. Muslims were also one of the groups reporting the highest levels of discrimination experiences, in the Mapping Social Cohesion surveys.

The attack on Islam as a religion has been a key feature of Islamophobia in Australia. During a public inquiry into multiculturalism in Australia in 2011–2012, there was a strong airing of virulent anti-Muslim and Islamophobic views in submissions and at a public hearing by Christian groups Endeavour Forum and Salt Shakers Inc., political parties such as the Christian Democratic Party, and other groups such as the Q Society, the Australian Defence League, and the Family Council of Victoria. The submissions and the statements at the public hearing painted a picture of Islam as an inherently violent religion; some said that it aimed to take over the country; that it was a threat to Christianity; that in Western countries where the Muslim population reached a certain percentage of the general population – for example, in Europe – massive social problems occurred; and some equated Islam with Nazism, with a representative from the Endeavour Forum claiming that it 'was a totalitarian political ideology akin to communism or fascism'. The fact that these ordinary citizens confidently made such assertions in a public forum, for the parliamentary record, indicated just how uncontroversial they believed their views to be (see Moran 2017, pp. 273–277). Australia also has a serious, festering problem with a numerically small but globally connected extremist white racist movement, with groups prominent online and in street demonstrations, including Antipodean Resistance and the now defunct United Patriots Front, whose former leader Blair Cottrell has been on occasion presented as a legitimate spokesperson in the mainstream media, interviewed in discussion panels on the ABC and Sky. These movements have a wide range of racial targets, but Islamophobia features prominently in their discourse and protest actions. There is also an anti-Islam political movement, Reclaim Australia, which has a strong Christian ideology, and has hosted rallies and demonstrations against 'Islamisation' in Australia and protested against the building of mosques.

Cainkar and Selod (2018) question the use of the term Islamophobia and argue for other ways to theorise the racist experience of Muslims in the West, taking as their main case study the US, with its major subgroups being Arabs, South Asians and African American Muslims. Drawing upon Omi and Winant's (2015) argument about different and competing racial projects, they argue for the particular racialising project involved in the 'War on Terror' since the September 11 attacks, but also note that this has continuities with the older US racial project of white supremacy, that has affected all racial groupings in the US, not just Muslims, and protected white racial interests. They argue for an intersectional approach, which references 'gender, communities of belonging, black Muslim experiences, class and sexuality' all framed by understanding this as a global white supremacist racial project. In fact, they argue that the racial project of the 'War on Terror' itself long pre-dated September 11 and is part of the US's long-standing 'terror industrial complex' (Cainkar and Selod 2018, p. 166):

> Because this racial project is grounded in the policies of empire . . ., and because its emergence was layered upon earlier racial and gender projects, its racialized subjects are positioned and identified in multiple intersecting ways, including by geography, skin color, clothing, gender, religion, and beliefs. There is no single racial naming of this made-up group of people, except that they are understood by the state and the public to be threats: terrorists and potential terrorists.

Islamophobia is also fundamentally shaped by gender, with particular constructions of Muslim women as repressed and unfree, and a powerful focus on women's forms of religious dress – veiling, burkas, niqabs, hijabs, etc. – that make them particular targets for public racial vilification, including by governments, politicians and media commentators, as well as street-based vilification, abuse and violence (Mirza 2013). Muslim males have been demonised as patriarchal, authoritarian and violent, as terror threats, and as religiously fanatical. As Ho (2007) has argued, these discourses of Muslims also rehearse old colonialist tropes, especially tropes of Western civilization 'saving' 'savage' women from their men.

## CONCLUSION

Maybe 'new racism' has been a misnomer after all. For, if nothing else, the history of racism is one of persistence in the context of change. Racisms transform continuously in new political, economic and social contexts. Nevertheless, the arguments about what is 'new' in contemporary forms of racism discussed in this chapter help us to understand the incredible persistence of racism, and the subtle ways that it has transformed, partly in response to the challenges of anti-racism, including the major movements that have agitated for change – including the new iterations emphasising the cultural and downplaying the biological (which nevertheless remains an important trace), the manoeuvrings of colour-blind racism, the new forms of racism emerging in postcolonial societies, and the transformation of prejudice and racism against Muslims, characterised as Islamophobia. It is clear from the discussion in this chapter that despite post-war anti-racism challenges, we have not moved to a post-racist era – far from it.

## REFERENCES

Ang, S. 2018, 'The "New Chinatown": The Racialization of Newly Arrived Chinese Migrants in Singapore', *Journal of Ethnic and Migration Studies*, vol. 44, no. 7, pp. 1177–1194.

Ang, S. 2021, 'The Myth of Migrant Transience: Racializing New Chinese Migrants in Mobile Singapore', *Mobilities*, vol. 16, no. 2, pp. 236–248.

Balibar, E. 1991, 'Is There a "Neo-Racism"?', in E. Balibar and I. Wallerstein, *Race, Nation and Class: Ambiguous Identities*, Verso, London, pp. 17–28.

Barker, M. 1981, *The New Racism*, Junction Books, London.

Bhatt, C. 2012, 'The New Xenologies of Europe: Civil Tensions and Mythic Pasts', *Journal of Civil Society*, vol. 8, no. 3, pp. 307–326.

Bonilla-Silva, E. 2014, *Racism Without Racists*, 4th edn, Rowman and Littlefield, Lanham, Maryland.

Bourgois, P. and Schonberg, J. 2009, *Righteous Dopefiend*, University of California Press, Berkeley, California.

Brubaker, R. 2017, 'Between Nationalism and Civilizationism: The European Populist Moment in Comparative Perspective', *Ethnic and Racial Studies*, vol. 40, no. 8, pp. 1191–1226.

Burke, M.A. 2016, 'New Frontiers in the Study of Color-Blind Racism: A Materialist Approach', *Social Currents*, vol. 3, no. 2, pp. 103–109.

Cainkar, L. and Selod, S. 2018, 'Review of Race Scholarship and the War on Terror', *Sociology of Race and Ethnicity*, vol. 4, no. 2, pp. 165–177.

Cheng, J.E. 2015, 'Islamophobia, Muslimophobia or Racism? Parliamentary Discourses on Islam and Muslims in Debates on the Minaret Ban in Switzerland', *Discourse & Society*, vol. 26, no. 5, pp. 562–586.

de Benoist, A. 1993–1994, 'Three Interviews with Alain de Benoist', *Telos*, 98/99, Fall, pp. 173–207.

Dikötter, F. 2008, 'The Racialization of the Globe: An Interactive Interpretation', *Ethnic and Racial Studies*, vol. 38, no. 8, pp. 1478–1496.

Doane, A.W. 2007, 'The Changing Politics of Color-blind Racism', *Research in Race and Ethnic Relations*, vol. 14, pp. 159–174.

Doane, A. 2017, 'Beyond Color-blindness: (Re)Theorizing Racial Ideology', *Sociological Perspectives*, vol. 60, no. 5, pp. 975–991.

Essed, P. and Muhr, S.L. 2018, 'Entitlement Racism and its Intersections: An Interview with Philomena Essed, Social Justice Scholar', *Ephemera: Theory & Politics in Organization*, vol. 18, no. 1, pp. 183–201.

Foner, N. 2015, 'Is Islam in Western Europe Like Race in the United States?', *Sociological Forum,* vol. 30, no. 4, pp. 885–899.

François, S. 2014, 'The *Nouvelle Droite* and "tradition"', *Journal for the Study of Radicalism*, vol. 8, no.1, pp. 87–106.

Fredrickson, G.M. 2002, *Racism: A Short History*, Scribe Publications, Melbourne, Victoria.

Garner, S. 2010, *Racisms: An Introduction*, Sage, London.

Garner, S. 2015, *A Moral Economy of Whiteness: Four Frames of Racializing Discourse*, Routledge, London.

Gilroy, P. 2000, *Against Race: Imagining Political Culture Beyond the Colour Line*, The Belknap Press of Harvard University Press, Cambridge, Massachusetts.

Goldberg, D.T. 2013, 'The Postracial Contemporary', in N. Kapoor, V. Kalra and J. Rhodes (eds), *The State of Race,* Palgrave Macmillan, Basingstoke, pp. 15–30.

Griffin, R. (ed.) 1995, *Fascism*, Oxford University Press, Oxford and New York.

Griffin, R. 2000, 'Between Metapolitics and Apoliteia: The Nouvelle Droite's Strategy for Conserving the Fascist Vision in the "Interregnum"', *Modern & Contemporary France*, vol. 8, no. 1, pp. 35–53.

Grosfoguel, R. and Mielants, E. 2006, 'The Long-Durée Entanglement Between Islamophobia and Racism in the Modern/Colonial Capitalist/Patriarchal World-System: An Introduction', *Human Architecture: Journal of the Sociology of Self-Knowledge*, vol. 5, issue 1, Article 2, viewed 15 May 2023, http://scholar works.umb.edu/humanarchitecture/vol5/iss1/2.

Hall, S. 2017, *The Fateful Triangle: Race, Ethnicity, Nation*, edited by K. Mercer, Harvard University Press, Cambridge, Massachusetts, and London.

Halliday, F. 1999, '"Islamophobia" Reconsidered', *Ethnic and Racial Studies*, vol. 22, no. 5, pp. 892–902.

Ho, C. 2007, 'Muslim Women's New Defenders: Women's Rights, Nationalism and Islamophobia in Contemporary Australia', *Women's Studies International Forum*, 30, pp. 290–298.

Kumar, D. 2020, *Islamophobia and the Politics of Empire; 20 years after 9/11*, 2nd edn, Verso, London.

Kumar, D. 2021, 'Rightwing and Liberal Islamophobia: The Change of Imperial Guard from Trump to Biden', *South Asian Review*, vol. 42, no. 4, pp. 408–412.

Lentin, A. 2011, 'What Happens to Anti-Racism When We Are Post Race?', *Feminist Legal Studies*, vol. 19, issue 2, pp. 159–168.

Lentin, A. 2012, *Racism: A Beginner's Guide*, Oneworld Publications, London.

Lentin, A. 2014, 'Post-Race, Post Politics: The Paradoxical Rise of Culture After Multiculturalism', *Ethnic and Racial Studies*, vol. 37, no. 8, pp. 1268–1285.

Lentin, A. 2020, *Why Race Still Matters*, Polity Press, Cambridge.

Meer, N. and Modood, T. 2008, 'On Conceptualising Islamophobia, Anti-Muslim Sentiment and Cultural Racism', in S. Sayyid and A. Vakil (eds), *Thinking Thru' Islamophobia, Symposium Papers*, Centre for Ethnicity & Racism Studies, University of Leeds, Leeds, pp. 34–39.

Miles, R. 1987, 'Recent Marxist Theories of Nationalism and the Issue of Racism', *The British Journal of Sociology*, vol. 38, no. 1, pp. 24–43.

Mirza, H.S. 2013, 'Muslim Women and Gender Stereotypes in "New Times": From Multiculturalism to Islamophobia', in N. Kapoor, V.S. Kalra and J. Rhodes (eds), *The State of Race*, Palgrave Macmillan, Basingstoke, pp. 96–117.

Modood, T. 1997, 'Difference, Cultural Racism and Anti-Racism', in P. Werbner and T. Modood (eds), *Debating Cultural Hybridity: Multi-Cultural Identities and the Politics of Anti-Racism*, Zed Books, London and New Jersey, pp. 154–172.

Moosavi, L. 2015, 'The Racialization of Muslim Converts in Britain and Their Experiences of Islamophobia', *Critical Sociology*, vol. 4, no. 1, pp. 41–56.

Moran, A. 2017, *The Public Life of Australian Multiculturalism: Building a Diverse Nation*, Palgrave Macmillan, Basingstoke.

Morning, A. 2009, 'Toward a Sociology of Racial Conceptualization for the 21st Century', *Social Forces*, vol. 87, no. 3, pp. 1167–1192.

Morning, A. 2011, *The Nature of Race: How Scientists Think and Teach about Human Difference*, University of California Press, Oakland, California.

Morning, A. 2014, 'And You Thought We Had Moved Beyond All That: Biological Race Returns to the Social Sciences', *Ethnic and Racial Studies*, vol. 37, no. 10, pp. 1676–1685.

Nelson, J. 2014, 'Place-Defending and the Denial of Racism', *Australian Journal of Social Issues*, vol. 49, no.1, pp. 67–85.

Nelson, J.K. 2015, '"Speaking" Racism and Anti-Racism: Perspectives of Local Anti-Racism Actors', *Ethnic and Racial Studies*, vol. 38, no. 2, pp. 342–358.

Nelson, J. and Dunn, K. 2017, 'Neoliberal Anti-Racism: Responding to "Everywhere But Different" Racism', *Progress in Human Geography*, vol. 41, no. 1, pp. 26–43.

Poynting S. 2020, '"Islamophobia kills". But Where Does It Come From?', *International Journal for Crime, Justice and Social Democracy*, advance online publication, viewed 15 May 2023, https://doi.org/10.5204/ijcjsd.v9i2.1258.

Rattansi, A. 2020, *Racism: A Very Short Introduction*, 2nd edn, Oxford University Press, Oxford.

Said, E. 1979, *Orientalism*, Vintage Books, New York.

Said, E. 1985, 'Orientalism Reconsidered', *Cultural Critique*, no. 1 (Autumn), pp. 89–107.

Sayyid, S. 2014, 'A Measure of Islamophobia', *Islamophobia Studies Journal*, vol. 2, no. 1, pp. 10–25.

Sayyid, S. 2018, 'Islamophobia and the Europeanness of the Other Europe', *Patterns of Prejudice*, vol. 52, no. 5, pp. 420–435.

Scanlon Foundation 2022, *Mapping Social Cohesion Reports, 2007–2022*, viewed 15 May 2023, <https://scanloninstitute.org.au/research/mapping-social-cohesion>

Stolcke, V. 1995, 'Talking Culture: New Boundaries, New Rhetorics of Exclusion in Europe', *Current Anthropology*, vol. 36, no. 1, Special Issue: Ethnographic Authority and Cultural Explanation, pp. 1–24.

Taguieff, P.-A. 1990, 'The New Cultural Racism in France', *Telos*, 83 (Spring), pp. 109–122.

Taguieff, P.-A. 1993–1994, 'From Race to Culture: The New Right's View of European Identity', *Telos*, 98–99 (Winter/Fall), pp. 99–125.

Taras, R. 2013, '"Islamophobia Never Stands Still": Race, Religion, and Culture, *Ethnic and Racial Studies*, vol. 36, no. 3, pp. 417–433.

Tsuda, T. 2022, 'Racism Without Racial Difference? Co-Ethnic Racism and National Hierarchies Among Nikkeijin Ethnic Return Migrants in Japan', *Ethnic and Racial Studies*, vol. 45, no. 4, pp. 595–615.

UN General Assembly 1948, *The Universal Declaration of Human Rights (UDHR)*, United Nations General Assembly, New York.

UN General Assembly 1965, *International Convention on the Elimination of All Forms of Racial Discrimination*, 21 December 1965, A/RES/2106, United Nations General Assembly, New York.

Velayutham, S. 2017, 'Races without Racism? Everyday Race Relations in Singapore', *Identities*, vol. 24, no. 4, pp. 455–473.

Wacquant, L. 2009, *Punishing the Poor: The Neoliberal Government of Social Security*, Duke University Press, Durham, North Carolina.

6

# THINKING WITH RACE, THINKING AGAINST RACE

How should sociologists deal with and theorise about race in the present? The typical sociological argument is that race is a social construction, forged and re-forged time and again within, and by, racism, and/or racialisation (Omi and Winant 2015; Miles and Brown 2003). Racial distinctions *do not* have their source in biological realities (races do not exist at the level of biology in some kind of nascent, more pure form) that then get refracted and rationalised into sociohistorical racial classifications, organised in a hierarchy in racist systems. The social construction reaches into biological understandings, reshaping human variation into categories of population (Morning 2014; Gilroy 2019).

But, how do sociologists proceed from there? Do they try to remove the category of race from sociological thinking? As early as the 1930s, social scientists were arguing that this is what social scientists and natural scientists *should* do. Influential social anthropologist Franz Boas rightly argued that social differences were the result of environment and culture, and that they could not be explained by a concept of biological race, which he rejected. In their widely read book of 1935, *We Europeans: A Survey of 'Racial' Problems*, biologist Julian Huxley and anthropologist Alfred Haddon argued that the race concept was hopelessly confused and scientifically wrong, and they argued for its replacement by 'ethnic group', better suited to signalling the cultural and social explanation for group sentiment and differences (Fenton 2003, pp. 54–57). The first UNESCO *Statement on Race* in 1950, which included among its authors sociologists, such as Morris Ginsberg (founding chairperson of the British Sociological

DOI: 10.4324/9781003267690-7

Association), and anthropologists, including Claude Lévi-Strauss, also argued for replacing the term race with ethnic group. Much later, in the 1990s, Stuart Hall, who also saw race as falling under the broader umbrella of ethnicity, since race was also in the field of cultural difference (Hall 2017, p. 85), nevertheless argued that we could not just do away with the biological connotations of race. In the US, he noted that there was well-founded resistance to race simply being replaced by an emphasis on ethnicity, noting the fear that 'the scale and enormity of racial oppression will be sidelined as it gets dispersed into the more segmented and generalized spectrum of differential incorporation and exclusion that is associated with ethnicity' (Hall 2017, p. 87). Moreover, he also argued that:

> the reason 'culture' and 'cultural difference' cannot be unproblematically substituted for 'race' and 'racial difference' as a way of holding in check the biologized signifier, which continues to secure the various meanings and discourses of race in place, is because the signifier of cultural difference – 'ethnicity' – is itself Janus-faced, contradictory, sutured, and stitched up, and as such is always in danger of sliding culture toward nature.
>
> (Hall 2017, p. 126)

How do we think with and against race? In this chapter I will discuss a range of arguments about how we should talk about and theorise race in the present, whether it can be replaced by other concepts, and what implications that has for the study of racism. My argument is broadly aligned with that of Stuart Hall, that we cannot just do away with race in sociological thinking, replacing it with another concept such as ethnicity. There are related issues concerning racial identities and how these should be approached both theoretically and as experienced identities, which I will discuss via Gilroy's arguments about 'planetary humanism' and related arguments by Appiah. I also discuss the implications for race and racism of demographic changes, including the rise of majority-minority populations and of 'mixed-race' populations. In the last part of the chapter, I discuss arguments from Emirbayer and Desmond's (2015) *The Racial Order* concerning the possibilities of emancipatory 'racial reconstruction'.

## THE STATUS OF RACE AS CONCEPT

Robert Miles has argued that race is not an *analytical* concept in sociology, and it should not be used that way, but it is a powerful idea that still has major social effects (Miles, interviewed in Ashe and McGeever 2011). He strongly critiqued the 'race relations' paradigm of sociological thinking about race that had been pioneered in the UK by John Rex and Michael Banton, which, he argued, used a concept of race that reinforced the idea in the public mind and among sociologists that races were real things, or real groups, with real social interests, meaning that 'races' competed over resources and social position in societies of domination (Miles 1989; Miles and Brown 2003). The key sociological analytical concept, Miles argues, is 'racialization', which is a process that can be historically traced and explained sociologically and in its particularity (see also Miles 1982, 1989; and Miles and Brown 2003) – the approach also taken by Omi and Winant (2015), as I discussed in Chapter 2. In this respect, Miles contrasted race with class. The latter is an analytical concept because, according to Marxist theory, it is created by the mode of production and because it is a structural feature of capitalist social formation (which race was not) (Miles 1982, pp. 157–158). Of course, as we saw in Chapter 1, Mills (1997) with his 'racial contract' theory and Cedric Robinson ([1983] 2000) seriously challenged this view and put race at the centre of the development of the capitalist system, a claim that has been given renewed emphasis by scholars arguing for racial or racialised capitalism – the ways that capitalism keeps developing its means of expropriation in the present, nationally, internationally and globally, by dividing populations up on racial lines, and exploiting them differentially in order to extract maximum profit, which is achieved through both formal and informal/illegal immigrant labour markets, as well as through a range of racially discriminatory financial practices (amidst a growing literature, see Bhattacharyya 2018; Virdee 2019; Issar 2021; Dawson 2016; Fraser 2016). As Nancy Fraser has argued, if we shift our attention from the direct relation between capital and wage labour, to examine the conditions in which that can occur – the possibilities of 'free labour' to be exploited by capital – we notice that there is a level of 'expropriation' that reveals the 'centrality of *racialized dependent labor* to capitalist society'. This allows us to see that capitalism is 'an institutionalized social order in which *racialized political subjection* plays a constitutive role', revealing 'capitalism's deep-seated entanglement with racial oppression' (Fraser 2016, p. 166). '"Race" emerges', she argues, 'as the mark that distinguishes free subjects from dependent subjects of expropriation' (Fraser 2016, p. 172). Capitalism requires an entire '*institutionalized social order*', the 'extra-economic arrangements' to support this distinction crucial to maximum extortion of profit (surplus value) (Fraser 2016, p. 173; italics in original).

Banton in his later writing, such as *The Idea of Race*, argued that social scientists might use the concepts of 'majority' and minority' instead of 'race' (Banton 1977, p. 7). Later still, Banton (2012, 2015) articulated a different position to that of Miles, claiming that 'race' was not useful at all as a term for thinking sociologically. Though 'race' was an ordinary language term, he argued that, for sociological explanation (for example, in the study of 'interpersonal relations'), it should be replaced by a term that signalled the influence of the continuum of skin colour and the ways that people made use of such differentiations of colour in social life; thus, a term such as 'colour differentiation' was more sociologically useful (Banton 2015). He argued that:

> Skin colour is a first order abstraction. It is visible and measurable. Race is a second order abstraction. It is neither visible nor measurable. Reference to 'racial' differences may have positive functions in the political realm, but attempts to use race as an analytical construct in sociological explanation only make the intellectual problem more difficult to resolve.
>
> (Banton 2012, p. 1128)

Nevertheless, Banton spent his whole career using terms such as race and racial in his many works. Moreover, how would 'colour differentiation' help with non-colour-coded forms of racism? Also, there are powerful reasons for sociologists to keep using the term race, and to keep it visible in sociological analysis, especially in its connection to racism, as Hall articulated.

Alana Lentin has argued that the 'race as a social construction' argument has only got social scientists so far. It has not undermined racism or racial thinking, nor has it resulted in the disappearance of racialised identities (Lentin 2020, p. 26; see also Hall 2017). Rather than stop talking about and emphasising race, Lentin reminds us, we need instead to become more 'race literate'. Lentin distinguishes two main groups in current debates about racism: 'race realists' who accept the 'reality' of race –she classifies these as racists, and included in this group are those who claim that race can be understood neutrally, as a range of differences based on genetics, drawing upon genetic indices (Lentin 2020, p. 21); and the 'race-critical anti-racists', who continue to highlight the connections between race and racism, and to challenge, critique and protest against racism. Between these stands an amorphous group that chooses to remain silent on race. Some of these people argue that even to talk about race is to engage in racism, and that talk of race and uses of it in sociology and other social sciences reinforces the false idea that race is real, arguing that it 'risks naturalizing and solidifying human distinctions' (Lentin 2020, p. 101). This group, like much of the white West, never or rarely listens to the voices of those who know directly about and experience racism, 'Black, Brown, Indigenous, Muslim and other racialized people', whose activists and intellectuals produce knowledge about racism and racialisation that is largely ignored by white-dominated public spheres and knowledge systems that continue to operate from a position of 'methodological whiteness' (Bhambra 2017) that treats their knowledges as inferior (Lentin 2020, p. 103).

Lentin claims that we can use race as an 'analytical tool' – it is not clear if this is an argument against the distinction that Miles made between race as idea and race as concept. Lentin (2020) does not share Miles's Marxist conception of race, but instead argues for a Foucauldian approach to thinking about race, explicitly rejecting the view that we should study racism as ideology (as in Miles, 1989). She argues that race is not something created by the 'ideology of racism':

> race itself is a technology rather than a category, that pre-exists the idea of the taxonomical system of biological 'races'. Race, from this perspective, should be understood as a project and a process elaborated by regimes such as colonialism and slavery, and within which structures and ideologies take shape over time.
>
> (Lentin 2020, p. 68).

Race, as a technology of rule, enables the proliferation of different regimes of governmentality: 'Race as ordering, as management, sedimentation, sifting, as correction and disciplining, as empowering some while causing others to buckle under that power has always relied on a plurality of processes' (Lentin 2015, p. 1403).

Here Lentin is drawing broadly upon Foucault's argument about racism from *The History of Sexuality Volume 1* (Foucault 1978), and his Collège de France lectures from 1975 to 1976, translated as *Society Must Be Defended* (Foucault 2003), linking racism to the new form of power that he termed 'biopower', emergent from the late eighteenth century, which was about promoting the healthy life of populations, and which also meant leaving segments of internal populations (internal, for example, to nations) and external populations (for example, in colonial possession) to 'die'. Race and racism provided this kind of power, which was ostensibly about 'giving' and promoting 'life', the rationale and justification for killing or allowing to die. This historically new technology of power, focused on whole populations, was central to the modern state's activities, so much so that 'modern racism' is 'state racism' (Foucault 2003, pp. 254–255). 'Once the State functions in the biopower mode,' Foucault (2003, p. 256) argues, 'racism alone can justify the murderous function of the State.' Foucault returns again and again in these lectures to the analogy of war, arguing that racism, once it becomes biological in the late eighteenth century, involves a new meaning of, and relationship to, war:

> But racism does make the relationship of war – 'If you want to live, the other must die' – function in a way that is completely new and that is quite compatible with the exercise of biopower. On the one hand, racism makes it possible to establish a relationship between my life and the death of the other that is not a military or warlike relationship of confrontation, but a biological-type relationship: 'The more inferior species die out, the more abnormal individuals are eliminated, the fewer degenerates there will be in the species as a whole, and the more I – as species rather than individual – can live, the stronger I will be, the more vigorous I will be. I will be able to proliferate.' The fact that the other dies does not mean simply that I live in the sense that his death guarantees my safety; the death of the other, the death of the bad race, of the inferior race (or the degenerate, or the abnormal) is something that will make life in general healthier: healthier and purer.
>
> (Foucault 2003, p. 255)

Stuart Hall also drew on elements of Foucault's thinking, and structuralism, when arguing that race is deeply sedimented in the discursive formation of modernity; that it structures whole signifying chains that establish racial/cultural/ethnic similarities and differences, in fact, acting as a kind of master signifier that can subtly change form and adapt in new situations. In his famous 1997 lecture, 'Race, the Floating Signifier', Hall argues against Appiah's position, articulated at the end of Appiah's essay on Du Bois (Appiah 1985), that we could ever get rid of the biological associations of race with, quoting from Du Bois, 'color, hair and bone', the biological trace of race (Hall 1997). Reflecting on that point in another lecture, Hall argued that this was not because race was 'real' or because it could fix itself to any kind of 'truth':

> It is because racial discourse is not a form of truth in any case, but rather a 'regime of truth' . . . The biological-genetic element functions to fix difference discursively all along the chain of equivalences in the racial system of representation. Thus, whatever its 'truth' in terms of scientific validity, it is through its discursive operations that race gives meaning to the world, makes a certain kind of sense of the world, constructs an order of intelligibility, organizes human practices within its categories, and thus comes to acquire real effects. To grasp this discursive functioning is to understand race as a sliding signifier.
>
> (Hall 2017, p. 81)

Paul Gilroy has studied closely, and for decades, the impact and deformations of racism, while also making a major contribution to the analysis of transatlantic black cultures, identities and cultural production, as well as challenging 'raciology' and racism. In the late 1990s and early 2000s, Gilroy started to argue for ways of thinking beyond race, which he termed 'planetary humanism' (Gilroy 2000). This thinking was also aligned with his thinking on 'convivialities', vernacular cosmopolitanism and multicultures, especially as lived in diverse urban spaces (Gilroy 2004). His articulation of 'planetary humanism' was partly inspired by his reflections on multiple, and diverse, uses of race from different social locations, including among black intellectuals, leaders and activists, which on occasion mimicked the worst traits of white supremacism, as in some of Marcus Garvey's arguments about purifying and standardising the black race and race separatism (Gilroy 2000, pp. 231–234). While recognising the power and importance of racial identities, including as forms of resistance against racism and as providing positive communal experiences, he also reflected on the Fascist and authoritarian tendencies of Black Atlantic political culture, including in Garveyism and in the Nation of Islam, and elements of black nationalism and Afro-centrism (with the latter claiming African superiority). Speaking of a utopian future, Gilroy (2000, p. 334) wrote that:

> I urge a fundamental change of mood upon what used to be called 'antiracism.' It has been asked in an explicitly utopian spirit to terminate its ambivalent relationship to the idea of 'race' in the interest of a heterocultural, postanthropological, and cosmopolitan yet-to-come.

In his recent speech when receiving the Holberg prize, 'Never again: refusing race and salvaging the human', Gilroy (2019) put this position forcefully. Reflecting on the terrible damage and historical disasters, including violence and genocide, caused by racism in tandem with nationalism and 'xenology', and witnessing the reinvigoration of ossified white racist identities, including via the vast expanse of the Internet, producing Alt-right multifaceted racism and neofascist trends as well as claims about 'white genocide' and the 'great replacement', he also responded to the 'seductive' 'ontological turn' in 'the study of race politics', which 'has become disastrously complicated by prospective nostalgia for the easy, essentialist approaches that were dominant when assertive cultural nationalism ruled the roost'. While his reassertion of the value of humanism involves utopian thinking, he argues that we must envisage futures beyond race, based in conceptions of common humanity. We must avoid the pitfall of imagining that perceptions of race and the alignment of groups and population with race are transhistorical phenomena. They are, and always have been, Gilroy argues, historical and contextual; and we are socialised into them. In their place, he envisaged different kinds of identities. In direct response to 'the certainties and moorings provided by racial sentiment', he wanted to locate and promote 'other kinds of ontological ballast' that 'can be found in forms of identification that, in opposition to reified identity, emerge from affinity and convivial contact, place, generation, sexualities and gender'. We needed to 'turn away from the defaulted racial ordering of life'. And this would have gains not only for those victimised and dehumanised by racial orders, but also for the racially dominant who would have their 'amputated humanity' repaired, a view that he associated with Frantz Fanon.

In the Holberg prize speech, Gilroy drew inspiration for this thinking from the versions of humanism on display when people faced natural and other disasters, where the 'composite of human frailty and interdependency . . . becomes visible', as well as from the black radical thinkers, such as Du Bois, Fanon, Césaire, Senghor, C.L.R. James, and black feminist thinkers, such as Anna Julia Cooper, who, while arguing about race and against racisms, pointed the way to planetary humanism in their articulation of 'agonistic humanism'. While their work was focused on vindicating black humanity, it also extended beyond that, 'enriched by exposure to cosmologies that do not consider individuality, subject formation, agency, temporality, property or groupness in exclusively European terms'. They provided us with a 'mix of resources [that] furnishes us with a compass we can use to locate newer and better understanding of the human – considered, "post-anthropologically" – that is, after the death of Man' (Gilroy 2019).

Gilroy has argued in a number of works that this humanism is also implicit in what he terms convivial relations:

> Conviviality is a social pattern in which different metropolitan groups dwell in close proximity, but where their racial, linguistic and religious particularities do not – as the logic of ethnic absolutism suggest they must – add up to discontinuities of experience or insuperable problems of communication.
>
> (Gilroy 2006, p. 40)

Noble (2013) argues that 'conviviality' is not about cosmopolitan types or individuals, but instead is about the cultivation of subconscious, cosmopolitan habits, everyday practices and solidarities, habituated through pragmatic living together where 'multiculture' becomes 'an ordinary feature of social life' (Noble 2013, p. 166, quoting Gilroy).

Gilroy's argument, like that of Appiah (1985, 1994, 2018), is not that we, as sociologists, as social scientists or as philosophers, can stop talking about racism and its depredations, and the suffering involved in racialised subjectivities, arranged in hierarchies by white supremacy. It would also seem that both Gilroy and Appiah are not claiming that, under current circumstances of racial inequality and injustice, we can stop altogether from using the term 'race' as we speak on these topics and challenge racism. It seems to be more of a call to racialised subjects to start to find ways to think themselves out of racialised selves, and not to give in to the false claims of race and what it means. Thus, at the end of his paper on the troubled life of the race concept in Du Bois' thinking, Appiah (1985) argued that, late in life, Du Bois reached a point in his thinking about his connection with a pan-African identity, where he should have taken the leap from thinking about difference as a question of racial essence (which persisted in Du Bois' thinking about race), and instead thought about civilisations without any recourse to racial or biological essences. In another essay, Appiah 'defended an analytical notion of racial identity', but worried 'about too hearty an endorsement of racial identification' (Appiah 1994, p. 135). He felt ambivalent about racial identification if it became too unitary, if it filled out the conception of individual (and by implication collective) identity. He worried about the 'imperialism' of racial or any singular identity, because each of us has much more than a racial identity:

> Racial identity can be the basis of resistance to racism; but even as we struggle against racism – and though we have made great progress, we have further still to go – let us not let our racial identities subject us to new tyrannies.
>
> (Appiah 1994, p. 134)

## BEYOND RACE?

The question of the possibility of ever being able to move beyond race is also a question of the context that the claim addresses, for the obvious reason that there is incredible diversity of racial situations throughout the globe; and also possibly some situations where other kinds of religious, caste, colour or other cleavages, that are not necessarily race-based, are more significant (Saharso and Scharrer 2022). A recent commentary series in *Comparative Migration Studies* tackled the question 'Beyond race?' and solicited responses from a range of scholars from different racial backgrounds, who specialised in the study of different parts of the world. They considered issues that included the impact of changing demographics (caused by mass migration flows, the expansion of mixed-race groupings), changing policies and changing racial movements. As one would expect, there were many variations in response to this posed question, including the outright rejection of the possibility in current circumstances.

Sawitri Saharso and Tabea Scharrer (2022), two scholars based in Europe, recognised in their initial framing article that what they had to say about race might look very different to the views of people from other places and from different racial backgrounds and experiences. For a start, the discourse of race was more often avoided in European contexts than in, for example, the US, with a preference for discussing 'ethnicity'. Their focus was on four main issues. First, there was changing demography, the combined result of immigration and greater interracial marriage and partnering, resulting in larger numbers of mixed-race people, and meaning the shift from white majority to minority-majority demographics in the US, Europe, Australia and New Zealand, predicted by scholars such as Eric Kaufmann (2019) to occur over the next one hundred years (much sooner in the US and New Zealand, according to Kaufmann). With such changed demography, would there emerge new cleavages other than race? Second, they raised the issue of the possible impact of the rise of mixed-race people on the viability of public policies, such as affirmative action, based on unitary racial categories. Third, related to changed circumstances, how would political mobilisation around race be affected? Fourth, more theoretically, they questioned the meaning of race as a category, and asked what going beyond race might mean? Was trans-race possible, for example – people choosing their own racial identity? Or would people transcend race altogether?

Saharso and Scharrer's (2022) answers to these questions were nuanced – for example, noting that expanding mixed-raciality might end up reinforcing white majorities, if large numbers of mixed-race people are drawn into white identity (as had happened in the past in the US with Jews and other 'white ethnics' and as Kaufmann (2019) in *Whiteshift* claims may happen). Also, mixed-race categories do not break down racial categorisation, but may just add other racial categories. The increasing public visibility and demographic signifi- cance of mixed races can result in white backlashes, including white populist movements. The implications of mixed race for affirmative action policies are also multifaceted – while people from mixed- race backgrounds might still experience the forms of racial discrimi- nation and disadvantages associated with minority race status, they may be greeted with suspicion if they do not show the right visible race markers (this has been a noted phenomenon for Indigenous people in Australia).

Saharso and Scharrer's (2022) discussion of social movements based on racial identities (such as Black Lives Matter) is also nuanced, discussing mainstream critiques (including from left and right), but also raising the possibility of broad-based social movements against multiple forms of injustice (racism, sexism, socioeconomic or class- based) that do not deny the relevance of meanings of identity claims. They conclude with a discussion of the possibilities of trans-race, using the example of Rachel Dolezal, a famous case in the US of a woman born into a white family claiming to be essentially black, despite her white body (see Brubaker 2016 for an extended analy- sis). At present, the prospects for 'choosing' or being accepted into a racial, or even an ethnic, category, without having some ancestral link to that category, still seem remote in most societies. Racial/ ethnic boundary making is different to what has been experienced for gender and sexual boundaries in some countries, where the idea that one might be born into the wrong biological body, making transgender possible, has at least some public acceptance.

Farida Fozdar (2022), an Australian scholar, began her contri- bution by reflecting on the hostile reception she received from another scholar when giving her paper on mixed-race experi- ences in Australia at a conference in New York, which revealed the high stakes of claims and arguments about mixed-race. Self-identifying as mixed-race herself (and making use of some autoethnography), she had discussed the relatively positive experi- ences of a small, qualitative sample of mixed-race migrant fami- lies in Western Australia (mainly a mix of European and Asian backgrounds) and how they negotiated race and cultural differ- ence in the sociocultural context of a multicultural settler soci- ety. Race was not a major concern within the families, and the children tended to feel positive about the way they were received outside their homes in society, not experiencing much overt racism and having a lot of positive experiences. The children tended to have cosmopolitan outlooks. Fozdar had suggested that this might reflect the impact of Australia's multicultural policies over more than four decades, leading to more positive views of and reactions to diversity. The scholar who challenged Fozdar, who had researched mixed-race experiences in Europe and the US, rejected this account of being mixed-race, arguing that the experience of racially mixed black families in the US and the UK was fundamentally shaped by white supremacy, structural racism and blocked social mobility. Fozdar went on in her article to explain the peculiarities of the Australian settler-nation's racial dynamics, its 'race blindness' that persists and is in fact supported by its multicultural policy – though the latter also meant that some forms of race and ethnic mixedness are valued and celebrated. Racial mixedness in Australia, and also in most other places, was very complex, and experiences, opportunities and social inclusion/exclusion differed, sometimes dramatically, depending on types of mixes and contexts, with some experiencing rejection and racism, while others were more at ease, proud of their mixedness and their connection to multiple peoples and worlds, seen also by society as a positive asset. There was no such thing as a characteristic mixed-race experience.

Thus, it was also difficult to draw political conclusions about the possible impact of race-mixedness, including how it might interact with or possibly help people to overcome racism, or move beyond rigid race categorisation. Jasmine Mitchell (2022), writing about the US and Brazil, questioned whether the rise of mixed-racial identity, which she termed 'multiraciality' indicates anything like moving beyond race. On the contrary, multiraciality can be an ideological tool used to maintain white supremacy. The success of multiracial public figures (political figures such as Obama or Kamala Harris, sportspeople, musical stars and other celebrities) can be used by those wanting to deny the ongoing significance of race and racial hierarchy to prove that societies have achieved racial progress or racial harmony. Moreover, in Latin America, 'racial mixture plays a fundamental role in . . . narratives denying racism' (Mitchell 2022, p. 2). 'Rather than undoing the continuance of race,' Mitchell (2022, p. 1) argued, 'constructions of multiraciality reinforce presumptions of racial difference and racialized ways of thinking.' She highlighted that there is a developing trend for mixed-race people to align with non-whiteness, rather than with whiteness, and that the phenomenon does not indicate a shift beyond racial consciousness in the US or Brazil, with their very different histories, but instead a hardening and reinforcing of race. However, this phenomenon may, she argued, lead to stronger non-white solidarity and an undermining of whiteness, denaturalising it as the desired norm.

Sayaka Osanami Törngren and Karen L. Suyemoto (2022), who self-identify and are ascribed as Asian or Asian American, reflected upon their research in Japan, Sweden and the US, and also argued against the claim that the phenomenon of race-mixedness indicated the potential of moving beyond race. This was because racism remained a global system of hierarchy and privilege, still dominated by whiteness and white supremacy, and that the meanings of race historically shifted but in relation to systemic racism. For this reason, it was also premature to talk of being able to move beyond race – such a movement would only be possible once racism was dismantled as a global, white supremacist system. In Japan, for example, which they argued had a racialised hierarchy with both historical and contemporary sources and manifestations, mixed-raciality led to ambivalent situations that were directly related to systemic racism. The colonial past meant that people of Chinese, Korean and other non-Asian Japanese backgrounds in Japan were racialised as second-class citizens, a subjection maintained multi-generationally via 'immigration control, economic exploitation, policing and unequal provision of rights' (Törngren and Suyemoto 2022, p. 4). Post-World War Two, the 'whiteness' of the West became a Japanese ideal, which has implications for different forms of race-mixedness: 'Mixed Japanese with Asian background, both consciously and unconsciously pass as Japanese (to avoid oppression) and mixed Japanese with Western phenotypes exercise their position as White (to gain privilege) in Japan' (Törngren and Suyemoto 2022, p. 5). In Sweden while some people who were phenotypically white but of migrant background (such as Poles, Yugoslavs, Finns and Italians) and 'mixed Swedes' could eventually 'pass' as majority Swedes, others further distant from phenotypical whiteness could not; the racial categorisation, division and hierarchy remained the same (Törngren and Suyemoto 2022, p. 7).

## RACIAL RECONSTRUCTION

Arguments about 'racial democracy' also address the theme of 'beyond race'. In their book *The Racial Order*, Emirbayer and Desmond (2015) posit that there are two extreme poles in current racial debate, or of 'normative reasoning in regard to race' – one is white supremacy and the other is the complete eradication of race. They argue for a position that veers towards the second pole, but does not go all the way. They suggest that there are three main formations that one could pursue for racial reconstruction in a positive sense, 'color blindness', 'multiculturalism/cosmopolitanism' and 'racial democracy'.

They see colour blindness, which has been discussed at some length in Chapter 5, as already the dominant ideology of the overcoming of race and racism in the post-civil rights era in the US. They reject this, not only on the grounds that it does not reflect the social realities of racial domination and, rather, denies their ongoing existence, but also on the grounds that it has a negative policy approach of just removing any mention of or consideration of race, even for practical purposes of trying to rectify the impact of past injustices that live on in the present. It thus has no way of fighting racial injustice, because it simply pretends that it does not exist anymore. In other words, colour-blind policy can do nothing to address and enhance the colour-blind ideal, which is that everyone would be treated equally as individuals, regardless of 'race' (Emirbayer and Desmond 2015, p. 294): 'Through an abracadabra act that transforms ethics into ontology (a way to live into how life is), color blindness demands an instant good society, one without history, where things are right and nothing is in need of restoration' (Emirbayer and Desmond 2015, pp. 295–296).

Multiculturalism or, in a more philosophical approach, cosmopolitanism, has more to recommend it. Unlike colour blindness, it recognises ontologies of difference, including cultural difference, and includes an ethic of respect for different expressions of life, and the possibility of different values. It is not just about individuals, but also concerns groups or collectivities (the latter more in its multicultural form, rather than cosmopolitanism). In its cosmopolitan versions (as articulated by Appiah, 2006), it encourages interest in engaging with and getting to know different others, fully appreciating their differences, and perhaps even being transformed by these encounters.

Emirbayer and Desmond make a similar critique as that made by other race scholars who criticise multiculturalism for placing so much emphasis on respecting diversity that little or no attention is paid to the past and ongoing effects of racism and racial domination, and to specific plans for tackling racism straight on. Here, it shares a failing with colour-blindness (Emirbayer and Desmond 2015, p. 301). It does not pay enough attention to the need to find practical ways of rectifying past racial injustice and overcoming continuing racial injustice.

The third formation is racial democracy, which, they argue, is the most plausible way of 'overcoming our racial problems' (Emirbayer and Desmond 2015, p. 291). Racial democracy has a strong concern with rectifying racial injustice, but that is not all that it does, because 'democracy, at least in its expansive, Deweyan sense, comprises not only justice, or even justice tempered by mercy and grace, but also self-realization, flourishing, and growth' (Emirbayer and Desmond 2015, p. 305). It is 'non-idealised' theory, unlike colour blindness, and to a lesser extent multiculturalism, which are idealised theories, in that they wish away current racial realities, including injustice and inequalities. It attempts to tackle head on exploitation and the individuals and groups that directly benefit from ongoing racial injustice. They illustrate, with the example of the urban black ghetto, that anti-poverty theorists often characterise in terms of '*lack*' of a range of resources, but which they argue is best understood as an example of exploitation that has immense benefits for capitalists such as property owners and landlords (Emirbayer and Desmond 2015, p. 304). This can only be rectified by tackling that exploitation head on (social movements have a major role here), including challenging its organisers and beneficiaries. Racial justice involves a radicalising of democracy, so that it creates and supports the conditions that directly challenge and eventually overcome racial domination and inequality.

Their book ends with a commentary on the 'means of racial reconstruction', that involves change at multiple levels – individual, interactional, institutional and interstitial. I will explain this in summary form and in some detail because it does represent an attempt to discuss how the racial order can be transformed in a positive way – and often racism scholars, pessimistic about the prospects of ever overcoming racism and racially dominating societies, do not address this; in fact, such scholars often point to the flaws, or the ongoing, hidden forms of racism evident in attempts to overcome racism.

In discussing individual change, Emirbayer and Desmond recognise the possible obstacles since they have given an account of unconscious, powerfully reproduced racial habituses (see my discussion in Chapter 4). However, they also point to the fact that the habitus, according to Bourdieu, is not 'eternal', in the sense of eternally reproducing itself in exactly the same form, but that dispositions can shift (Emirbayer and Desmond 2015, p. 313). The habitus is always related to ongoing experiences and, in addition, there can be misalignments between habitus and field (Bourdieu showed these in some of his works), which also raise possibilities for creative, individual habitus changes. Change can come about through inserting oneself into new, multiracial interactions and environments, from informal settings such as interaction with racially different neighbours to more formal interactions such as joining anti-racism organisations (Emirbayer and Desmond 2015, p. 314). Bonilla-Silva (2014) has similarly suggested that whites could enact everyday anti-racism by taking deliberate steps to move out beyond their 'white habitus' to engage more deeply and regularly with non-white others.

The second example is the personal change that comes about through reflecting on 'misfirings' in 'critical moments', where one's habitus does not seamlessly reproduce practices, but one must reflect on what to do, how to be, in certain contexts and situations:

> Potentially this involves reconstructing one's ways of thinking, perceiving, feeling, and acting – for instance, in racial life, questioning one's sense of ethnic superiority; one's erotic fantasies toward the racial Other; one's fear of confirming demeaning stereotypes; or one's tendencies toward self-exclusion, the self-denying verdict that 'this is not for the likes of me'.
> (Emirbayer and Desmond 2015, p. 314)

The ongoing critical self-questioning to overcome racist feelings, thoughts and actions should not be only an internal individual monologue, but rather should be conducted in dialogue with others, such as friends, lovers, family, and in social movements – one requires sources of response in order to effect change, and to change patterns of racially dominant action (Emirbayer and Desmond 2015,

p. 316). However, change to the racial order cannot be achieved simply by individuals changing.

Change at the interactional level involves things such as challenging racist assumptions in moments of interaction, like a white person challenging another white person's racist claims, so that white solidarity is broken down and a space is opened for change. This is a disruption to the normal working of the racial order – it is disruptive and confrontational, rather than simply educative (Emirbayer and Desmond 2015, p. 318). It can also occur in interaction between non-white others across racial lines and challenges to stereotypes and beliefs that non-white others have about other non-white others. Here, at this level, Emirbayer and Desmond also discuss the shift in the US from affirmative action policies in the 1980s to diversity training in organisations – while they do not dismiss diversity training outright, they are critical of the ways that it individualises differences – which undermines understandings of the dominative structures involved in interaction across differences, built on centuries of racial oppression – and also because it has been shown that diversity programmes have not changed racial diversity at managerial levels, which remain white-dominated. This has also been shown to be the case for Australia, which has embraced 'diversity and inclusion' models within its broad multicultural policy framework, but where the top leadership roles across companies, universities, the governments and government bureaucracies are dominated by white people (and by white males) significantly beyond their proportion in the population (Working Group on Cultural Diversity and Inclusive Leadership 2018).

Racial democracy must also be fought for at the institutional level – economy/workplace, state (government, courts, policing and prisons), cultural production institutions (such as the arts, media, etc.), and also the institutions in the field of civil society (including housing, schooling and the family). This also follows the broad contours of Jeffrey Alexander's (2006) argument in *The Civil Sphere* about the multilevel operation of processes of 'civil repair', including the civil repair involved in dealing with complex, systemic racism that impedes the universalising tendencies of the civil sphere. The larger institutional structures profoundly shape habituses, as well as social interaction, and thus racial change must occur at the institutional level to achieve racial democracy. Mechanisms include the ever-important anti-discrimination laws that have been enacted since the 1960s, as well as the affirmative action programmes (which have been challenged and undermined, especially by colour-blind advocates, since the 1980s). Citing the moral egalitarianism philosopher Elizabeth Anderson (see, for example, Anderson 2010), they argue that a compelling case can be made for affirmative action in terms of the power of integrative effects on overcoming segregation and negative stereotyping and allowing racialised groups to participate fully in a democratic society, enjoying full access to mainstream resources. They also point to William Julius Wilson's argument about policies that have a 'hidden agenda' of addressing racial disadvantage, that anti-discrimination and affirmative action do not necessarily address (because they tend to enhance the opportunities of more privileged sections of racially dominated groups, see Wilson 1978, 1987), by enacting policies that are apparently not racially based, but are addressed to a generalised 'truly disadvantaged' section of populations that, nevertheless, have a significant proportion of non-white members. Examples include job creation schemes in economically depressed areas. Notably, Wilson re-addressed these ideas in an article (Wilson 2011) revisiting his famous book *The Declining Significance of Race* (Wilson 1978). Reflecting on the retrenchment of anti-discrimination and affirmative action policies in the 1980s as a result of white backlash, and on the ongoing evidence of major levels of racial disadvantage, Wilson (2011) argued that he now saw the need for both class-based and race-based policies, such as affirmative action, in order to deal with racial inequalities and racial justice. He stated he would now place 'much greater emphasis on the need to *strongly* and *continuously* embrace, as well as advance, both race- and class-based solutions to address life chances of people of color' (Wilson 2011, p. 67).

Emirbayer and Desmond also discuss symbolic reclassification and its importance at the institutional level. Phenomena here include the legacies of racial signification apparent in state-based classifications used for censuses, immigration quotas, etc., and rules around English speaking, as well as dress codes and other racialised cultural codes that reflect white racial criteria, assuming that this is universal rather than racially coded. The racialised separations of the 'sacred' and the 'profane' enact 'consecration and denigration', which are racially damaging, but which can be 'negated by efforts at symbolic reclassification'.

Finally, they discuss the need for 'moral *re*regulation' which means 'the hammering out of new structures of moral expectations and constraints (regarding race relations) at the institutional level' (Emirbayer and Desmond 2015, p. 325; italics in original), decided through processes of expansive democratic decision-making (following the model laid out by Durkheim (1958) in his argument about occupational groups as moral educators and regulators, in *Professional Ethics and Civic Morals*).

Change at the interstitial level refers to the crucial role of social movements and other kinds of organisations (such as settlement houses historically, and such as the contemporary Christian evangelical 'urban monastery movement', operating in poor, racially mixed urban areas across the US), as well as loosely formed 'publics', aimed at racial social reform, which occur in various forms such as via the Internet, on the street, in clubs, churches and townhalls, and organised social movements, to the extent that they directly challenge, address and combat racism, racial domination and racial inequalities. Emirbayer and Desmond (2015, p. 328) recognise that there is a problem for these locally based initiatives as they struggle to effect change at the national level. Interstitial actions include demonstrations, strikes and boycotts, and racial uprisings. Such political struggle is fundamental for the social change required for racial democracy. Some multiracial interstitial organisations, including, for example, multiracial workers unions, model in their organising structures and actions the multiracial democracy that they aim to achieve.

## CONCLUSION

The broad conclusion that emerges from the discussion in this chapter – including the debates about how or whether we can ever move 'beyond race', and whether any significant societal and demographic changes (e.g., the rise of majority-minority populations and of 'mixed-race' populations and identities) are pushing us in that direction – is that continuing systemic racism means that we must keep race and its workings *in view*. Thus, as Stuart Hall argued, we cannot just do away with race in sociological thinking, replacing it with another concept such as ethnicity. For the present, we cannot do without the term race, which is required in order to retain focus on the impacts of racism. How we think about the status of that term is another question. The Foucauldian approaches that see 'race' as a technology of governmentality emphasise both its deep entrenchment in the modern West for the last few centuries and also that its work continues in deep and subtle ways, even as ideological constructions of race shift. Thus, it cannot be easily dislodged, or people inoculated against its pernicious influence. Racialisation theories emphasise how race is constructed and reconstructed in contested terrain involving different racial projects. This allows for the possibility of more positive constructions of race, though these are always tested and threatened by the weight of historical forms of racist hierarchy, and the more deadly constructions of race associated with white supremacy.

How we approach and theorise racial identities, but also how we experience and think about these identities, as individuals and within collectivities, was addressed through the utopian, future-oriented thinking of Paul Gilroy about 'planetary humanism' as well as by Appiah who questioned the construction of race and racial identities that ultimately rely upon assumptions about racial essences. Both recognised the resistance qualities of some racial identities while also warning about how their rigid adoption can lead to other tyrannies of identity. Finally, I considered the prospects of possible movements beyond racism argued by Emirbayer and Desmond (2015), of the possibilities of emancipatory 'racial reconstruction' via a vision of 'racial democracy' that accepts that people will continue to experience racial identities while societies continuously work towards individual and group thriving, and social justice for all, through collective social action challenging racism at all levels of society.

## REFERENCES

Alexander, J.C. 2006, *The Civil Sphere*, Oxford University Press, Oxford.

Anderson, E. 2010, *The Imperative of Integration*, Princeton University Press, Princeton, New Jersey.

Appiah, K.A. 1985, 'The Uncompleted Argument: Du Bois and the Illusion of Race', *Critical Inquiry*, vol. 12, no. 1, pp. 21–37.

Appiah, K.A. 1994, *Race, Culture, Identity: Misunderstood Connections, The Tanner Lectures on Human Values*, University of California at San Diego, California.

Appiah, K.A. 2006, *Cosmopolitanism: Ethics in a World of Strangers*, Penguin Books, London.

Appiah, K.A. 2018, *The Lies That Bind: Rethinking Identity*, Profile Books, London.

Ashe, S.D. and McGeever, B.F. 2011, 'Marxism, Racism and the Construction of "Race" as a Social and Political Relation: An Interview with Professor Robert Miles', *Ethnic and Racial Studies*, vol. 34, no. 12, pp. 2009–2026.

Banton, M. 1977, *The Idea of Race*, Tavistock Publications, London.

Banton, M. 2012, 'The Colour Line and the Colour Scale in the Twentieth Century', *Ethnic and Racial Studies*, vol. 35, no. 7, pp. 1109–1131.

Banton, M. 2015, 'John Rex's Main Mistake', *Ethnic and Racial Studies*, vol. 38, no. 8, pp. 1369–1381.

Bhambra, G.K. 2017, 'Brexit, Trump, and "Methodological Whiteness": On the Misrecognition of Race and Class', *The British Journal of Sociology*, vol. 68, issue S1, pp. 214–232.

Bhattacharyya, G. 2018, *Rethinking Racial Capitalism: Questions of Reproduction and Survival*, Rowman & Littlefield, London.

Bonilla-Silva, E. 2014, *Racism Without Racists*, 4th edn, Rowman and Littlefield, Lanham, Maryland.

Brubaker, R. 2016, *Trans: Gender and Race in an Age of Unsettled Identities*, Princeton University Press, Princeton, New Jersey.

Dawson, M.C. 2016, 'Hidden in Plain Sight: A Note on Legitimation Crises and the Racial Order', *Critical Historical Studies*, Spring, pp. 143–161.

Durkheim, E. 1958, *Professional Ethics and Civic Morals*, trans. C. Brookfield, The Free Press, Glencoe, Illinois.

Emirbayer, M. and Desmond, M. 2015, *The Racial Order*, University of Chicago Press, Chicago, Illinois.

Fenton, S. 2003, *Ethnicity*, Polity Press, Cambridge.

Foucault, M. 1978, *The History of Sexuality, Volume 1*, Pantheon Books, New York.

Foucault, M. 2003, *'Society Must Be Defended': Lectures at the College de France, 1975–76*, trans. D. Macey, edited by M. Bertani and A. Fontana, Picador, New York.

Fozdar, F. 2022, '"This Is Not How We Talk About Race Anymore": Approaching Mixed Race in Australia', *Comparative Migration Studies*, vol. 10, no. 11, pp. 1–14, viewed 15 May 2023, https://doi.org/10.1186/s40878-022-00285-1.

Fraser, N. 2016, 'Expropriation and Exploitation in Racialized Capitalism: A Reply to Michael Dawson', *Critical Historical Studies*, Spring, pp. 163–178.

Gilroy, P. 2000, *Against Race: Imagining Political Culture Beyond the Colour Line*, The Belknap Press of Harvard University Press, Cambridge, Massachusetts.

Gilroy, P. 2004, *After Empire: Melancholia or Convivial Culture?*, Routledge, London and New York.

Gilroy, P. 2006, 'Multiculture in Times of War: An Inaugural Lecture Given at the London School of Economics', *Critical Quarterly*, vol. 8, no. 4, pp. 27–45.

Gilroy, P. 2019, 'Never Again: Refusing Race and Salvaging the Human,' Holberg Lecture, University of Bergen, Norway, 4 June 2019, viewed 15 May 2023, https://www.newframe.com/long-read-refusing-race-and-salvaging-the-human/.

Hall, S. 1997, 'Race, The Floating Signifier', Transcript, Media Education Foundation, Northhampton, viewed 15 May 2023, www.mediaed.org.

Hall, S. 2017, *The Fateful Triangle: Race, Ethnicity, Nation*, edited by K. Mercer, Harvard University Press, Cambridge, Massachusetts, and London, England.

Issar, S. 2021, 'Listening to Black Lives Matter: Racial Capitalism and the Critique of Neoliberalism', *Contemporary Political Theory*, vol. 20, no. 1, pp. 48–71.

Kaufmann, E. 2019, *Whiteshift: Populism, Immigration, and the Future of White Majorities*, Abrams Press, New York.

Lentin, A. 2015, 'What Does Race Do?', *Ethnic and Racial Studies*, vol. 38, no. 8, pp. 1401–1406.

Lentin, A. 2020, *Why Race Still Matters*, Polity Press, Cambridge.

Miles, R. 1982, *Racism and Migrant Labour*, Routledge and Kegan Paul, London.

Miles, R. 1989, *Racism*, Routledge, London.

Miles, R. and Brown, M. 2003, *Racism,* 2nd edn, Routledge, London.

Mills, C.W. 1997, *The Racial Contract*, Cornell University Press, Ithaca and London.

Mitchell, J. 2022, 'Back to Race, Not Beyond Race: Multiraciality and Racial Identity in the United States and Brazil', *Comparative Migration Studies*, vol. 10, no. 22, pp. 1–17, viewed 15 May 2023, https://doi.org/10.1186/s40878-022-00294-0.

Morning, A. 2014, 'And You Thought We Had Moved Beyond All That: Biological Race Returns to the Social Sciences', *Ethnic and Racial Studies*, vol. 37, no. 10, pp. 1676–1685.

Noble, G. 2013, 'Cosmopolitan Habits: The Capacities and Habitats of Intercultural Conviviality', *Body & Society*, vol. 19, nos 2&3, pp. 162–185.

Omi, M. and Winant, H. 2015, *Racial Formation in the United States*, 3rd edn, Routledge, New York.

Robinson, C. [1983] 2000, *Black Marxism: The Making of the Black Radical Tradition*, University of North Carolina Press, Chapel Hill, North Carolina, and London.

Saharso, S. and Scharrer, T. 2022, 'Beyond Race?', *Comparative Migration Studies*, vol. 10, no. 4, pp. 1–14, viewed 15 May 2023, https://doi.org/10.1186/s40878-021-00272-y.

Törngren, S.O. and Suyemoto, K.L. 2022, 'What Does It Mean to Go Beyond Race'? *Comparative Migration Studies*, vol 10, no.9, pp. 1–17, viewed 15 May 2023, https://doi.org/10.1186/s40878-022-00280-6.

Virdee, S. 2019, 'Racialized Capitalism: An Account of its Contested Origins', *The Sociological Review*, vol. 67, no. 1, pp. 3–27.

Wilson, W.J. 1978, *The Declining Significance of Race: Blacks and Changing American Institutions*, University of Chicago Press, Chicago, Illinois.

Wilson, W.J. 1987, *The Truly Disadvantaged: The Inner City, The Underclass and Public Policy*, University of Chicago Press, Chicago, Illinois.

Wilson, W.J. 2011, 'The Declining Significance of Race: Revisited & Revised', *Daedalus*, vol. 140, no. 2, pp. 55–69.

Winant, H. 1998, 'Racism Today: Continuity and Change in the Post-Civil Rights Era', *Ethnic and Racial Studies*, vol. 21, no. 4, pp. 755–766.

Working Group on Cultural Diversity and Inclusive Leadership 2018, *Leading for Change: A Blueprint for Cultural Diversity and Inclusive Leadership Revisited*, Australian Human Rights Commission, Canberra.

# CONCLUSION

Racism has been and continues to be a major form of domination, organising societies across the globe. It has been structured by an over-arching white supremacy that continues to shape its experience and drive its effects, locally, nationally and globally. Racism delivers benefits for some (phenotypically white people), and discriminates against and shapes the lives of many non-white, racialised others in negative and often devastating ways. Beginning as a European invention, racism became modular (as Anderson [1983] 2006 argued for nationalism), and now finds complex iterations throughout the globe, including in non-white societies. Though the white/black binary still dominates the organisation of race and racism in the world, as discussed in this book there are also non-colour-coded forms of racism in postcolonial and other non-white dominated countries (even if 'whiteness' is also still part of that story). Work in this area has been neglected, but in this book I have discussed some of this research, in places such as China (in Chapter 3), Singapore and Japan (in Chapter 5).

There is now a vast literature on racism. In this book I have attempted to chart a way through important ways of arguing about and theorising racism. My aim has been to emphasise that the study of racism should be a mainstream concern of the social sciences, especially sociology, because its workings are central to the ways that societies have been organised over the last few centuries, as systems of domination. Though racism involves many forms of violence, I have not explicitly focused on explaining manifestations of extreme racist violence and ideology, as, for example, in contemporary extremist movements. This is also an important site for research, but it should not be treated as the main way that racism works or is expressed.

DOI: 10.4324/9781003267690-8

Rather, I have focused on the mainstream nature of racism, in order to explain how it works systemically, and in mundane ways, being reproduced over time, even as it takes on new forms (as discussed in Chapter 2 and Chapter 5).

As I argued in Chapter 1, racism is a modern phenomenon, intricately connected with the movement of modernity, shaped by capitalism (or racial capitalism), imperialism, colonialism, the transatlantic slave trade, and the forms of thinking, including ways of classifying humans and discourses of liberty, equality and democracy that gradually emerged and consolidated as the Enlightenment spread its political, cultural and social effects in the eighteenth and nineteenth centuries. Though race had many meanings that changed as race thinking developed across the centuries, it eventually congealed as a vision of a hierarchy of types, with white Europeans at the top and all others ranked on different levels. This typology became a powerful ideology supporting regimes of discrimination and oppression, and the justification for European imperialism, colonialism (including settler-colonialism) and slavery.

Racism spread its tentacles in many different directions, also inspiring resistance, including from the black radical tradition of scholars discussed in this book. Racism was challenged in the twentieth century, especially after the horrors of the Holocaust became symbolically associated with a now discredited racism (see Alexander 2002, 2006), and in the wake of the post-war decolonisation movements. The United Nation's (UN) member states were determined to prevent a repeat of the organisation of racial discrimination that had resulted in genocide during World War Two. The UN Charter itself, setting up the UN in 1945, involved anti-racist elements – it made clear that one of its central strategies was promotion of respect for human rights and fundamental freedoms for all 'without distinction as to race, sex, language, or religion'. *The International Convention on the Elimination of All Forms of Racial Discrimination* (UN General Assembly 1965) was aimed at anything that was racially discriminatory in 'purpose or effect' (Banton 1996).

That said, before the Holocaust and World War Two the racist depredations of colonisation by Europe across the previous several centuries, including the economically lucrative slave trade, have been highlighted and stressed by the radical black tradition, including Du Bois in his voluminous works. Anti-colonial thinkers such as Césaire

(1972) and Fanon (1968) emphasised the direct connections between European colonialism and the racist anti-Semitism leading to the Holocaust in Europe. They have been followed by many others, such as Cedric Robinson ([1983] 2000) with his argument about racial capitalism, and Charles W. Mills (1997) with his argument about the racial contract (discussed in Chapter 1).

Though 'race', as I have argued, has no foundation in biology, it is at the same time a lived reality – there are racial and racist subjectivities organised by racism which help to reproduce racism, as I argued in Chapter 4, where I drew upon the psychoanalytically informed social theory of the Frankfurt school, other psychoanalytically informed approaches, including the works of Kovel and Fanon, and sociological theories of discursive formation and subjective positioning, ending with a discussion of future possible non-racist white identities. Race takes its place alongside other key concepts of descent and ancestry, such as ethnicity and nation, which also blur into each other (Fenton and May 2002; Hall 2017). Sociologists cannot simply replace the term race with an alternative such as ethnicity, because when doing so it becomes very hard to theorise adequately about racism. Though it would be a good thing if societies had transformed in such ways that 'race' was no longer a significant source of identity experiences, and the structuring of access to resources, to life chances and opportunities, we are a long way from achieving this situation, even if such imaginings beyond race are worthy thought experiments and hopeful, utopian strivings (as discussed in Chapter 6).

Racism is a complex phenomenon to study and explain. 'Part of the complexity of analysing the historical impact of racism,' Solomos and Back (1996, p. 57) have argued, 'is that it is often intertwined with other social phenomena, and indeed it can only be fully understood if we are able to see how it works in specific social settings.' Stuart Hall (1980) made a similar point when arguing for the way that race and racism are articulated in social formations with multiple levels. In addition, there is never one racism, always context-specific racisms, Hall argued. This also indicates the ways that we have to think about racism intersectionally in the broadest of senses, an approach I outlined in Chapter 2, drawing upon a diverse range of thinkers including key black feminist scholars such as Angela Davis, Kimberle Crenshaw, Audre Lorde, Patricia Hill Collins, bell hooks,

Floya Anthias and Nira Yuval-Davis. This theme was also taken up in Chapter 3, when exploring the interconnections between race, racism, nation and nationalism. There I argued that race and racism had in many historical circumstances and situations fed into and underpinned nationalism, always expressed through visions of sexuality, which racism and nationalism also aimed to control, in order to produce racially/nationally healthy populations (as argued by Foucault). Reflecting on the current explosive and global phenomenon of right-wing populist nationalism, I argued that these intersections needed to be thought through carefully, including historically, and argued against the claim that all forms of nationalism are inherently racist.

Faced with the ongoing, systemic nature of racism, including the ways that it has transformed itself in reaction to new political and social conditions (as outlined, for example, in Chapter 5), it might seem that anti-racism is futile, always being undermined by new ways for racism to work its way through society. Reflecting on post-civil rights racism, Winant (1998, p. 764) noted that:

> Confronting racism in such a situation is difficult. It is a moving target, a contested terrain. Inevitably, as a society, as political movements and as individuals, we have to make lots of mistakes; we have to see our action and our thought, our praxis, in pragmatic terms. Because racism changes and develops, because it is simultaneously a vast phenomenon framed by epochal historical developments, and a moment-to-moment experiential reality, we can never expect fully to capture it theoretically. Nor can we expect that it will ever be fully overcome. That does not mean, however, that we are free to desist from trying.

Thus, even those critics, many of whom have been discussed in this book, who have argued that racism is as pervasive as it has been in the past, or even in some respects worsened under neoliberal conditions, do not necessarily abandon the hope of fighting against racism. In fact, their persistent work as scholars revealing the often hidden workings of racism implies a political hope that racism can be challenged and overcome, despite the fierce resistance of those who benefit from racism. For example, Eduardo Bonilla-Silva (2014), who has so fiercely challenged the claim that we are in a post-racial era, and instead argued that there is a new racism that helps reproduce a structural racism that is insidious and reproductive of high levels of racial inequality across all domains of social life (discussed in Chapter 5), nevertheless does not give in to overwhelming pessimism. Instead, he argues that, just as the older Jim Crow racism had been transformed, so too the new racism could be challenged. In the final sections of *Racism Without Racists* he even challenges white people to personally engage in practical action to recognise, respond to and make changes to their segregationist social lives, to the friendship groups and neighbourhoods that they are embedded in, in white spaces (Bonilla-Silva 2014).

In his lengthy analysis of the successes of the American civil rights movement in effecting a major transformation of racial domination in American life, Alexander (2006, pp. 384–385) cautions against underestimating the nature of that achievement of anti-racist struggle:

> Our distance from that earlier time, and our awareness of the deep problems of racial exclusion that remain, often make us see the Civil Rights movement as less than it was. In fact, its impact was extraordinary. The civil rights laws of 1964 and 1965, and the organizational interventions that accompanied them, forced significant change in virtually every noncivil sphere of American life, from corporations to universities, from higher education to popular culture, from the choice of residence to participation in political parties, and to the very structure of the state.

This movement also inspired other social movements, and guided their forms of action and protest: the more recent women's movement, the protest movement against the Vietnam War, movements of other Indigenous, ethnic and racial groups aimed at achieving or extending civil rights, and even later movements for prisoners, for sexual/gay rights, and for disability rights. Alexander argues that for a range of reasons the mass civil rights movement fractured. The late 1960s and 1970s saw the rise of more militant, revolutionary and polarising political leaders such as Malcom X and movements such as Black Power, Black Liberation and the Black Panthers, that contributed to the fracturing of the civil rights movement, and the drift of white people away from its political causes. There was a white political backlash in the late 1960s, and reaction against achieved civil rights, and anti-discrimination and affirmative action policies (the latter gradually pared back especially in the 1980s). Nevertheless, anti-discrimination and affirmative action policies in the 1970s continued to spread through various levels of society, achieving important effects and opening up new economic and educational opportunities for African Americans and other non-whites. The black middle class that it had helped to create moved away from the urban ghettos, which became terrible places of abandonment, where the 'truly disadvantaged' lived, as captured by William Julius Wilson's (1987) evocative phrase, and analysed by other scholars including Wacquant (1998, 2009) and Elijah Anderson (2012). The association of such 'black urban ghettos' with crime, violence, poverty, unemployment, broken families and drugs produced powerful stigmatising effects ('territorial stigmatization' in Wacquant's 2007 account), that associated the 'black ghetto' with all blacks, including the middle classes, who have to constantly prove themselves to avoid that stigma in white society (Anderson 2012). This form of racism and racist stereotyping contributes to the links between mass incarceration of blacks and the terrible police violence that inspired Black Lives Matter.

In the period while I was writing this book, the Black Lives Matter movement went global, with masses of people from a wide range of ethnic, racial, class, gender, sexual and age backgrounds out protesting in the streets in many different countries, marching, demanding justice on a range of racial inequalities, especially against ongoing institutional/structural/systemic racism and violence. In Australia, Black Lives Matter found a huge resonance with Indigenous people, who staged mass street protests against the continuing racially disproportionate levels of incarceration of Indigenous people and the high number of deaths in custody, the taking away of Indigenous children from their parents and communities under welfare and child protection policies, and other symptoms of the structural racism that has characterised Australia as a settler-colonial state.

As with the civil rights movement, activists and scholars in the Black Lives Matter movement have appreciated the importance of multiracial, multi-class, multi-ethnic coalition building, while being led by young black activists (Dawson 2016). There has been recognition of the fundamental importance of anti-racism to be led and guided by those who have experienced the impact of racism (Brownhill 2020), rather than by white people who, while also having a major role in challenging racism, including their own unconscious racism, need to listen hard to the voices of the oppressed.

The challenge of changing racist structures, systems, ideologies and subjectivities is immense, as decolonisation scholars remind us. Anti-racism must also involve other forms of decolonisation, including the decolonisation of public space, demanded by movements such as 'Rhodes Must Fall' in South Africa, and the removal of colonialist statues and names in many parts of the world, including the settler-colony of Australia – a widely publicised example being the removal of the statue of slave trader Edward Colston from a Bristol street in the UK and its dumping in the harbour in June 2020. As Mbembe argues, we need to decolonise public spaces in order to make them truly democratic, inclusive public spaces. This requires the removal and repudiation of all colonial iconography:

> The decolonization of buildings and public spaces includes a change of those colonial names, iconography, i.e., the economy of symbols whose function, all along, has been to induce and normalize particular states of humiliation based on white supremacist presuppositions.
>
> (Mbembe 2015)

More broadly, the immense work required for the remaking of society as a racial democracy, as discussed in Chapter 6 via the work of Emirbayer and Desmond (2015), and to make the world a place free of and beyond racism, involves not only social movements, but sociologists and other social scientists. For these reasons, the study of racism remains central to sociology and the social sciences.

## REFERENCES

Alexander, J.C. 2002, 'On the Social Construction of Moral Universals: The "Holocaust" from War Crime to Trauma Drama', *European Journal of Sociology*, vol. 5, no. 1, pp. 5–85.

Alexander, J.C. 2006, *The Civil Sphere*, Oxford University Press, Oxford.

Anderson, B. [1983] 2006, *Imagined Communities: Reflections on the Origins and Spread of Nationalism*, 2nd edn, Verso, London.

Anderson, E. 2012, 'The Iconic Ghetto', *ANNALS, AAPSS*, vol. 642, July, pp. 8–24.

Banton, M. 1996, *International Action Against Racial Discrimination*, Clarendon Press, Oxford and New York.

Bonilla-Silva, E. 2014, *Racism Without Racists,* 4th edn, Rowman and Littlefield, Lanham, Maryland.

Brownhill, L. 2020, 'The Emancipatory Politics of Anti-Racism', *Capitalism Nature Socialism*, vol. 31, no. 3, pp. 4–15.

Césaire, A. 1972, *Discourse on Colonialism*, trans. J Pinkham, Monthly Review Press, New York.

Dawson, M.C. 2016 'Hidden in Plain Sight: A Note on Legitimation Crises and the Racial Order', *Critical Historical Studies*, Spring, pp. 143–161.

Emirbayer, M. and Desmond, M. 2015, *The Racial Order*, University of Chicago Press, Chicago, Illinois.

Fanon, F. 1968, *Black Skin, White Masks*, MacGibbon and Kee, London.

Fenton, S. and May, S. 2002, 'Ethnicity, Nation and "Race": Connections and Disjunctures', in S. Fenton and S. May (eds), *Ethnonational Identities*, Palgrave Macmillan, Basingstoke, pp. 1–20.

Hall, S. 1980, 'Race, Articulation and Societies Structured in Dominance', in UNESCO (ed.), *Sociological Theories: Race and Colonialism*, UNESCO, Paris.

Hall, S. 2017, *The Fateful Triangle: Race, Ethnicity, Nation*, edited by K. Mercer, Harvard University Press, Cambridge, Massachusetts, and London.

Mbembe, A. 2015, 'Decolonizing Knowledge and the Question of the Archive', Public Lecture, Wits Institute for Social and Economic Research (WISER), University of the Witwatersrand (Johannesburg), viewed 15 May 2023, https:// wiser.wits.ac.za/system/files/Achille%20Mbembe%20%20Decolonizing%20 Knowledge%20and%20the%20Question%20of%20the%20Archive.pdf.

Mills, C.W. 1997, *The Racial Contract*, Cornell University Press, Ithaca, and London.

Robinson, C. [1983] 2000, *Black Marxism: The Making of the Black Radical Tradition*, University of North Carolina Press, Chapel Hill, North Carolina, and London.

Solomos, J. and Back, L. 1996, *Racism and Society*, Macmillan, Basingtoke.

UN General Assembly, *International Convention on the Elimination of All Forms of Racial Discrimination*, 21 December 1965, United Nations, Treaty Series, vol. 660, p. 195, available at: https://www.refworld.org/docid/3ae6b3940. html [accessed 5 August 2023].

Wacquant, L. 1998, 'Inside the Zone: The Social Art of the Hustler in the American Ghetto', *Theory, Culture & Society*, vol. 15, no. 2, pp. 1–36.

Wacquant, L. 2007, 'Territorial Stigmatization', *Thesis Eleven*, no. 1, pp. 66–77.

Wacquant, L. 2009, *Punishing the Poor: The Neoliberal Government of Social Security*, Duke University Press, Durham, North Carolina.

Wilson, W.J. 1987, *The Truly Disadvantaged: The Inner City, the Underclass and Public Policy*, University of Chicago Press, Chicago, Illinois.

Winant, H. 1998, 'Racism Today: Continuity and Change in the Post-Civil Rights Era', *Ethnic and Racial Studies*, vol. 21, no. 4, pp. 755–766.

# INDEX

INDEX

white habitus 113–115
white power 48
white racial frame 55–57, 60–61
white supremacy: in contemporary
context 178; global racial hierarchy
of nations 8; historical context 30
whiteness: historical Caucasian type
20–21; subjectivities of racism
94–95, 108–110, 117–119

Williams, Raymond 3
Wilson, William Julius 172, 183
Winant, Howard 7–8, 29–31, 46,
53–55, 58–59, 118, 156, 181
Wolfe, Patrick 25–26

xenology 161

Yuval-Davis, N. 6–7, 42

Milton Keynes UK
Ingram Content Group UK Ltd.
UKHW022146101123
432360UK00008B/92